T0331842

Interactive Textures for Architecture and Landscaping:
Digital Elements and Technologies

Mikael Wiberg, Umea University, & Uppsala University, Sweden

INFORMATION SCIENCE REFERENCE

Hershey · New York

Director of Editorial Content:	Kristin Klinger
Director of Book Publications:	Julia Mosemann
Acquisitions Editor:	Lindsay Johnston
Development Editor:	Julia Mosemann
Publishing Assistant:	Deanna Jo Zombro
Typesetter:	Deanna Jo Zombro
Production Editor:	Jamie Snavely
Cover Design:	Lisa Tosheff

Published in the United States of America by
Information Science Reference (an imprint of IGI Global)
701 E. Chocolate Avenue,
Hershey PA 17033
Tel: 717-533-8845
Fax: 717-533-8661
E-mail: cust@igi-global.com
Web site: http://www.igi-global.com

Library of Congress Cataloging-in-Publication Data

Wiberg, Mikael, 1974-
  Interactive textures for architecture and landscaping : digital elements and technologies / by Mikael Wiberg.
       p. cm.
  Includes bibliographical references and index.
  Summary: "This book addresses the phenomenon called "interactive architecture that challenges artists, architects, designers, theorists, and geographers to develop a language and designs toward the "use" of these environments"--Provided by publisher.
  ISBN 978-1-61520-653-7 (hardcover) -- ISBN 978-1-61520-654-4 (ebook) 1. Architecture and technology. 2. Texture in architecture. 3. Materials--Technological innovations. 4. Surfaces (Technology) 5. Human-computer interaction. 6. User interfaces (Computer systems) I. Title.
  NA2543.T43W53 2010
  720.1'05--dc22
                                           2009053473

British Cataloguing in Publication Data
A Cataloguing in Publication record for this book is available from the British Library.

All work contributed to this book is new, previously-unpublished material. The views expressed in this book are those of the authors, but not necessarily of the publisher.

Table of Contents

Preface .... **vii**

Acknowledgment .... **xii**

On the Texture of This Book: A Reading Guide .... **xiv**
The Structure of This Book xxvi
Perspectives on the Audience of This Book xxxv
The Value of This Book and its Main Contributions xxxviii
Research Challenges: Textures and New Materiality xlv
References xlvi

Section 1:
Motivation: Current Thinking Outside The Box

Section 1 Introduction
A Pre-Interaction Reflection: The Breakdown of the Box

Chapter 1
Interaction 1
From Desktop Computing to Ubiquitous Computing to Everyware 2
From Computers to Users to Persons to Inhabitats 14
From Interfaces to Interaction 17
From Communities of Practice to Combinations of Professions 41
A Post-Interaction Reflection: The Return of Boxes 43

Towards Clutter or Texture? 43
References 48

Chapter 2
Textures Matters! **54**
Deconstructing the User Interface 61
Discovering Textures 63
Articulation of Textures 65
Meaningful Environments 66
Reading and Rewriting Textures 70
References 71

Chapter 3
A New Architecture? **72**
Traditional Architecture 73
The Basics of Architecture 74
Architecture and the Built Environment 76
Towards a New Architecture 78
Physical and Digital Materials 80
New Environments 81
Reflection: Interactive Textures and the Sciences of the Artificial 88
References 90

Section 2:
Foundations: Elements, Textures and Architecture

Section 2 Introduction
Beyond Boxes: Basics That Matter

Chapter 4
Enabling Technologies **95**
New Materials and Elements 95
Architectural Thinking on Elements 98
Compositions 98
Interactive Textures 99
Textures in Details: The Making of the New 101
References 111

Chapter 5
Theorizing Interactive Textures **112**
Blending Architecture and Interaction Design 112

Textures and Representations..114
Towards a Theory of Textures 115
Textures as Navigational Aids...122
Interaction with and Through Textures..124
References 125

Chapter 6
Interactive Architecture **128**
From Digital Elements to Interactive Textures....................................129
From Textures to Architectures 130
From Architectures to Environments 135
Towards Living Systems: Interactive Architecture and Landscaping..............136
References 138

Section 3:
Character: Cases and Concepts

Section 3 Introduction
Making Cases and Seeing with New Eyes

Chapter 7
Five Cases: From Mobile Devices to Interaction Landscaping
and the City **142**
Case 1. Mobility: Supporting People Moving Around in Places.....................143
Case 2. Focusing on Places and Public "Input Gates" 145
Case 3. Focusing on Places and Public "Output Gates"..........................149
Case 4. Totally Interactive Environments 152
Case 5. Everyday City Textures: Times Square, New York 161
Five Different Cases: Some Concluding Remarks................................168
References 170

Chapter 8
Interaction through Textures **171**
P3-Systems (People-to-People to Geographical Places) 172
Discovering the Interactive Texture..173
Interacting vs. Being (User Vs. Inhabitant)..174
Public Interaction Rituals..174
Conventions for Interaction with and Through Interactive Textures...............177
Putting "Interaction Knowledge" into the World................................178
The IT- ("Interaction through Textures") Framework.........................179
References 182

Section 4:
Exploration: There is No Box

Section 4 Introduction
Getting Real and Realizing Where to Go

Chapter 9
Interactive Architecture and Interaction Landscaping......................... 187
IT as Embedded Element... 188
IT as Infrastructure and Installed Base 189
Lifehacking... 190
Interaction Landscaping 191
References 195

Chapter 10
Conclusions... 196
A Digital World 196
A New Agenda.. 197
Temporal Rooms and New Spatial Engagements 199
References 200

About the Author 201

Index.. 202

Preface

Our built environment is currently undergoing a transformation in terms of digitalization. Today, computers are *attached*, or *embedded* in our physical environment and *accessed* through e.g. RFID, 3G, WiFi and Bluetooth, *manipulated* via e.g. embedded public interactive displays and tangible user interfaces (TUIs), through *interaction modalities* including e.g. gestures, movements, positioning techniques, voice commands, etc. In these modern environments we also carry with us small mobile computational devices capable of communicating with the infrastructure, or the *digital elements* of the built environment, to e.g. make phone calls, unlock doors, schedule meetings, or access the Internet.

Embedded computers in our built environment have so forth mainly been installed for *functional purposes*, e.g. to support us in automatically open up doors for us at shopping malls, control the heating in our houses, and so on. More recently however researchers, designers, and artists have started to explore how digital technology could be used as a design material to reshape our build environment into interactive environments or "interaction environments" in support of *social interaction, play* and *experiences*. Through the blend of digital technology, sensors and media with public places new forms of digitally enhanced environments are brought into our reality. Today, researchers, designers, artists and architects have started to address, and approach this development through the development of concepts including e.g. *ubiquitous computing, embodied interaction, interactive architecture, responsive environments, media places, hybrid spaces, ambient intelligence,* and *digital art installations*.

These new interactive environments are often portrayed as being responsive, active, sensitive, and in a constant dialogue with us as users or inhabitants. While this trend started out with quite simple and small-scale examples of so called TUIs (tangible user interfaces) in which a user can interact with, and manipulate, digital material though the interaction with physical objects, this trend is now developing on a large scale basis due to the development of new innovative materials (Materio, 2007) or *transmaterials* (Brownell, 2005; 2008), i.e., physical material with interactive characteristics, and with current movements towards the creation of ubiquitous computing landscapes realized through e.g. interactive wall installations, mobile devices and small size computers. This trend is captured in terms like ambient intelligence (e.g. Lindwer, et al., 2003; Aarts, 2005; Gárate, et al, 2005), smart environments (e.g. Siegemund, 2005; Das & Cook, 2006), interactive environments (Pinhanez & Bobick, 2003) and interactive architecture (e.g. Zellner, 1999; Kolarevic, 2003). Malcolm McCullough (2004) has argued in the book "Digital ground" that this change towards fully interactive environments has fundamental implications for both the area of architecture as well as computing as we used to know it.

This book addresses this relatively new phenomenon called "interactive architecture", i.e. the current blending of building materials with interactive components which challenges us as artists, architects, designers, IT theorists, and geographers, to develop our language and designs towards the "use" of these environments, articulating both what it means to interact in these new modes of place, and framing interaction with and through so called "interactive architecture" (e.g. Oosterhuist & Xia, 2007; Bullivant, 2005; Bullivant, 2007).

Interactive architecture can be described as an emerging field of research in the borderland of architecture, art installations, public performance, and novel use of digital technologies. Some researchers have used alternative terms such as "responsive environments", "responsive architecture", or "performative architecture" (e.g. Bullivant, 2006; Kolarevic & Malkawi (2005)), while other have labeled the integration of digital technologies in built environments as "hybrid spaces" (e.g. Zellner, 1999) to address a development towards a complete blend of our physical and digital world, and to address a development in which the traditional physical and social public domain is being supplemented by zones, places and subcultures that transcend the local to interlink with the translocal and the global (Rheingold, et.al., 2007). In this current development, I will take as an important point of departure current literature which describes, analyses and theorize *the ongoing integration of digital technologies in our built environment* (e.g. Cai & Abascal (2006); Margolis & Robinson (2007) and Greenfield, 2006).

Further on, this book builds upon a conceptualized understanding of the integration of architecture and digital technologies as "Media spaces" to address how digital technologies enable us to spatially stretch places, connect places, and connect to other human beings across geographical distances (e.g. Morley, 1995), integration of architecture and digital technologies as new media and the digital transformation of public places (Drucker & Gumpert, 1996), and the creation of so called "Media districts" (Indergaard, 2004). In this book this is further explored through the concepts of *temporal rooms* and *spatial communication*.

In this book "interactive architecture" is approached from a multifaceted viewpoint, with its two focal roots in the specific fields of interaction design and architectural literature. In this undertaking the introduced notion of "Interaction through textures" will serve as a unifying analytical concept capable of putting an emphasis on our built environment from an architectural standpoint, while keeping the nature of interaction at the center of our attention. Further on, the notion of "textures", as referring to "the feel, appearance, or consistency of a surface" is a concept borrowed from the field of architecture and material science with similarities with the concept of "interfaces" in interaction design. These important similarities that can help to create a conceptual link between these two fields and that is the main objective with this book. Further on, the "through" dimension of "Interaction Through Textures" addresses the interactive dimension of the new materials and textures that modern interactive architecture rely upon, thus adding an interaction design perspective to architectural thinking, while at the same time working as a concept well established in the area of interaction design (see e.g. the book *Through* the Interface" by Susanne Bødker, 1990).

As this book sets out to illustrate, textures are ubiquitous, and the "skins" of our everyday world, and they serve a number of different purposes as reference points, filters, surfaces, enablers, and extensions of human actions. As we attempt to seamlessly blend digital technology into our physical world the issue of texture, and how to work with texture from a standpoint that integrate an interaction design perspective with an architecturally rooted perspective will be one of the core challenges for the years to come.

Interactive textures will enable architects, and interaction designers to rethink the fundamentals of our surrounding with these new dimensions in mind. Welcome to a new world!

REFERENCES

Aarts, E. (2005). Ambient intelligence drives open innovation. *Interactions, 12*(4), 66-68.

Brownell, B. (2005). *Transmaterial: A Catalog of Materials That Redefine our Physical Environment*. Princeton Architectural Press.

Brownell, B. (2008). *Transmaterial 2: A Catalog of Materials That Redefine our Physical Environment*. Princeton Architectural Press.

Bullivant, L. (2005). *4dspace: Interactive Architecture, Architectural Design*. Wiley-Academy.

Bullivant, L. (2006). *Responsive environments – Architecture, art and design*. V & A Contemporary Publications.

Bullivant, L. (2007). *4dsocial: Interactive Design Environments, Architectural Design*. Wiley-Academy.

Cai, Y., & Abascal, J. (2006). *Ambient intelligence in everyday life*. Springer-Verlag.

Das, S., & Cook, D. (2006). Designing and Modeling Smart Environments. In *Proceedings of the 2006 International Symposium on World of Wireless, Mobile and Multimedia Networks WOWMOM '06*. IEEE Computer Society.

Drucker, S. & Gumpert, G. (1996). The regulation of Public Social Life: Communication Law Revisited. *Communication Quarterly, 44*(3), 280-96.

Gárate, A., Herrasti, N., & López, A. (2005). GENIO: An ambient intelligence application in home automation and entertainment environment. In *Proceedings of sOc-EUSAI '05*. ACM Press

Greenfield, A. (2006). *Everyware – The dawning age of ubiquitous computing*. Berkeley, CA: New Riders.

Indergaard, M. (2004). *Silicon Alley - The Rise and Fall of a New Media District*. Routledge.

Kolarevic, B. & Malkawi, A. (2005). *Performative Architecture – Beyond instrumentality*. UK: Spon Press.

Kolarevic, B. (2003). *Architecture in the digital age – Design and manufacturing*. Taylor & Francis.

Lindwer, M., Marculescu, D., Basten, T., Zimmennann, R. Marculescu, R., Jung, S., & Cantatore, E. (2003). *Ambient intelligence visions and achievements: linking abstract ideas to real-world concepts*. IEEE Xplore, IEEE.

Margolis, L. & Robinson, A. (2007) Living Systems – Innovative materials and technologies for landscape architecture. Birkhäuser.

Materio (2007). *Material World 2: Innovative Materials for Architecture and Design*. Birkhäuser.

McCullough, M. (2004). *Digital Ground – Architecture, Pervasive Computing, and Environmental Knowing*. Cambridge, MA: MIT Press.

Morley, D., & Robins, K. (1995). *Spaces of identity: Global media, electronic landscapes and cultural boundaries*. Routledge.

Oosterhuist, K. (2007). *iA #1 Interactive Architecture*. Rotterdam: Episode Publishers.

Pinhanez, C., & Bobick, A. (2003) Interval scripts: a programming paradigm for interactive environments and agents. *Personal and Ubiquitous Computing, 7*(1), Springer-Verlag.

Rheingold, H., et al. (2007). *Open 11: Hybrid Space*. NAi Uitgevers/Publishers.

Siegemund, F., Floerkemeier, C., & Vogt, H. (2005). The value of handhelds in smart environments. *Personal and Ubiquitous Computing, 9*(2).

Zellner, P. (1999). *Hybrid Space – New forms in digital architechture*. Thames & Hudson.

Acknowledgment

It is almost a cliché to say that the writing of a book is not a one man's job. Nevertheless, that is absolutely true, and I would therefore like to thank several important persons to me for their involvements and contributions to making this book happen.

First of all, I would like to thank my lovely wife Charlotte for all your love, support, creative discussions, patience and encouragements during the time that it took to write this book. As you already know for sure, I couldn't have done this without you! ;-)

Following from this, and as the author of this book, I would like to acknowledge the help of all involved in the collation and review process of the book, without whose support the project could not have been satisfactory completed. A special note of thanks goes also to all the staff at IGI Global, whose contributions throughout the whole process from inception to the initial idea to final publication have been invaluable. A special thanks goes to the publishing team at IGI Global, in particular to Julia Mosemann for her genuine interest in this book, and for keeping the project on schedule.

A special sponsorship acknowledgement goes to the research project that has funded this work (i.e. the "xID 2.0 – Interaction Design in Extreme Environments" project funded by the EU Target 2 structural funds).

I would also like to direct a special thanks to all of my colleagues at the department of Informatics at Umeå University, and to all of my colleagues at Umeå Institute of Design, Umeå university, Sweden for all your support, feedback and creative discussions that we have had throughout this project! A special thanks also goes to Peter Kjaer, rector at Umeå School of Architecture, Umeå university for our interesting and thoughtful discussions around architecture as social intervention processes. Another special thanks goes to Erica Robles, NYU for our always-inspiring research collaborations on e.g. the aesthetics of computational materiality. Our collaboration over the last two years has also left special imprints on the ideas outlined in this book. Thank you. I would also like to thank my new colleagues at the department of Informatics & Media at Uppsala University for good comments related to the notion of texture as introduced in this book.

In closing, I would also like to thank my great parents Britt and Ulf, and my sister Marie for always being there for me. And at last, but definitely not at least I would like to thank our two fantastic kids Viktor and Wilma for always being a huge source of inspiration, and for always asking and pinpointing the things that no one else would think about. You're just so great!

Mikael Wiberg, PhD
Professor, Department of Informatics & Media, Uppsala University, Sweden
Research Director, Umeå Institute of Design, Umeå University, Sweden

September, 2010

On the Texture of This Book:
A Reading Guide

In this section I provide a guide on how to read this book – from what it appears to be in terms of surface appearance and structure, but also in relation to its deeper messages. As such, this section present the "texture" of this book, as a relation between the appearance of the book (in terms of text, chapters, sections, examples, etc) and its deeper materials from which it is made, including an understanding of IT as a material that enable a new technology-enabled society.

This new book is in fact my second book about a new technology-enabled society in the making. In my first book "The Interaction Society" (Wiberg, 2004) I pinpointed a very important shift in the way we use IT in our modern society. The book "The Interaction Society" marked out an important shift from IT being mainly used as a tool for calculations, transactions, etc. towards IT as a tool for communication and social interaction in between people. In the first book I therefore proposed that IT should rather be understood as an acronym for "Interaction Technologies" than an acronym for "Information Technologies" (Wiberg, 2004, p. 4).

In this second book a new statement is made. IT needs to be better integrated in our physical world. We can now see that IT is heavily integrated in our social lives, and in our everyday communication and interaction patterns (typically through all the blogs, twitter feeds, etc. that has become so popular over the most recent years). The next big wave for IT development is therefore maybe not in this area. IT will of course continue to develop and become more adjusted to our social lives, but I believe that one of the largest challenges now, in order to fit technology into our everyday lives, is also about understanding how to integrate IT in our physical world, i.e. to integrate IT into the very architecture of our build environment.

Looking into the constant stream of new "call for papers" to conferences and journals within the broad field of IT research there are several themes emerging. One theme is of course heavily related to the general theme of my first book, i.e. themes related to IT and social interaction. However, there is also another theme possible to identify right now. This second theme is about "urban informatics", "ICT & The City", "Ambient Information Environments", and "Interactive Architecture". All of these are pointing in one interesting direction, and all of these are pointing towards one interesting research question: *How do IT integrate itself with our built environment?* Or, if rephrased as a design questions then it could be formulated as: *How can we find new ways to scaffold our thinking on how to better integrate IT with our built environment?*

Today, we can see a lot of practical examples of both good and bad integrations of new digital technology in our physical world. We find embedded digital technologies in our homes, ranging from the computer that controls the fridge, to the wall mounted LCD, Plasma or LED TV. We also find a lot of digital technology in public places, ranging from traffic signals to restaurants. The picture (Figure 1) illustrates one such good example of IT as integrated in a public physical space. This picture is from a hamburger restaurant in which four frames with information about the menu has been installed as an integrated part of the indoor architecture. Worth noticing here is that the two frames to the left are traditional light boxes with color printed paper adds about the menu in the front of the boxes. Alongside of these two are two additional frames. However, these two frames are in fact computer displays.

Figure 1. Two computer displays (the two frames to the right) integrated in the physical environment

Given an interest in understanding IT integration in physical space this is a quite good example that can work as an illustration of how traditional interaction design thinking could have framed this design in comparision with the texturation approach to interaction design and architecture as presented in this book.

In traditional interaction design an explicit focus is of course set on the digital technology and how to interact with the technology. Some core concepts from the area of interaction design are to work with the user and how to design the interactive experience. *Attention, experience* and the notion of a *user* are as such central concepts in interaction design. Sometimes the focus on experiences is further framed as *experience design* (e.g. Shedroff, 2001; Battarbee, 2003; Forlizzi & Ford, 2000) and in terms of attention that is also typically framed by concepts like *presence* (e.g. Lee & Nass, 2003), or *immersion* (e.g. Sheridan, 2000).

However, in the restaurant case as outlined about it is not only a question of interaction design, and the concepts of users, attention and experience design are not applicable to this situation in which the people who are coming to this place see themselves more as just people or maybe as guests to this restaurant, but for sure, they do not see themselves primarily as "users" of a computer system. And it is not the interaction with the displays mounted above the counter that they want to engage themselves with, and it is not that interaction they are focused on "experiencing". Instead, their focus in on the experience of the whole environment as a wholeness, typically referred to as "the atmosphere" of this particular place which is about the impression of every aspect of the surrounding simultaneously taken into account, i.e. an impression that do not distinguish the computer system from the rest of the built environment.

If we now consider this particular example from the restaurant and if we look into how the IT is integrated as part of the environment, if we look into how it is present, but still remains in the background of our attention as to become part of the wholeness and part of the overall impression some aspects are emerging. I like to think about these aspects as signs of how the digital technology is *texturized* in a physical environment.

From a texture perspective there are many things that can be said about these displays in this physical environment if focusing on the "in-betweeness" of the physical and the digital, i.e. how the two are integrated into one integrated design. Just to give a few examples of this:

If studying the interior design in Figure 1 in detail one can see that the design of the digital displays has been nicely adjusted to the physical environment in several different ways. The backlights of the computer displays are adjusted as to, in terms of brightness, color, and contrast, match the backlight in the traditional light boxes. The computer displays has the same sizes, forms and frames as the light boxes. There are no visible cables or other indicators that these are in fact computer displays. Instead, the signal cables have been equally hided or embedded as the rest of the electricity system in this environment. The computer displays have also been mounted alongside the light boxes as to assemble them into one coherent part of the interior. If we also focus on the process behind this installation we can easily imagine how the integration of the digital in this particular environment was planned on an equally detailed level as e.g. the planning and installation of electricity and heating protection cover for the spotlights nicely installed in the sealing of the restaurant.

From the perspective of this book this is a quite good and illustrative example of how we can work with new digital textures in our built environment. In this book, these textures are labeled "interactive textures". Of course, the interactiveness of these displays is somewhat low. These displays do not rely on any actions taken by a user. In fact, a lot of questions arise from this case if only addressing it from an interaction design perspective. Are the displays interactive or not? Does it matter? To say that they are "potentially interactive" is that an answer? Under what circumstances could these displays be interactive? And what would the purpose be of having these displays as interactive surfaces? How could more interactivity added to these displays be useful or meaningful to the people inhabiting this place?

This book is not an attempt to answer, or even address these questions. Simply because they are all typical, narrow, and technology-driven questions in which there seem to exist an underlying idea that more advanced technology and more interactivity is always better. Instead, this book is an attempt to move "out of the box" in terms of a narrow focus on digital technology as a product, and instead move into a position where digital technology is understood more as a digital material which can be used in the creation of architectural spaces. That, however, requires a broader approach to this phenomenon. Given one such approach another set of questions might arise from this case including questions like: when these displays become fully blended into our physical world, when will we notice this blendedness? When will the technology reveal itself to us? Will it be in technological breakdowns only, or can it dynamically distinguish itself from its blendedness as to present itself, its functionality and its computational power? In which cases? And what would trigger blending vs. distinguishing? Another set of questions might range from the core question of whether or not it matters that the displays are digital (from an environment inhabitant perspective) to the ultimate question of whether or not there is a need to maintain a conceptual separation between physical and digital in our everyday world. In this book a unified approach that integrates the digital and the physical, or interaction design and architecture, is a starting point for a deeper understanding of how we might interact with and within the built environments of a future that is partly already here and partly already happening.

When we blend the digital with the physical it is reasonable to imagine that what we typically consider as the raw model for interaction is changing. This is not strange, since the raw model of interaction that we have comes from the individual use of a desktop computer typically used in a somewhat private space (an office cubicle, or e.g. in the home). That is why the first part of this book is devoted to the very phenomenon of interaction since it is the glue that connects us as social beings to the world of computers. Still, these new textures have the potential of scaffolding various kinds of both synchronous and asynchronous interactions with and through these textures. A potential to scaffold both the people present in the environment, as well as the potential of scaffolding remote updates and interaction with dispersed people in relation to the location in which the textures are located. That is why I, in this book define interactive textures as *"digitalized materials, physically manifested, and capable of representing information and potentially also to scaffold interaction".*

While this case was a good example of IT as integrated or "texturized" into a physical space there are of course also a lot of bad examples out there. Figure 2 illustrates one such installation as an illustrative example of modern technology loosely texturized in physical space although some efforts and good intentions have preceded this particular installation.

In Figure 2 a new modern clock has been installed at the very location of an old clock that used to be elegantly texturized in the overall interior of this space. As illustrated in Figure 2 the whole wall is in fact also a wall painting and as such a

Figure 2. Modern clock installation at the very location of an old analogue clock

piece of art, or at least an artistic architectonic element, which adds to the oceanic atmosphere of the swimming hall in which it is located.

If looking at this installation from an interaction design perspective, with a focus on this new object, we can see several things. The new clock shows the correct time, and the clock is in fact radio controlled which means that it is the same time displayed on all of the clocks in this building. This in turn enables centralized administration of the clocks. Further on, the white clock with black numbers and black hour hand and minute hand makes it easier to see what time it is compared to the old clock due to the bigger contrast between white and black compared to blue and black.

These are all good arguments for this new clock, and these are traditional arguments from the area of interaction design (related to the old questions in interaction design that has to do with accurate information, accessibility/usability, and system maintenance). Still, it is sort of obvious that some additional perspective is missing here. Somehow, it feels like the clock is not integrated or adjusted to the location where it is installed.

If we now move into the perspective as presented in this book, i.e. into a perspective in which we keep one eye on the creation of wholeness which looks into the total appearance of how materials work together in the creation of a space, and one eye on the details when it comes to how different materials are integrated or aligned to one another another set of issues appear if studying the clock case above. Given a texturation perspective we can see that the design and the form factor of the clock is not aligned with the theme of this space. Further on, the new clock is not integrated with the wall. It has just been quickly installed *on* the wall (without even removing all of the details of the old integrated clock, and without even making sure that it is placed in the exact center of the old clock). This package of issues leads to the fact that the new clock appears, and presents itself on this wall as a separate object and not as part of the total design of the interior.

This example with the clock is on the one hand a good example that illustrates the texturation approach as presented in this book. One the other hand, it is also a good example of how this complementary approach that integrates interaction design thinking with a perspective rooted in architecture as presented in this book can be of practical help for analyzing and understanding technology integration in context. This relate to a set of important messages in this book.

- To a large extend we have not treated IT as an architectural element or as a design material.
- We have to a large extent failed to integrate IT in our physical world, and
- We need a language to address the dimensions of IT integration into our physical world as to scaffold our design thinking in this area.

In this book I set out to address this set of messages through the specific research question concerning IT integration in our physical world as outlined above in search for new ways of thinking about and conceptualizing IT as integrated in, not only our social and cultural world, but also in our physical world.

There has of course been previous work conducted along this line of thinking including e.g. contextual design (e.g. Beyer & Holtzblatt (1998)) in which one question concerns design of the digital in relation to the physical context. However, in this book no separation is made between the digital and the physical context. Instead, those are just two different materials in the creation of wholeness, i.e. in the creation of meaningful places and spaces for people to inhabit. If the separation is removed then of course context is no longer an outside parameter possible to design *in relation to.* Instead, *context is part of the design.*

This is a very important starting point for this book. Given this starting point I would argue that is not a narrow book in computer science or informatics. Although it has to do a lot with the development of IT that is not the main focus for the book. Nor is this a traditional book in architecture. The book also takes a specific point of departure in our built environment, but it is important for the reading of this book to understand that the whole book is really about the meeting between IT and architecture with a special interest in, and focus on, the things emerging in between these two entities. Thus, to fully appreciate this book the reader should think about Computer Science and Informatics, especially interaction design, one the one hand, and traditional architecture capable of describing our built environment on the other hand, as two fundamental cornerstones and points of references and points of departures for the kind of intellectual journey this book is providing into an area where no distinction is made between the physical and the digital, and between digital and traditional material.

Figure 3. The "Dynamic Facade" created by architect Giselbrecht + Partner ZT GmbH. Typically known as the Kiefer Technic Showroom in Bad Gleichenberg, Austria

In this book, one of the core ideas are that this line of reasoning scale from the small scale room, as the restaurant example above, to full scale architecture, and Figure 3, i.e. the Kiefer Technic Showroom in Bad Gleichenberg, Austria created by architect Giselbrecht + Partner ZT GmbH work as one good example of this reasoning at the scale of the building. It also works as a good example of this current phenomenon in which architecture and interaction design is starting to blend to the point where no meaningful separation can be made between architecture and interaction design. Instead, the meaningfulness appears through the texture of the building in which it communicate to the world around it that it is both a physical building, but also a dynamic computational object and therefore in capacity of dynamically changing its appearance or texture.

This book is a book focusing on these new textures and the new computational materials that enable IT to literary weave itself into the materials of our everyday world until it is indistinguishable from it as so elegantly formulated ones by Mark Weiser (1991), one of the most important pioneers in the area of ubiquitous computing. Mark Weiser was also the co-founder of the idea of "calm technology" in which computational power remains in the background of our attention, integrates itself in our physical world, but still remains constantly ready to scaffold us with computational power whenever we need it. As formulated by Weiser & Brown (1996):

"The most potentially interesting, challenging, and profound change implied by the ubiquitous computing era is a focus on calm. If computers are everywhere they better stay out of the way, and that means designing them so that the people being shared by the computers remain serene and in control. Calmness is a new challenge that UC [Ubiquitous Computing] brings to computing. When computers are used behind closed doors by experts, calmness is relevant to only a few. Computers for personal use have focused on the excitement of interaction. But when computers are all around, so that we want to compute while doing something else and have more time to be more fully human, we must radically rethink the goals, context and technology of the computer and all the other technology crowding into our lives. Calmness is a fundamental challenge for all technological design of the next fifty years. (Weiser & Brown, 1996, p.7).

In line with this thinking this new book builds upon this pioneering work and adds to it a very important aspect, i.e. the fundamental concept of *texture* as a novel approach to address not only the relation between the human and the computer as in the case with calm computing, but equally important, the relation between the computer and the context in which it is implemented. Since the mainframe computers until now most computers are not integrated into the physical environment "until it is indistinguishable from it". Instead, computers are typically self-contained objects that that tend to distinguish themselves from any theme, form, or purpose with a built environment, ranging from the Internet PC in the hotel lobby to the large time and temperature display mounted on outdoor walls of large buildings.

In this book texture is proposed as a concept that can help us to see the details in our physical environment, see how materials are integrated into architectonic compositions, and how computational power could be integrated with equal elegance into these build environments. An important point of departure for this book is thus to "think outside the box", i.e. to leave the conceptualization of the computer as a "box", and the conceptualization that a computer always needs to be a box (either in the form of a desktop computer, a laptop, or a small mobile device), and instead work with a conceptualization of the computer as a material, or as a computational material (ref). The advantage with a material perspective is that we are used to think about materials as something we can work with, and to think about materials as something that we can form, and configure into a piece that works together with other materials that together forms a whole, an object, or even a whole building. Therefore, a point of departure in *IT as material* is important. Following this line of reasoning to importance of texture start to make itself clear. When we set our focus on compositions of materials we also need an understanding of what the composition will look like, and we need a concept that can backtrack the relation between material properties and the appearance of a surface or an object in our everyday world. Here is where the notion of texture comes into play.

In this book this notion of texture is rooted in the theoretical work and definitions within the field of material science (e.g. Randle & Engles, 2000) as well as rooted in the architectural strand of literature (e.g. Ching, 2007) in which "texture" is typically defined as *"the feel, appearance, or consistency of a surface"* (a definition also used by Oxford dictionary).

Computer displays are typically thought of as surfaces, but to further scaffold our thinking on how the notion of texture can help us to see how computational power can be integrated in our physical world this book expands this concept into "interactive textures" in an attempt to start to treat computational material (Vallgårda & Redström, 2007) as just one material amongst others, and as a way to open up a discussion on how computational materials, as a new texture, could be integrated with other, maybe more traditional textures as to form new architectural spaces in which no separation is made between computational materials and other materials.

In this book I define interactive textures as *"digitalized materials, physically manifested, and capable of representing information and potentially also to scaffold interaction"*. These new textures are part of larger constructions of intertwined physical, social and digital materials (Robles & Wiberg, 2010). Interactive textures enable the physical to communicate remote information, and it enables a physical space to become active, query-able, and connected. Further on, it enables the digital to situate and manifest itself in the physical world, i.e. as an integrated part ranging from a small object, or a room, to a full-blown architecture.

In particular, this book is about these new interactive textures and how these could be used in architecture. As this section has described this is with a focus on architecture in terms of built environments, and not on architecture in terms of "computer architecture", although such digital architectures of course are a vital aspect in any creation and execution of computer applications. However, this is an important distinction that the reader should bear with him/her throughout the reading of this book.

The book also has a focus on landscaping. This focus is two-folded, and it is important to keep this dual focus in mind throughout the reading of this book. On the one land, the focus is on the new physical landscapes that new computational materials and thus new interactive textures and new interactive architecture (Bullivant, 2005; Addington & Schodek, 2005) enable. One the other hand, the focus is also on the digital landscapes that people are creating which are also present in the modern cityscape. This is a landscape that might be harder to observe immediately and by anyone. Still, how people configure devices and different sets of IT artifacts into larger systems, and how they install and configure applications and services as to work for them across these digital assembles as part of their everyday lives is a landscaping activity that needs to be taken into account when addressing how IT is becoming integrated in our lives, in the society, and in the modern cityscape.

The focus on landscaping further implies an interest in not only the landscape as a fixed reality, but also in the process through which the landscape is constantly changing, reconfigured and adjusted through human actions and interactions, i.e. landscape as the process of landscaping.

The focus on landscaping is further on a straight-forward implication from recent research within the fields of computer science, informatics, human-computer interaction, interaction design, etc which all have paid special attention to questions related to the design and use of e.g. ambient intelligence, smart environments, ubiquitous computing, and pervasive computing (e.g. Ruyter & Aarts, 2004; Pousman & Stasko, 2006; Robertson, Mansfield, & Loke, 2006; Sengers, 2004) areas which partly deals with integration of IT in our built environment in one way or another.

If we concretize this reasoning we can see that the "built environment" can for instance be a room that can stand as a model for "physical surrounding". Rooms are part of buildings. One room can actually work as a building, but typically a building consists of a collection of rooms that together with outdoor walls and an exterior forms a building. Buildings are further on part of the modern landscape, and if a large set of buildings are built within close range of each other we can start to talk about a city and the cityscape. This book has an interest in this spectrum, scaling from IT integration in one particular room, to the size of the building, but also ranging from the building to the public spaces created outdoors in between the buildings, in the form of meeting spots, passages or as any other kind of resource for the commons.

In this book the notion of "landscape" is defined as the *visible features* of an area of land, including *physical elements* such as landforms, living elements of flora and fauna, abstract elements like lighting and weather conditions, and human elements like human activity and *the built environment*.

This definition of "landscape" contains three aspects of special importance for the reading of this book as indicated in italic above. First, it addresses the visible features. This makes this focus on landscapes and landscaping activities closely related to the notion of texture as used in this book. Second, this definition focuses especially on *physical elements* and their form, and not only on experiences which also connect the focus on landscape to the focus on materials and elements in this book. Third and finally, this definition connect to *the built environment* which in this book is the definition of architecture used throughout the book which makes it heavily connected to the focus on architecture as well.

When it is said in the definition of landscape that it is about the visible features of an area of land it is also important to reflect upon who is seeing these features, what are the features being seen, and whether or not everyone can see the same landscape, or if we all have our own interpretation of our surrounding and from that interpretation are capable of extracting different views of the landscape, or even different landscapes. This is partly a philosophical and ontological question closely related to e.g. phenomenological reasoning about whether or not there exist one world outside of us, or if we, to a large extent construct the world inside of us through the experience of the world and through our interpretations of what we experience (Borgmann, 1999; Heidegger, 1977).

From a more practical viewpoint landscapes are typically for everyone. Anyone can see their present surrounding and anyone can make their own interpretation of the surrounding. Some people see some aspects of the world, and some people see other aspects. Sometimes this is phrased as "in the eye of the beholder...", meaning that it is not only the objective world but also that world as understood by an observer. The skill of observing can further on be different from person to person. Some things are easier to see for some people. A trained eye can see other things, or see things differently, and a trained eye can see wholeness, patterns, and details. A trained eye can see the textures in the surrounding, and it can see how compositions of materials form the appearance of objects, places, surfaces and even larger architectural elements. The intention with this book is partly to give the reader some conceptual tools to see these things. Even though it might not be a straightforward path from having access to these concepts to a clear view the intention with this book is at least that these concepts can help people to train their own "eye" for how we read the world around us.

In the modern city we have access to the physical landscape around us including the buildings, the streets, and means of transportation, and we have access to various kinds of private and public places. But in the modern city we also have access to a digital landscape that is simultaneously available to us. While going on the bus downtown one can now surf the web, check the balance of the bank account, or stay in touch with friends and family without leaving the bus seat. With appropriate technology at hand and with the right skills anyone can access and navigate the digital landscape. Still, it is equally hard for the untrained "eye" to see, access, navigate and use the digital landscape. Of course, it is somewhat easy to see computers, including both hardware and software. However, it is harder to "see" the connections made across this highly networked landscape that enable transactions, channels, information flows, synchronization, data transfer, etc. However, with the current movement towards design and use of ambient information environments, interactive architecture and ubiquitous computing these two landscapes are merging, becoming blended, and becoming one. Through the digitalization of the city new landmarks are created in the digital landscape with its origins and roots in the physical world, and new digital imprints are making themselves visible throughout the city (Croon Fors & Wiberg, 2010).

From a more philosophical viewpoint, and as further described in the end of this book, the new landscape forming in-between the physical, the social and the digital is also to a large extent a temporal landscape. As part one of this book will describe in detail interaction with the digital is very much about the interplay in-between the human and the computational material, and is also very much about temporality. As such, the first part of this book with a focus on interaction and temporality connects to the forth and final part of this book in which I shift perspective from traditional spatial geography to a new temporal geography scaffold by the notions of *temporal rooms* and *spatial engagements*. In doing so, the question of temporality is framed both in relation to interaction, but also in relation to spaces and landscapes. As can be seen from the structure of this book temporality is first discussed from the perspective of interaction in which the notion of temporal form (Mazé & Redström, 2004) is acknowledged as an important perspective to understand interaction design. And then, in the end of the book temporality is discussed from a landscape and landscaping point of view in which issues of timing, timeliness, and rhythm makes the connection back to the center piece of this book, i.e. to new textures and to traditional architecture in which temporality related concepts including datum, rhythm, repetition, time and process are all classical concepts which now comes back into the picture again capable of also addressing the temporal aspects of new interactive textures. This meeting of the spatial, the temporal, the physical and the social, that is the overall scope of this book.

In outlining the overall idea on how to read this book I have now walked through the main conceptual cornerstones of the book in the order they are introduced and covered in each part of this book. In detail I have moved from the concept of interaction, via textures, to architecture and landscapes, to finally end up in landscaping and temporal rooms, which again takes us back to the beginning of the book. As such, it closes the circle, at the same time as it gives us a chance to also reflect upon this current development – i.e. how IT is becoming texturized in our everyday lives, in our cities, and in the architecture of the everyday.

Having outlined the cornerstones of this book including the focus on interaction, textures, architecture and landscaping the next section presents the overall structure of this book as to present how these different cornerstones are introduced, and how each part of the book follow upon each other, and an introduction to the different chapters of the book.

THE STRUCTURE OF THIS BOOK

This book consists of 10 chapters that relate to four overall themes or parts of this book. The four parts are labeled: (1) *"Motivation: Think Outside the Box"*, covering the general idea that we should focus on the temporal form emerging out of the interplay between people and computational material, and that we need to look into cases in which there is no longer only self-contained objects or "boxes" in the world typically labeled "computers" but in fact, to also rethink how computing is blending itself with our physical and social world. Computation and interaction with and through computational material are today found "outside" these boxes as computers are becoming materially and socially *embedded* and *ubiquitously* accessible. This first part of the book introduces the notion of *texture* as to address these two lines of development and how it might lead to the formation of new environments and a new architecture. The second part is labeled: (2) *"Foundations: Elements, Textures and Architecture"*. This part covers the ideas fundamental to building a conceptual deck for addressing a complete blending between the physical, the digital and the social for the purpose of establishing the notion of interactive textures that adds to the areas of interaction design and architecture, and also sets the theoretical ground for an area that can exist in between these two. The third part of the book is labeled: (3) *"Character: Cases and Concepts"* covering four of my own empirical research projects in which we have explored a range of texturation approaches – from the digital landscape mapped onto social mobility in the physical world to wall-size displays mounted in a physical space to create new forms of architecture. In this part the theoretical concepts outlined in part two is used to highlight these cases followed by a theoretical exploration of the notion of *interaction through textures* as one of the bearing concepts for this book. The forth and final part of this book is labeled (4) *"Exploration: There is no box"*. In this final part of the book I discuss the idea of interactive architecture in relation to the concept of "interaction landscaping" which I propose as a concept to address how people constantly configure their digital landscapes and how this might blend with the physical landscape. Further on, I discuss the general conclusions that can be drawn from this book and a new agenda for research and development that correspond to this current development.

From a structural point of view, the four parts of this book can be read independent of each other, but these parts can of course also be read as a single book from the first page to the last. As outlined above, the first part of this book is labeled *"Motivation: Think Outside the Box"*. This first part introduces the reader to this emerging field of computation, how it is becoming blended into our physical world, and how we might frame interaction in, with and thorough the new textures that modern information- and interaction technologies enable. As described above, the second part of the book is labeled *"Foundations: Elements, Textures and Architecture"*. This second part of the book takes on a more conceptual, analytical, and theoretical perspective in an attempt to bring out and provide some answers to questions like e.g. what characterizes these new environments?, how does it differ from traditional, non-digital, environments, and how has this been discussed in the literature? Further on, this second part of the book provides some analytical frameworks, and analytical tools for going about analyzing how modern information technology enables new interactive textures and new interactive architectures and which issues it puts in the foreground. The third part of the book is labeled *"Character: Cases and Concepts"*. This third part is devoted to practice and as such devoted to empirical cases that let us see the examples and illustrations of these new phenomenon and digital technologies as they integrate themselves in our physical world. Finally, the forth part of the book labeled *"Exploration: There is no box"* let us take a look around the corner to see what the future holds for us. Shortly speaking, it is about the cutting edge of how IT is becoming integrated in our society in a number of different ways, spanning from concrete integration in physical space to temporal integration in our everyday routines or life-rhythms.

Next follows a brief introduction of the 10 chapters in this book and how they relate to each of the four parts of the book as outlined above. As the following short descriptions of each chapter will show, the chapters in this book cover many different theoretical concepts which taken together contribute to the formulation of a vocabulary to address an emerging area in-between architecture and interaction design. I like to think about this area in terms of new textures and to think about this vocabulary as parts of a texturation theory in the making.

Let me now present the 10 chapters that taken together forms the body of this book. As described above, the first part of the book has the title "**Motivation: Think Outside the Box**". This first part of the book consists of the first three chapters in the book. As an ingres to this first part of the book called "A pre-interaction reflection – the breakdown of the box" I first start out with a general reflection around "the box" as a traditional framing of computers and how this box is now breaking down everywhere.

In chapter 1 called "*Interaction*" I then take "the breakdown of the box" as a point of departure for moving our thinking away from the boxes, and more in the direction of why interaction matters and why we should focus on interaction as a core element in any digital design project. As already outlined above there is an increasingly need to understand interaction as this turn-taking dance between man and machine, and even more importantly to understand interaction as a form that grows out of this interplay and how this dynamic form can be set through the process of interaction design. This first chapter makes the case that there is a need to understand what kind of different *relations* that we can have with the digital and that we can in fact form the character of this meeting. Interaction with the digital does not always need to be immersive, attentative and active, but it can also be more ambient and this chapter describes this current movement "out of the box" from desktop computers to ubiquitous coming and everyware as well as it describes the current movement from the traditional notion of users to a notion of inhabitant and why this might be an important distinction to make when addressing use of computational resources in an, if not already present, nearby future.

If we think about the movie Minority Report in which Tom Cruise is playing the lead character we can get a quite good idea of why interaction matters, and why we need to focus on this dance between human and machine, and not only pay attention to technology or human capabilities. In this movie Tom Cruise is interacting with a transparent wall size display using only a pair of interactive gloves. The interface is gesture based and filled with graphically pleasing, and animated functionality. However, it is not the half transparent display with the graphical interface, nor is it the interactive glows enabling Tom Cruise to interact with the interface that has made this particular scene from this movie so famous. Instead, it is the almost seamless and fluid interplay between the human and this wall size display that has caught the attention of the audience. This is probably due to the fact that the form of the interaction itself is so clear in this particular scene.

In the end of this first chapter there is also a discussion introduced concerning the design professions needed for the creation of future computational environments. From the area of participatory design (e.g. Muller, et. al., 1991; Törpel, 2005; Watkins, 2007; Fisher, 2008) we have learned that in IT-projects it is important to work in close collaboration with the intended users of a new system. Still, and even though the user side of this collaboration has been acknowledged in detail the same level of details have not been explored on the designer side of it. Instead, in most participatory design projects it has been assumed that the notion of "designers" is equal to e.g. programmers, interaction designers, information architects, system developers or something similar and it has not been addressed in detail. Instead, all design professions have been gathered under the general label of "designers". In this book the notion of "mixtures of professions" is introduced as to put a specific focus on the different design professions needed in the design of new interactive textures as implemented and highly situated as architectural elements, and as fully integrated in physical, social and cultural contexts.

Before moving on the chapter 2 of this book the discussion around boxes is re-introduced through the two sections "*A Post-Interaction Reflection: The Return of Boxes*" in which I discuss the trend towards new digital devices, and "Towards Clutter Or Texture?" in which I discuss appropriation of new technologies in relation to two approaches to structure our thinking around these new ecologies of computational materiality.

Chapter 2 of this book is called "*Textures Matters!*" and in this chapter the notion of "texture" is introduced in detail. The chapter starts with a critique of the graphical user interface as a working model for describing interaction with computational material when we're facing the recent developments towards ubiquitous, ambient, and embedded computing. As we leave the desktop computing paradigm and the computational becomes part of the physical we can move away from interfaces on surfaces (typically digital screens) and instead direct our focus on interfaces as integrated in any material, in any object and in any form. To grasp this movement the notion of texture is introduced to enable us to address new computational materials where the digital make use of the properties of physical materials to manifest instances for interaction, and where the physical is bent from static spatial form to new dynamic temporal forms through the power of the computational. In this chapter, this discovery and articulation of textures is highlighted and further outlined in terms of its implications for design of meaningful environments, and for the reading and rewriting of textures enabled and situated in-between the physical and the digital.

In chapter 3 called "*A New Architecture?*" I take one step back to review the most classical terms and concepts used and developed within the field of architecture. In this chapter the basics in traditional architecture are presented including the most fundamental concepts of points, lines, planes and volumes. In this chapter architecture is presented as a design approach to our built environment. Architecture is further presented as a way of understanding and analyzing our environment. In this chapter a discussion is also introduced on architecture as spatial form making in relation to architecture as temporal form making, and architecture as the crafting of social intervention processes. From this point of departure this chapter then introduces the argumentation from chapter 1 and 2 in saying that the blending of the physical and the digital into new transmaterials, and in the forming of new material practices, might also enable a new architecture to start growing. As we adopt new materials that integrate both physical and digital properties new environments can be imagined and realized which in turn sets a new agenda for architectural development. The chapter ends with a discussion on how these new interactive textures not only adds to the field of architecture, but also adds to the design space of possibilities in the sciences of the artificial, i.e. in research aimed at defining and designing preferred social, cultural and material contexts.

As outlined above, the second part of this book has the title "**Foundations: Elements, Textures and Architecture**". This second part of the book consists of the following three chapters of this book, i.e. chapter 4, 5 and 6. In chapter 4 called *"Enabling Technologies"* new materials are first discussed as one important foundation for interactive textures. Following upon this the architectural notion of elements is introduced as to contextualize the role of materials in architectural thinking. With a theoretical foundation established around materials and elements, the chapter then moves on to the introduction of the notion of compositions as to start a discussion on the structuring of new materials into larger architectural elements and built environments.

In chapter 5 called *"Theorizing Interactive Textures"* I further process the concepts introduced so far in this book into models and descriptions capable of defining, describing and analyzing how now interactive textures enable new spaces and how these new textures work as mediators between the world of human activities and the world of materials. In this chapter the notion of textures is related to the notion of representations, a term typically used in the areas of systems design, computer science, informatics, and interaction design to denote the "skin" or texture for a set of information. Further on, this chapter outlines a preliminary theory of new textures and discusses compositions of new textures in relation to notions of wholeness, appearance, value ground and design. The chapter then discusses textures as navigational aids from the perspective of how our surrounding work as sign and symbols, and how we use these textures in our everyday lives. As media gets blended into our everyday lives, tweaking themselves into new material constellations we get embedded computational power in the materials that we for long have read as "our reality". This reality sits in-between the virtual and the real, in-between the digital and the real making products of materiality meet with services of virtuality. In this chapter a discussion is introduced on how we might relate to these new textures in terms of interaction with and through the computational "skin" of our built environment.

While chapter 5 takes on a theoretical approach to the fundamentals of interactive textures in an attempt to work through this fundamental element another approach is introduced in chapter 6. Whereas chapter 4 and 5 looked into the details of enabling technologies and new interactive textures, chapter 6 take us through the fundamental structures and principles of the new wholenesses enabled and created through the complete integration and blending of the physical and the digital.

Making the transition smooth from a focus on details, enabling technologies and materials to issues of wholenesses the chapter starts with a section covering the spectrum from digital elements to interactive textures.

Having outlined the relation between digital elements and interactive textures chapter 6 then moves on to elaborate upon the relation between textures and architecture. While texture denotes the new surfaces, and the way in which digital technology becomes integrated in our physical world, thematically, functionally, and literary, then architecture is about the social processes and social spaces these new textures enable. The whole chapter follows this line of reasoning, moving from the small scale to the larger scope. Step by step, a systematic exploration of how new materials link to built environments, and how built environments form larger complexes situated in-between the physical, the social, the cultural and the digital. Accordingly, the next part of this chapter introduces the relation between architecture and environment in the context of interactive textures, and from this position the chapter ends with a discussion focused on the notion of "living systems" (ref) and how it unifies current perspectives within the area of interactive architecture with similar lines of thinking within landscape architecture.

The third part of this book has the title "**Character: Cases and Concepts**". This third part of the book consists of chapter 7 and 8 of this book. As outlined above, this third part serves the purpose of both providing concrete and empirically based examples of the textures addressed in this book (chapter 7) as well as it works as a bridge towards a more analytical and conceptually informed understanding of these textures as they become integrated in our digital, physical, social and cultural world.

In more specific terms, chapter 7, in this book called "*Five Cases: From Mobile Devices to Interaction Landscaping and the City*" provides us with five different empirical cases. Each case fills an important role in making the argumentation and practical demonstration of the limits, scope and character of digitalization "outside the box" of traditional computing. From one perspective, each of the empirical cases as introduced in this book works as a stand-alone example of how our surrounding is becoming digitalized. At the same time, and from the viewpoint of interactive textures as being the general theme for this book, the five cases are intended to be read as one complete narrative covering a movement from mobile digital devices to digital technology as integrated in the physical "skin" of our built environment, i.e. as an important enabling ingredient of any interactive architecture. A story that starts in one idea, in one exploration, and in one demonstration of digital integration in our physical and social world, and with a first point of departure taken in the notion of mobility, t then develop into a story which systematically grows and develops over the five different cases.

The first case introduced in chapter 7 is called "Case 1. Mobility: Supporting People Moving Around In Places". As a starting point for this story that will take us from mobile technologies to digital technology as integrated in our physical environment this particular example introduces a research project that I conducted during the years of 2000-2004. This particular research project included the development of the RoamWare system (Wiberg, 2001), a mobile system aimed at supporting mobile co-located groups in moving in-between physical and virtual meetings. As outlined in this chapter, the RoamWare system relied on relative location for a proximity-based service capable of generating an interaction history of buddy lists as the establish a bridge from co-located physical meetings to further online communication within a group of people. Following upon the description of the RoamWare system this chapter continues with descriptions of four additional mobile systems developed during this project all aimed at elaborating the role of the mobile in relation to the surrounding. These descriptions include a review and discussion around the FolkMusic system (Wiberg, 2004), a mobile peer-to-peer system for proximity-based music sharing, the MoveInfo system (Wiberg, 2008), a concept design for having mobile access to computational resources in the physical surrounding. The Negotiator system (Wiberg & Whittaker, 2005), a mobile phone based prototype developed for experimenting with the managing of availability in the interaction landscape. And finally, Midgets (Wiberg, 2007) as a design concept for application mobility across heterogeneous interaction landscapes.

The second case presented in chapter 7 is called "Case 2. Focusing on Places and Public Input Gates". This second case introduces a research project that I conducted in 2005 called WorldPortal (further described and elaborated upon in Wiberg & Stolterman, 2008). This second case moves the story forward from completely mobile technologies to a semi-mobile technology in the form of a physical installation with mobile Internet access. Through this second case introduced the discussion moves in the direction of the situating, and the manifestation of the computation in our built environment and it evoke a discussion about interaction with physical, although also computational installations, i.e. interactive textures, in public places.

Moving on from this second case, then the third case that I introduce in chapter 7 is called "Case 3. Focusing on Places and Public Output Gates". Whereas the World-Portal project was very much about experimenting with active input from people to a computational texture as manifested in a public place, this case introduces a design project run in 2007 in which we designed and installed an integrated public display outside of the ICEHOTEL in the far north location of Jukkasjärvi in Sweden. In this case, we experimented with the output aspect of integrated digital technology in a public place. More specifically, this case tells the story of how online data about a physical location can be brought back to that particular site, and be made available to the public followed by the outlining of the pros and consequences of closing that loop of physicality and online data about that physical space. As this chapter illustrate, the closing of the loop is technically easy, but hot always the most feasible approach to engage people in a certain location.

In the forth case called "Case 4. Totally Interactive Environments" as introduced in chapter 7 I move the story in the direction towards a research project that I ran in 2008-2010 in which we continued to work in close collaboration with ICEHOTEL on IT as an architectural design material. Throughout this project we elaborated with IT as not only being about its full integration in the physical environment, but in fact becoming an essential aspect of what defines the environment, a state in which the digital work in full interplay with the physical to the extent that the removing of the physical from the digital would be hard, if even possible if still wanting to keep the sense and overall architecture of the place intact.

As for a contrast to this somewhat futuristic case then the fifth and final case called "Case 5. Everyday City Textures: Times Square, New York" provides a somewhat different perspective in relation to the notion of texture and digital integration in our physical environment. In this case there is no fifth research prototype being introduced and described. Nor does it contain any research site or case study in the normal sense. Instead, this fifth case serve the purpose of being a reality check in terms of taking a look around, and to see what's actually out there in terms of new textures, and digital technologies, and to reflects upon the current development in a modern city from the perspectives of textures and adoption and integration of new digital technologies in our everyday world. As a suitable location for one such observational study this book targets Times Square in New York City, i.e. one intense area, both in terms of social activities in a city area, but also in terms of city development and adoption of new digital textures as part of the cityscape.

Having outlined these five research cases this chapter ends with a section in which I elaborate upon these cases in relation to the story these cases are telling as a reflection of over 10 years of research within this area. The chapter acknowledges some important trends related to: IT and the Internet (including the current development from products to services), IT and the physical world (including the development from functions to an aesthetics of the computational), and a reflection on mobile IT from the perspective of access to the virtual world in the physical world and vice versa.

Having worked through these different empirical cases then chapter 8 called "Interaction Through Textures" takes on a more theoretical account in an elaboration on the relation between humans, places and digital technology. The chapter starts with a discussion around the P3-framework (Jones, et. al., 2004) that deals with the relation between people, and between people and places from the viewpoint of digital technology. The chapter then moves on to a discussion about the discovering of interactive textures followed by a discussion of interacting with vs. being in relation to interactive textures. This discussion re-introduces the discussion initiated in chapter 1 on the notion of users vs. inhabitants, but now from the perspective of interactive textures rather than from a futuristic idea of ambient intelligence. Having re-introduced this discussion the chapter sets out to address the question about how to relate to this new texture in public spaces in a section devoted to public interaction rituals. Here, I introduce this discussion as the ultimate test since public interaction is not only about a relation between man and machine, but also about the acting out of interaction in public, i.e. on the public stage, thus potentially also in front of an "audience" from a Goffman (1959) based perspective.

The acting out of interaction in public space is challenging and in this chapter I also address this challenge in relation to the notion of conventions and how we might work with conventions for interaction design focusing on interaction with and through interactive textures. Following this line of reasoning, this chapter continues with a discussion on the embedding of "interaction knowledge" in the world.

The chapter ends with a theoretical take on interaction and textures and in doing that I propose the "IT (Interaction through Textures)-framework" as a conceptual frame for thinking about the intertwining of the physical and computational, and how we might interactive with and through these new computational resources and elements of our everyday world.

As outlined above, the fourth and final part of this book is called "**Exploration: There is no Box**". This final part of the book consists of the last two chapters of this book, i.e. chapter 9 and 10.

In chapter 9 called "*Interactive Architecture and Interaction Landscaping*" I discuss IT as an embedded element in our everyday world, followed by a discussion on IT as infrastructure and installed base and the implications from these arguments for the field of research growing in-between architecture and interaction design. As a contrast to this discussion on installed base, standards and infrastructure, which is heavily focused on structures, this chapter also introduces another current trend that seems to contradict with these stabilizing structures, i.e. the current lifehacking movement. From a point of departure taken in this bottom-up movement the chapter moves on to also introduce the notion of "interaction landscaping" as to elaborate our thinking on how people use computational resources. The chapter presents a modeling of the interaction landscape include a lens of 6 different usages that defines interaction landscaping including 1) the service landscape (concerned with offered use), 2) Drift (related to change in use), 3) Workarounds (denoting change of use/the alteration of use), 4) The Do it yourself trend (capturing invention of use/establishment and initiation of specialized use), 5) Service combinations (as dealing with the integration of use), and finally 6) Service sharing (as the "extragration" of use).

In this chapter I then move on to a discussion on the difference between design and landscaping as general approaches, followed by a discussion on top-down vs. bottom-up development of the interaction landscape and the establishment and manifestation of interactive textures in our built environment. Ultimately, the chapter sets out to question whether the texturing of digital technology in our built environment is only an issue for designers and architects, or whether in fact, it is a response to the technological imperative as it work its way across the modern society.

In the process where the digital texturizes itself into our modern society we can identify several trends following this movement. In the end of this chapter I work through these trends including the movement from the *digital imperium* to the *nano-use* as being part of a larger movement in this book elaborated through the phrasing of this process as the "long-tailing of interaction". This "long-tailing of interaction" further includes the movements "from monuments to moments", "from the giants to the gigahertz" and "from the individual to the masses" as important aspects of the growing bottom-up framing and re-framing of the digital, which I have decided to generally refer to as interaction landscaping.

In the 10ᵗʰ and final chapter of this book with the simple, clear and straightforward title *"Conclusions"* I try to re-location my line of thinking as developed throughout this book into a new position from which I am setting out to reflect upon the more general implications of this piece of work. In this chapter I do this through the three sections called 1) "A digital world", in which I reflect upon the ongoing digitalization of our society, 2) "A new agenda" as to address a space that both grows out in-between the physical and the digital, and more generally in-between the areas of architecture and interaction design, as well as forms itself around these two dimension creating a new space that do not situate itself in-between, but rather demonstrate itself as a new and important area of study. Here, it is suggested in this chapter that a new agenda and vocabulary is needed to address this space. Finally, the last section 3) "Temporal rooms and new spatial engagements" works as a tool to once again rethink the meaning and implications of new technology as it continues to develop and engage our modern society.

PERSPECTIVES ON THE AUDIENCE OF THIS BOOK

There are many different ways in which a book can speak to an audience, and there might be very different reasons for an audience to be interested, and pay attention to a particular book. Furthermore, in many cases there is not just one narrow or coherent audience for a particular book. Rather, and to the contrary, many different persons might be interested in very different aspects of a book, or show an interest in a book because of its certain topic, presentation, description, or framing of a particular phenomenon.

Accordingly, and from my perspective, this book might be read in several different ways depending on you as a reader of this work. From my own perspective, this book can be read, at least from a practical, theoretical, and educational perspective, as a scholarly work, or just as a resource for creativity and inspiration. In this section I will try to describe and outline my intended audience for each and one of these perspectives.

Starting off with the straightforward practical perspective I truly believe that this book might work as guide for advancing our understanding around current aspects of digitalization in our society with a specific focus directed toward the ongoing materialization of the computational as it manifest itself in our built environment.

While this book is foremost research oriented in its scope we should at the same time bear in our minds that research is in many cases also about historical reviews aimed at making foresights for the future, and about going back in history to be able to point at ongoing change processes in our society, i.e. to also contribute to our practical understanding of here and now. As to exemplify this for a moment we can notice how the research field of "tangible bits", a field ultimately focused on the integration of the physical and the digital, now, 13 years after its first research agenda was ones formulated and declared, has found its way out to the public.

Back in 1997 two visionary researchers, Hiroshi Ishii and Brygg Ullmer from MIT Media Lab in Cambridge, MA published their seminal paper "Tangible bits: towards seamless interfaces between people, bits and atoms" (Ishii & Ullmer, 1997). Their pioneering work set the agenda for a research area focused on the blending of the physical and the digital with a specific focus on what they called "tangible user interfaces" (or simply TUIs).

Today, 13 years later, I am just returning back home from the TEI (Tangible & Embedded Interaction) international conference held at the MIT Media Lab in Cambridge. This conference gathered around 200 researchers from all around the world to discuss and further our thinking, proofs of concepts and theories in this area. Today, on 29 January 2010 as I am returning back from this conference I pick up a copy of the Wired magazine at Newark International Airport. This current issue includes the central article "Atoms are the new bits". To me, this is a clear indication that the message is now out in the public sphere.

This book is for people interested in the enabling character of new materials. To further elaborate on the bridging of the physical and the real, the virtual and the real we can for instance notice how Amato (1997) in the book "Stuff" makes no separation between materials used to create digital devices and other materials used for any other purpose in the words. Clearly, the message is spreading as these two materials are coming together (atoms and bits).

The ongoing integration of the physical and the digital, the traditional and the new, is what this book is about and its intended audience for this book is assumed to be found in this area of interest. The indications for this integration happing right now is not, however, something that can only be spotted in the literature. Instead, this book is just reporting from the field about a clear integration process as it spans across our modern society. A recent and very practical example of this integration of the old and the new can be found in the New York University Book Store (see

Figure 4. Shelves with Aurdino kits, sensors, and electronic parts next to shelves of books in the old Book Store at Steinhardt School of Culture, Education, and Human Development, New York University

Figure 4). Here, traditional paper course books share the bookstore space with modern electronics components (including e.g. arduino boards, LEDs and various kinds of sensors, including e.g. stretch sensors, bend sensors, touch sensors, pressure sensors, and light sensors).

From a related, although more philosophical perspective this book is also intended for people interested in the ideas and philosophies forming around the integration of the physical and the virtual, the digital and the real. In this book a combination of future oriented perspectives, as the one formulated by William Gibson below meet similar thoughts as formulated within this field of research, e.g. by professor Hiroshi Ishii, founder and director of the MIT Media Lab in Cambridge, MA, USA.

As stated by the science-fiction writer William Gibson:

"One of the things our grandchildren will find quaintest about us is that we distinguish the digital from the real, the virtual from the real. In the future, that will become literally impossible."

In a similar way, professor Hiroshi Ishii (2008) has formulated that:

"At another seashore between the land of atoms and the sea of bits, we are now facing the challenge of reconciling our dual citizenships in the physical and digital worlds"

In this book, the proposed concept *Interaction through Textures* picks up this thread and provides the reader with a concise theoretical foundation valuable for anyone interested in understanding the potential and impact of interactive architecture and IT as an integrated material in our everyday world where no distinction is made between the physical and the digital, the virtual and the real.

Due to the scale of this ongoing development, ranging from the current development of small computational objects and how these manifest themselves in the physical world, to full-scale architecture and the computational textures emerging in the modern cities of today, to the multitude of complex ways in which the digital and the physical becomes intertwined and how this intertwines influences our modern society I would personally say that there should be a broad audience for this book.

Then again, from a scholarly, theoretical, or intellectual perspective this book is for anyone that seeks to enrich his or her thinking and understanding on how the complexity of the current blending of our physical built environment with modern computational materials – ranging from traditional information technologies to recent developments in e.g. ubiquitous computing, mobile devices, and ambient intelligence - not only provide us with new ways of accessing and interacting with information and other persons, but ultimately it challenge us in our thinking on integration of the physical and the digital.

From an educational perspective this book is for undergraduate and master students from a wide range of backgrounds studying e.g. classes in e.g. traditional architecture, or any subject related to new digital materials including e.g. courses in Human-Computer Interaction (HCI), Computer-Supported Cooperative Work (CSCW), interaction design, Computer-Mediated Communication (CMC), history of technology, media studies, etc. A broad range of professionals, including e.g. designers, architects, artists, hardware- and software developers, and technology users will hopefully also find this book useful, and so will graduate students who are moving into this area from related disciplines.

Furthering the scholarly perspective on this textbook, it could accordingly also serve as an intellectual tool for anyone interested in furthering our understanding of the ongoing digitalization of our built environment, our culture, and our society, and how the removal of the physical-digital distinction can be addressed and further conceptually framed given the theoretical backbone suggested in this book – i.e. texture.

THE VALUE OF THIS BOOK AND ITS MAIN CONTRIBUTIONS

The value of any book is relational. Typically relational both in terms of how well it speaks to, or manage to relate to, its intended audience, and reader, as well as in relation to current trends in our society, and how it manage to address, question, or in any other way relate to some aspects of our everyday lives.

While several books have provided good overviews of this emerging area of digital integration in our physical and social world, and have collected several illustrative examples of this current development, this book provides a theoretical basis for reflections, and for analysis of this emerging area. With a point of departure taken in traditional architectural thinking, combined with concepts that reflect the recent developments in the area of interaction design, this book creates a conceptual bridge between these two professions as to address this development from not only a perspective that highlights development of our built environments or a perspective focused upon the current digitalization but instead a perspective that integrate these two into one new and unique approach to this area.

From a scholarly perspective, the academic work reported in this book represents a perspective in which the uniqueness of this book appear as, and boils down to, a three-folded approach to sense-making around the current digital integration in our physical world.

First of all, this is a unique book since it is the first book published with an explicit focus on materiality from the perspective of digital technologies integrated in physical and social contexts. The notion of materiality also opens up new perspectives and an interesting discussion on how we might envision crafting of physical-digital compositions. Further on, the notion of texture enables us not only to discuss the relation between material properties and appearance, but also the appearance of one texture related to other materials in the formation of wholeness.

Related to the issue of materiality which brings texture into a richer framework on how physical-digital compositions are also embedded in a larger physio-social context we should also acknowledge the importance of an historical perspective on materials and how they form and enable new social practices. This importance of an historical perspective has also been further elaborated upon by Farelly (2009):

"To understand how to use materials effectively, a designer needs to have an understanding of precedent or how materials have been used historically and an awareness of innovations in material application. Both can provide a useful way to develop a range of design approaches." (Farrelly, 2009)

History provides perspectives, making us think and reflect on the present from the horizon of the past. As such, history teaches us about the present by connecting the today appearing with the matters of yesterday. From the historical bootstrap of this paper what we have learned is 1) to always make sure to have a good sense and focus on the materials used in any composition, and 2) that the crafting out the relations between material properties is related to the appearance of the wholeness, i.e. the relation between material and materiality. This unifying understanding of materiality that reaches back to material properties, via material appearance and further into a unified totality of materiality is further elaborated on by Lazzari (2005) that compares materiality with the human body from the aspect on how to read this as a relational unified unit of analysis:

"Material objects render palpable infinite kinds of relations, sensations, thoughts, and actions, most of which do not occur before our eyes, as archaeologists know so well. But this sort of paradox of presence through absence that things foreground can be compared to bodily symptoms: they are not the superficial expression of some inner, essential state, but they are the state of affairs itself" Lazzari (2005)

The notion of *"materiality"* this character of being material and composition of matter is typically and according to Oxford Dictionary defined as: *"1. the matter from which something is or can be made. 2 items needed for doing or creating something. 3 cloth or fabric. Materiality is 1. consisting of or referring to physical objects rather than ideas or spirit. 2 important; essential; relevant.".*

Materiality is heavily related to the physical world, in which compositions of materials forms larger structures of meaningful wholes. Simultaneously, materiality seems to transcends the merely material (Miller, 2005 extending into the shaping of the social (Graves-Brown, 2000; Miller, 2005). Miller (2005) the material might even serve as a basis for understanding the social making the material and the social inseparable, and in doing so we may refute the very possibility of calling anything immaterial, and we may want to refute a vulgar reduction of materialism to simply the quantity of objects (Miller, 2005, p. 4). In similar terms Lazzari (2005, p. 126) describes the dual character of matter, being simultaneously animated and inanimated. Following this line of thinking Suchman (2006) and Orlikowski & Scott (2008) introduce "sociomateriality" to challenge the assumption in contemporary Information Systems research that digital technology, work, and organizations should be conceptualized separately, and advances the view that there is an inherent inseparability between the technical and the social, in which materiality is a "recursive relationship between people and things (Lazzari, 2005). In fact, their work on the notion of "sociomateriality" re-introduces the classical debate in Information Systems research on the relation between the social and the technical, historically framed as the socio-technical perspective (e.g. Hirschheim and Klein, 1989). The advantage of the notion of sociomateriality to not distinguish between the social and the technical bridges an ontological gap between the social and the technical world previously upholded by the socio-technical perspective:

"Typically, a paradigm consists of assumptions about knowledge and how to acquire it, and about the physical and social world. As ethnomethodological studies have shown such assumptions are shared by all scientific and professional communities. [...] it is natural to distinguish between two types of related assumptions: those associated with the way in which system developers acquire knowledge needed to design the system (epistemological assumptions), and those that relate to their view of the social and technical world (ontological assumptions)". (Hirschheim and Klein, 1989).

Through the establishment of "sociomateriality" as an epistemological contribution this notion also unified the two worlds – the social, and the technical - on an ontological level. Following this unifying perspective Barad (2007) coined the term *onto-epistem-ology* as to further to indicate the impossibility to separate the ontological from the epistemological. In a similar way, Haraway (1991) uses the term material-semiotic, and Barad (2007) material-discrusive in order to indicate how the natural and the cultural, the material and the discursive, are inextricably intertwined, i.e. sociomaterial (Suchman, 2006).

In parallel we are now facing a second wave of ontological separation. While there seems to be a development in new perspectives to unify the ontological relation between the social and the material (being it merely physical, or partly digital), it is in this book argued that we need a similar unifying epistemology to approach and understand the relation between computational appearance, i.e. the aesthetics of the computational materiality, and the materials from which such materiality's are made, i.e. we need a vocabulary of computational materiality's capable of addressing, and crafting out, not only the relations between the human, the social and the computational (as so elegantly structured via e.g. the notion of "performing the perception" as the aesthetics of interaction, recently proposed by Dalsgaard and Hansen, 2008), but we also need a relational language that speaks to computation as a whole, across its material and immaterial properties, from the symbolic to the graspable, from the immaterial to the physically present and materialized. We think of this relational notion (epistemology) in terms of "texture" as a new ontological ground or mechanism to further our thinking on computational materiality, simultaneously viewing this as an important piece of theory to unify the social, the technical, the physical and the digital.

In concrete terms, we see different strands of evidences of a growing interest in the materiality of computation that signifies a shift in the modes of strategizing bridges across the physical-digital divide. This, we believe, is a "material turn" in interaction design (Robles & Wiberg, 2010).

Most evident in research on smart materials, interactive textures, and tangible interfaces is the recent developments in material science that fuel and inspire this development through making available a complete range of new dynamic materials including e.g. translucent concrete, shock-absorbing foam, thermochromic ink and e.g. nitinol wire, extending the scope of interaction design, from primarily a matter of graphics design to not only transcend into the physical world, but in fact fully incorporating and thereby redefining it as part of the interaction design canvas.

These two strands of development fuel a conversation filled with examples where no separation is *made,* or to that extent *meaningful* or even *possible,* between the physical and the digital. Current academic work in this area further demonstrates the "material turn" through the desire to begin treating the computer as just another material. Bdeir (2009) gives voice to a more general interest in *"bring[ing] electronic devices down to a material used in the design process by imagining electronic parts on the same level as paper, cardboard, and other materials found in design shops".* No longer content to rapidly prototype the computational with the non-computational, the designers are moving towards stripping away distinctions altogether. Similarly, Vallgårda and Redström (2007) read the computer as a material, analyzing the substances from which it is made, its surface, and structure, and then utilizing these properties as a springboard for discussing the potential properties of "composite computational materials" similar to the concept of "transmaterials" (Brownell, 2005; 2008).

This shift in the prioritization of the computational as material indicates the emergence of an aesthetic position of manifesting relations between the physical and the digital, between material composition and computational properties, and across computational materiality's, remarkably different from that of the Weiserian vision of ubiquitous computing, with its regard for pushing the computational towards disappearance in relation to the physical world.

Following this trend of a new materiality we can now witness how a range of everyday materials including e.g. felt (Reiger, 2007) and clay (Reed, 2009) are being re-imagined as substrates that can be invested with computational properties. The result is an activation of properties, always already there, that can be interacted with and experienced in wholly new ways. A large number of researchers are beginning to consider how a range of new materials – from shape memory alloys and fabrics to smart fluids that deform when exposed to current – might transform interaction design. This "material turn" indicates a kind of communal reaching towards a vocabulary for describing the management of material properties within a computational framework, i.e. within a relational language of computational materiality.

Explicit theorizing about computing through a material lens is also beginning to surface. On the one hand, Löwgren and Stolterman (2004) suggest that information technology is in fact a material without properties. As pinpointed by Vallagård & Redström (2007) that would paradoxically make it hardly qualify as a material. But, from Vallagård & Redström´s perspective what Löwgren and Stolterman (2004) are hinting at is the way in which information technology seems to exist in-between the material and the immaterial, with properties so flexible it almost can take on any form imaginable thus paradoxically in itself, and through its application serving the objective of ontologically unifying the physical and the digital, the material and the computational.

Following from this recent development in the area of computational materials designers are now beginning to address more basic material properties across a broader range of substrates. This more fundamental treatment has proven rather powerful for generating new design insights at a variety of scales, including the architectural. Shutters (Coelho & Maes, 2009) a computational re-design of a common building element, louvers, is not merely another example of embedding digital functionalities within a traditional object. On the contrary, Shutters manifests and materializes the interaction design concept of "soft mechanics", a move away from hard structural joints and towards soft forms. By viewing the architectural in the context of computing, they re-consider as well the material properties of the origi-nally material form. The result is a new kind of re-forming texture for apertures on louvers.

This strategy of moving towards a complete unification of digital and physical materials into a coherent composition has inspired a range of useful techniques in the repertoire of interaction design – from sensors and context-aware computing to ambient and calm computing.

Tangible computing, perhaps best characterized by Ishii & Ullmer (1997) and the Tangible Bits as it manifests the larger research program on atoms and bits begins with the premise of bridging the digital and the physical. Paradoxically though, while talking about digital and physical materials as one, or to that extend unifications of atoms and bits keep them apart. And this upholding of one such dis-tinction is also to uphold a design space preoccupied with bridging this divide. To let go of the fundamental distinction between the physical and the digital, between the virtual and the real begs the question, what, then, kind of design space might emerge? Here we foresee e.g. the crafting of new materials situated in-between, at the same time unifying and transcending the digital and the physical. We view this crafting out of new materials as part of a larger conversation around a new materiality which reaches beyond typical interaction design questions on how to apply a certain material for any given purpose or application, but instead we seek to reach into the new computational materials *per se* for the purpose of crafting out an understanding of these materials, and to organize our thinking on how one such understanding might be capable of resolving some of the relations between computational material appearance and material properties, this in turn to fuel a larger conversation about a new materiality that to a large extent constitute our modern society, in this book – we propose one such initial concept to initiate this conversation, i.e. texture.

However, in order to start addressing this distinction, and to ontologically and epistemologically address the current divide we need a language or vocabulary (Löwgren & Stolterman, 2007; Krippendorf, 2005) enabling as to not only describe what we're seeing, but also help us in re-framing the seemingly obvious as to further unveil the more integrated aspects of new materiality's i.e. to then disrupt any per-spective that upholds current distinctions between the digital and the physical and instead aim for the development of concepts capable of speaking relational across any material assemblage from perspectives and scales ranging from e.g. product design to full scale architecture.

Similar to contemporary research on the "aesthetics of interaction" (e.g. Graves Petersen, Hallnäs and Jacob, 2008; Dalsgaard & Hansen, 2008; Rullo, 2008; Red-ström, 2008; Wright, Wallace and McCarty, 2008) who have initiated an in-depth scholarly dialogue that advocates a vocabulary that speaks to the relation between the social and the computational material, thus opening up an interesting discussion on how we as humans relate to computational materiality, this book seek to establish an encompassed vocabulary with a point of departure taken in the notion of texture to speak fluently in guiding physical-digital compositions at any scale of design.

Secondly, and speaking about different scales of design projects, this is a very unique book since it takes on the question on how to fully integrated digital technology in our built environment at the scale of architecture.

The exploration around IT as an important material and how it changes the very nature of architecture is a focal concern for this book. Further on, and from the opposite viewpoint, this integration of digital technology in our built environment also changes our relation to IT. From being a focal technology occupying our attention this strand of development now re-situate digital technology in the periphery, blended into the everyday textures of the cityscape. While this movement is on one sense a manifestation of the latest developments in the area of digital technology that enable us to design new dynamic surfaces, a much wider question has to do with the basic relations that exist between materials and architecture as a more fundamental and deeply historically rooted issue. As formulated by Farrelly (2009):

"Materials create an ambience and provide texture or substance to architecture. To understand how to use materials effectively, a designer needs to have an understanding of precedent or how materials have been used historically and an awareness of innovations in material application. Both can provide a useful way to develop a range of design approaches." (Farrelly, 2009)

This quote is indeed a multidimensional one in that it addresses not only the relation between materials, texture and architecture, but it does further on link the importance of historical perspectives on new material innovations and how it relates to the craftsmanship of doing design.

Related to this, and as a third and final uniqueness, this book dwells into this craftsmanship from the perspective on how a design is not only a thing for designers, but instead a process better described in terms of landscaping in which the inhabitants of the city and the new interaction landscapes provides continuously keep developing and adjusting the landscape according to their needs and their activities. As such, the city architecture, including its digital textures keep developing creating a modern history of digital integration as new interactive textures.

From this perspective, the point of departure taken in this book in new materials as a step away from a pure social analysis of technical development paradoxically brings this conversation right back into that debate. However, the perspectives offered by the notions of materiality and texture puts as in a new, exciting and more advanced position in regards to how we could view digital technologies, emerging social practices and our everyday physical world as one solid object of study.

RESEARCH CHALLENGES: TEXTURES AND A NEW MATERIALITY

There are of course a number of research challenges that follows from an object of study framed as being about the intertwines of our physical, social and digital everyday.

Having set the focus on how digital technologies gets integrated in our physical world we need more empirical studies describing new dynamic materials in use from the perspectives of how the digital not only blends into the physical world from a functional and aesthetical perspective, but also how it blends into our social everyday, forming new social practices, and how it scaffolds and enable new social activities.

We also need to do experimental hands-on research with these new materials. I.e. to try them out, experiment with those materials and discover these new material properties from the perspective of design.

Another research challenge includes the further development of the theoretical perspective proposed in this book in which no distinction is made between the physical and the digital. This development also needs to be complemented with research into methodological approaches to further study and generate new knowledge about IT is integrated in our physical and social world. This will be heavily related to finding new ways ways to structure our thinking as to address this new wholeness (i.e. an ontological and theoretical challenge).

Following this line of reasoning, another challenge has to do with the development of a relational language that can enable us to talk about these new materiality's that transcends the physical into the digital and vise versa. In this book this is viewed as not only a conceptual challenge, but also a semantic one in terms of developing a language around the notion of texture to address issues working across material properties and material appearances, and across the scale ranging from raw materials to complex constructs of material assemblages.

From a broader perspective the unification of the physical, the social and the digital will have a great impact on how we explore and make analysis of our modern society, and it is likely that this proposes research challenges that moves us in the direction of a need for research in the areas of e.g. a new sociomateriality (Orlikowski & Scott, 2008), research into the ethics of things (Introna, 2009), historical backdrops as to organize our thinking around an archeology of materiality (Meskell, 2005) as to in different ways capture the sociocultural aspects of materials, as to scaffold our thinking with the important implications that we need to know given the history of materials in use, in design, and as just materials.

REFERENCES

Addington, M. & Schodek, D. (2005) *Smart materials and technologies for the architecture and design professions*. New York: Elsevier, Architectural Press.

Amato, I. (1997). *Stuff – The materials the world is made of.* New York: BasicBooks.

Barad, K. (2007). *Meeting the Universe Halfway – Quantum Physics and the Entanglement of Matter and Meaning*. Durham & London: Duke University Press.

Battarbee, K. (2003). Defining Co-experience. In *Proceedings of Conference on Designing Pleasurable Products and Interfaces, 23-26 June, Pittsburgh* (pp. 109-113). ACM.

Bdeir, A. (2009). Electronics as material: littleBits. In *Proc. TEI 2009* (pp. 397-400). ACM Press.

Beyer, H., & Holtzblatt K. (1998). *Contextual Design*. San Francisco: Morgan Kaufmann Publishers

Borgmann, A. (1999). Holding on to Reality: The Nature of Information at the Turn of the Millennium. Chicago and London: University of Chicago Press.

Brownell, B. (2005). *Transmaterial: A Catalog of Materials That Redefine our Physical Environment*. Princeton Architectural Press.

Brownell, B. (2008). *Transmaterial 2: A Catalog of Materials That Redefine our Physical Environment*. Princeton Architectural Press.

Bullivant, L. (2005). *4dspace: Interactive Architecture, Architectural Design*. Wiley-Academy.

Ching, F. (2007). *Architecture: Form, Space, and Order*. New York: John Wiley & Sons, Inc.

Coelho M., & Maes, P. (2009). Shutters: A permeable surface for environmental control and communication. In *Proc TEI 2009* (pp. 13-18). ACM Press.

Croon Fors, A. & Wiberg, M. (in press). Digital Materiality as Imprints and Landmarks: The case of Northern Lights. *International Review of Information Ethics*.

Dalsgaard , P., & Koefoed Hansen, L. (2008). Performing perception—staging aesthetics of interaction, *ACM Transactions on Computer-Human Interaction (TOCHI), 15*(3), 1-33.

Dalsgaard , P., & Koefoed Hansen, L. (2008). Performing perception—staging aesthetics of interaction, *ACM Transactions on Computer-Human Interaction (TOCHI), 15*(3), 1-33.

Farrelly, L. (2009). *Basics Architecture: Construction + Materiality.* AVA Publishing.

Farrelly, L. (2009). *Basics Architecture: Construction + Materiality.* AVA Publishing.

Fisher, G. (2008). Challenges and Opportunities for Distributed Participatory Design (DPD). In *Proceedings of CHI 2008*, April 5-April 10, 2008, Florence, Italy. ACM Press.

Forlizzi, J., & Ford, S. (2000). The Building Blocks of Experience: An Early Framework for Interaction Designers. In *DIS 2000 Conference Proceedings* (pp. 419-423).

Goffman, E. (1959). *The Presentation of Self in Everyday Life.* GardenCity, NY: Doubleday.

Graves Petersen, M., Hallnäs, L., Jacob, R. (2008) Introduction to special issue on the aesthetics of interaction. *Transactions on Computer-Human Interaction (TOCHI), 15*(4).

Haraway, D. (1991). A Cyborg Manifesto: Science, Technology, and Socialist-Feminism in the Late Twentieth Century. In D. Haraway (Ed.). *Simians, Cyborgs, and Women. The Reinvention of Nature* (pp. 183-201). New York: Routledge.

Heidegger, M. (1977). *Question Concerning Technology and Other Essays.* New York: Harper & Row.

Hirschheim, R. & Klein, H. (1989). Four paradigms of information systems development, *Communications of the ACM, 32*(10), 1199–1216.

Introna, L. (2009). Ethics and the speaking of Things. Theory, Culture & Society, 26, 25-46.

Ishii, H. & Ullmer, B. (1997) Tangible bits: Towards seamless integration interfaces between people, atoms, and bits. In *Proc. CHI 1997* (pp. 234-241). ACM Press.

Ishii, H. & Ullmer, B. (1997) Tangible bits: Towards seamless integration interfaces between people, atoms, and bits. In *Proc. CHI 1997* (pp. 234-241). ACM Press.

Ishii, H. (2008). Tangible bits: Beyond pixels. In *Proceedings of the Conference on Tangible and Embedded Interaction.* ACM Press.

Jones, Q. et al., (2004). People-to-People-to-Geographical-Places: The P3 Framework for Location-Based Community Systems. In *J. Computer Supported Cooperative Work, 13*(3-4), 202-211.

Krippendorff, K. (2005). *The semantic turn: A new foundation for design.* CRC Press.

Lazzari, M. (2005). The Texture of Things: Objects, People, and Landscape in Northwest Argentina. In L. Meskell (Ed.), *Archeologies of Materiality.* Blackwell Publishing.

Lee, K. M., & Nass, C. (2003). Designing social presence of social actors in human computer interaction. In *Proceedings of the SIGCHI Conference on Human Factors in Computing Systems* (Ft. Lauderdale, Florida, USA, April 05 - 10, 2003), CHI '03 (pp. 289-296). New York: ACM.

Löwgren, J, & Stolterman, E. (2007). *Thoughtful interaction design: A design perspective on information technology.* Cambridge, MA: MIT Press.

Löwgren, J. & Stolterman, E. (2004). Design av informationsteknik: Materialet utan egenskaper. Studentlitteratur AB. Lund, Sverige.

Mazé, R. & Redström, J. (2004). Form and the Computational Object. In *Proceedings of CADE 2004*, (Malmö, Sweden)

Meskell, L. (Ed.) (2005). *Archeologies of Materiality.* Blackwell Publishing.

Miller, D. (Ed.) (2005). *Materiality.* Duke University Press.

Muller, M., Blomberg, J., Carter, K., Dykstra, E., Halskov, K., & Greenbaum, M. (1991). Participatory design in Britain and North America: Responses to the "Scandinavian Challenge." In *Proceedings of CHI '91 - the SIGCHI conference on Human factors in computing systems: Reaching through technology.* ACM Press.

Orlikowski, W., & Scott, S. (2008) Sociomateriality: Challenging the Separation of Technology, Work and Organization. *The Academy of Management Annals, 2*(1), 433–474.

Pousman, Z. & Stasko, J. (2006) A taxonomy of ambient information systems: Four patterns of design. In *Proceedings of AVI '06 - the working conference on Advanced visual interfaces.* ACM Press.

Randle, V., & Engler, O. (2000). *Introduction to Texture Analysis: Macrotexture, Microtexture, and Orientation Mapping.* Singapore: Gordon and Breach Science Publishers.

Redström, J. (2008). Tangled interaction: On the expressiveness of tangible user interfaces. *Transactions on Computer-Human Interaction (ToCHI), 15*(4).

Robertson, T., Mansfield, T., & Loke, L. (2006). Designing an immersive environment for public use. In *Proceedings Participatory Design Conference*, Aug 2006, Trento, Italy. ACM Press.

Robles, E., & Wiberg, M. (2010). Texturing the "material turn" in interaction design. In *Proceedings of the Fourth International Conference on Tangible, Embedded, and Embodied Interaction* (Cambridge, Massachusetts, USA, January 24 - 27, 2010), TEI '10 (pp. 137-144). New York: ACM.

Rullo, A. (2008). The Soft Qualities of Interaction. *Transactions on Computer-Human Interaction (TOCHI), 15*(4).

Ruyter, B., & Aarts, E. (2004). Ambient intelligence: visualizing the future. In *Proceedings of AVI '04 - the working conference on Advanced visual interfaces* ACM Press.

Sengers, P., et al (2004). Culturally Embedded Computing. *Pervasive Computing, 3*(1).

Shedroff, N. (2001). *Experience Design.* Indianapolis, IN: New Riders Publishing.

Sheridan. T. (2000). Interaction, imagination and immersion some research needs. In *Proceedings of the ACM symposium on Virtual reality software and technology (VRST '00)* (pp. 1-7). New York: ACM.

Suchman, L.A. (2006). *Human–machine reconfigurations: Plans and situated actions.* Cambridge, UK: Cambridge University Press.

Törpel, B. (2005). Participatory design: a multi-voiced effort. In *Proceedings of CC '05 - the 4th decennial conference on Critical computing: between sense and sensibility.* ACM Press.

Vallgårda, A., & Redström, J. (2007). Computational composites. In *Proceedings of CHI '07 - the SIGCHI conference on Human factors in computing systems.* ACM Press.

Watkins, J. (2007). Social Media, Participatory Design and Cultural Engagement. In *Proceedings of OzCHI 2007*, Nov 2007, Adelaide, Australia.

Weiser M. & Brown, J. S. (1996). The coming age of calm technology. In P.J. Denning & R.M. Metcalfe (Eds.), *Beyond Calculation: The Next Fifty Years of Computing.* New York: Springer Verlag.

Weiser, M. (1991). The computer of the 21st century. *Scientific American, 265*(3), 66-75.

Wiberg, M. (2001). RoamWare: An Integrated Architecture for Seamless Interaction In between Mobile Meetings. In *Proceedings of GROUP 2001, ACM 2001 International Conference on Supporting Group Work*, September 30-October 3.

Wiberg, M. (2004). FolkMusic: A mobile peer-to-peer entertainment system. In *Proceedings of the Thirty-Seventh Annual Hawaii International Conference on System Sciences, HICSS37.* Hawaii, USA.

Wiberg, M. (2007). Midgets: Exploring the Design Space for Truly Liquid Media. In *Proceedings CMID '07, 1st international conference on cross-media interaction design* - 22-25 March, Hemavan, Sweden.

Wiberg, M. (2008). Re-Space-ing Place: Towards Mobile Support for Near Diagnostics. In D. Hislop (Ed.), *Mobility and Technology in the Workplace*. Routledge.

Wiberg, M. (Ed.) (2004). *The Interaction Society: Practice, Theories, and Supportive Technologies*. Hershey, PA: Information Science Publishing.

Wiberg, M., & Stolterman, E. (2008). Environment interaction: Character, Challenges & Implications for Design. In *Proceedings of the SigMobile and ACM conference "MUM 2008 the 7th international conference on Mobile and Ubiquitous Multimedia."* ACM Press.

Wiberg, M., & Whittaker, S. (2005). Managing Availability: Supporting Lightweight Negotiations to Handle Interruptions. *ACM Transactions of Computer-Human Interaction (ToCHI), 12*(4).

Wright, P., Wallace, J., & McCarthy, J. (2008). Aesthetics and Experience-Centered Design. *Transactions on Computer-Human Interaction (TOCHI), 15*(4).

Section 1
Motivation: Current Thinking
Outside the Box

Pre–Interaction
Reflections:
The Breakdown of the Box

There are I guess different approaches to kick-start a book. One way is to picture a future scenario and then step-by-step illustrate by going from chapter to chapter just how far we have come in relation to this future scenario. Another approach is to take one step back in an attempt to provide some perspective on the current development of today. This book is advocacy for this second strategy.

Moving back in time to the mid 60th we situate ourselves right in the middle of a period heavily occupied with the construction of "the box", i.e. the computer or the computing machinery which we today label PC, desktop computer, laptop, or even netbook. People like Alan Kay and Douglas Engelbart pioneered this development in their development of the computer and laid the ground for the computational box. Their work did however not only cover the realization of the computational box, but also the design of various input/output peripherals that could be attached to the box. Moving along this line of development the term "interaction modalities" was soon framed to talk about different interactional approaches to "the box" as a way of accessing the computational from the world outside of the box, in a sense creating ways from the outside to the inside of the box.

After the establishment of "the box" followed a whole movement in terms of development projects related to the crating of new "virtual" worlds within the box. This development has been referred to as e.g. VR - Virtual Reality, online communities, and virtual worlds.

Right now we are facing a third important phase in the development of our approach to computational power. Instead of building "the box", or building worlds within "the box" we can, through the current development towards *ubiquitous computing* recognize the first signs of the "breakdown" of the box. Behind this development is Weiserian goals of making the computer disappear into the background of our attention, taking it to the level of abstraction where it gets absorbed into the world that up until now has been distinguished from "the box" and has been about everything outside of "the box".

In a sense Mark Weiser turned "the box" inside out through the formulation of the ubiquitous computing vision. No longer should we strive to build worlds within "the box". Instead, we should draw computers out of their boxes, out of their "electronic shells" and let computational power blend into our everyday lives:

"Indeed, the opposition between the notion of virtual reality and ubiquitous, invisible computing is so strong that some of us use the term 'embodied virtuality' to refer to the process of drawing computers out of their electronic shells." (Weiser, 1991).

This goal of moving computational power out of the box is now happening with digital services in "the cloud", grid computing, internet access everywhere, and embedded computational power mounted inside almost any everyday object – ranging from the electronic shaver to any modern car.

With this development we can notice a movement of applications and services re-placing themselves outside of the box. In a sense, and as a pre-interaction reflection we might now face the breakdown of the box as we used to think about the computational. In this pre-interaction reflection I first started out with a general reflection around the work in the 60th to establish "the box" and how this has become the stable way of framing computers. Now, however, the box is breaking down everywhere. We have a current movement going from desktop computers towards ubiquitous computing. In this movement "the box" loses its focal position. Given this movement an important question remains, i.e. "If "the box" is breaking down, and the computational becomes part of our everyday lives, then when is left?". My short and clear answer to this question is basically - "interaction". Having that answer in place we do however now need a better understanding of interaction from this viewpoint and better knowledge about interaction from the viewpoint of texturized computational power and design. The first chapter in this book is therefore devoted to this important issue, i.e. the modeling of interaction as a form element in itself.

Chapter 1
Interaction

Interaction is a core element of any digital design – or design of "the digital". Interaction provides us with the tools and ways of using, manipulating, changing and developing digital material. While interactivity deals with a specific character of digital technology as a dynamic material, interaction also includes the human in the loop, i.e. the interaction with digital technology as an interactive material. In international research areas like Human-Computer Interaction (HCI), or Interaction Design (IxD) we can notice that interaction is a core aspect of the object of study. Still, most research conducted in these areas are concerned with either human factors or design of computer support in HCI or "Design" as a specific approach to IT in the field of Interaction Design. Similarly, in sub areas of research like "Mobile Interaction Design", or "Social Interaction Design" the focal object of study is "mobility" or "social behaviors" rather than a focus on the character of interaction *per se*.

In this first chapter I specifically set out to elaborate on the notion of *interaction* as a fundamental concept for understanding the current development of IT-use as a movement from desktop computing to *everyware* (Greenfield, 2006) including the movement from mobile to ubiquitous computing.

Here, interaction is viewed as the multitude of intersectional processes between humans and digital technologies that enables computer supported actions to be undertaken.

DOI: 10.4018/978-1-61520-653-7.ch001

In doing so, this first chapter introduces and describes the rise of Ambient Informatics and present Mark Weisers vision of ubiquitous computing as a point of departure for addressing the essence of interaction, and as a point of departure for the construction of *interaction through textures* as an analytical framework for understanding interaction with and through interactive architectures.

FROM DESKTOP COMPUTING TO UBIQUITOUS COMPUTING TO EVERYWARE

Since the introduction of the Personal Computer (PC), in the mid 80´s, i.e. the "PC era" we have witnessed a tremendous development in the area of digital technology. In just 20 years the computer has transformed from being a slow, clumsy and stationary unit to become a lightweight, mobile, and instantly accessible device that has found its way into our everyday lives (Greenfield, 2006). Today, the modern computer is so highly interwoven and blended into our everyday lives, activities, routines, hobbies, and leisure hours that we have started to use terms like *embedded, ubiquitous* and *pervasive* computing to describe this disappearing character of modern IT. This development was predicted 15 years ago by Mark Weiser who stated that: *"For ubiquitous computing one of the ultimate goals is to design technology so pervasive that it disappears into the surrounding"* (Weiser, 1991) and in his paper "The computer for the 21st century" he continue to argue that: *"the most profound technologies are those that disappear. They weave themselves into the fabric of everyday life until they are indistinguishable from it"*.

Today and in a foreseeable future this trend is likely to continue. Many of our surrounding everyday physical environments are changing character as they get blended with new digital material. They are becoming increasingly interactive in a way we have not earlier experienced. These new interactive environments are often portrayed as being responsive, active, sensitive, and in a constant dialogue with us as users or inhabitants. While this trend started out with quite simple and small-scale examples of so called TUIs (tangible user interfaces) in which a user can interact with, and manipulate, digital material though the interaction with physical objects, this trend is now developing on a large scale basis due to the development of new *transmaterials* (Brownell, 2005), i.e., physical material with interactive characteristics, and with current movements towards the creation of ubiquitous computing landscapes realized through e.g. interactive wall installations, mobile devices and small size computers. This trend is captured in terms like *ambient intelligence* (e.g. Lindwer, et.al., 2003; Aarts, 2005; Gárate, et.al., 2005) *smart environments* (e.g. Siegemund, et.al., 2005; Das & Cook, 2006), *interactive environments* (Pinhanez, & Bobick, 2003) and *interactive architecture* (e.g. Zellner, 1999). Malcolm Mc-

Cullough (2004) has argued in his book "Digital ground" that this change towards fully interactive environments has fundamental implications for both the area of architecture as well as computing as we used to know it.

While it sure has been a fast moving transformation concerning the role, form and function of the computer over the last 20 years this transformation do, on the other hand, have some milestones that can be extracted from this process.

In the mid 80s the focus was very much directed towards the computer *per se* and how to develop it to fit human needs including the development of the graphical user interface (GUI) and better input and output devices (including better screen resolution, the mouse, WIMP (Windows, Icons, Menus and Pointers) de facto standards for GUIs, etc. While this focus on the development of the computer itself was successful there were some voices raised about the danger of applying a machine-centered orientation to life instead of a person-centered view (Norman, 1993). In line with this argument a lot of attention were given to the area of human-computer interaction (HCI) in which a human-centered approach was adopted to guide the design of new digital technologies.

From this point the area of HCI has developed in all different kinds of directions and today there are subfields of research and development into any aspect of computing including e.g. novel input devices, gestures, VR, mobile devices, wearable computing, computer graphics, sound design, etc. and into all different kinds of application areas including e.g. pervasive games, e-health, office work, transportation, education, process industry, etc, etc. With all this technology available it becomes important not only to focus on the human according to the human-centered approach, or the computer, but to address what kind of *interaction* that we should arrive at, and to develop an approach to arrive at a preferred interaction between humans and computers. With interaction in mind the chosen approach were *design*, and in 2002 the current efforts made in this area were published by Preece, et.al., (2002) in the book Interaction Design which summarized and provided valuable insights into the design of digital interactive systems and a design-oriented approach to interaction technologies.

We have also seen a broadening of the scope from an initial focus on the individual to collaborative aspects of interaction or interaction technologies in areas like CSCW – Computer Supported Cooperative Work and CMC – Computer Mediated Communication, and in recent studies of the interaction society (Wiberg, 2004) in which interaction technologies has been considered as being part of a bigger interaction landscape, i.e. as an important infrastructure for modern social interaction. While the field of CSCW opened up for a distinct focus on our social world, i.e. "the turn to the social" as formulated by Grudin (1990) and how to design digital products and services in line with observations of how people communicate, collaborated and coordinate their activities the notion of the interaction society function as a concept that describes how these technologies have now found their way out of the research and development labs and have become an integrated part of the textures of our everyday lives.

In the same way as digital technology has found its way into our everyday social world we can now witness a similar process as this technology gets completely integrated in our physical world. Now, when this trend hits the modern society with its full potential we can seriously start to talk about a digital ground for our society (McCullough, 2004) and *everyware* as a general notion for *"The Dawning Age of Ubiquitous Computing"* as formulated by Greenfield (2006).

What we see in front of us now is an evolving interaction landscape. A landscape with physical, social and digital connotations that provides architects and interaction designers with new challenges and opportunities for designing our built environment.

At the same time we can witness individuals everyday activities directed towards the remodeling and reconfiguration of this evolving interaction landscape. In the book *Digital Ground: Architecture, Pervasive Computing, and Environmental Knowing* the author Malcolm McCullough (2004) provides us with many valuable insights related to the interaction landscape of today by combining the trend towards ubiquitous computing with knowledge from the area of architecture. In doing so, he outlines a field of computing that holds the potential to restructure physical space and our relation to it. A field that will quickly become an important area of study for anyone interested in architecture, planning, and urban design.

With this point of departure and with the interaction society already in place, in which e.g. mobile phones, mobile email, social networking services, mobile blogs, etc. is a natural part of how people come together we can really start to talk about "social city design" not only from a traditional viewpoint, but also from a point of view of interactive architecture as the *planning for interaction* perspective, and interaction landscaping as the *interaction in the making* perspective.

If then taking a step back again to reflect upon the current development it is one trend that surface more than other, i.e. the trend towards ubiquitous computing. This concept is right now surfacing in almost any computer related context. But what does it mean? If checking the term "ubiquitous" it has its origin from the modern Latin word "ubiquitas" in which "ubique" stands for "everywhere". So, what is it that is "everywhere"? Well, from my point of view I think that we need to consider this concept in several different contexts including:

1. Mobile computing
2. Internet
3. Embedded computational power
4. Interaction

Mobile computing enables us to carry computational power with us everywhere. And mobile computing is now almost everywhere[1]. On the other hand, it also makes good sense to think about the Internet in terms of being ubiquitous. Today, web pages can be accessed from any location on our planet and from a wide range of different platforms and devices. By 2007 over 798 million people around the world accessed the Internet or equivalent mobile Internet services such as WAP and i-Mode at least occasionally using a mobile phone rather than a personal computer (http://en.wikipedia.org/wiki/Mobile_phone).

But of course, the Internet of today is not only about web pages and email, but in fact an infrastructure or communication material that has found its way into a wide range of software applications and physical devices.

Google Earth is one good example of this trend (see Figure 5). Google Earth is a software application that is partly a software application that you install on your computer, and partly an Internet service.

However, the term "ubiquitous" might also refer to embedded computational power in everyday physical objects and devices, or even "embedded internet" in traditional analogue objects. The nowadays-popular "internet radio" device like The Vooni Internet Radio (www.vooni.com) is just one example (see Figure 6).

Another example is the Roku Soundbridge (www.roku.com). An internet radio devices that can be connected to the home stereo to play internet radio on a regular stereo set. A Soundbridge can also via a WiFi network connection stream music from any online music library on any computer on the same network as the Sound-

Figure 5. Screenshot of the Google Earth application

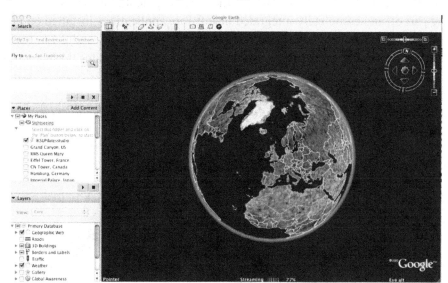

Figure 6. The Vooni Internet radio (www.vooni.com) and the Roku Soundbridge (www.roku.com)

bridge and play the music through any ordinary stereo equipment. Following this line of development we can see several examples of embedded internet services in e.g. alarm clocks, mobile phones, cars, refrigerators, etc. The combination of real-time information, embedded computational power, but all this still manifested in physical objects is a trend that has just started and a first sign of the digitalization of the textures of everyday life. In a nearby future it is very likely that we will see more examples of this blend of the digital with the physical and the Ambient Orb and the Ambient Umbrella might be two good examples of this trend.

The Ambient Orb (see Figure 7) tells its user about changes in the stock market through changes in the color of the physical Orb. Similarly, the Ambient Umbrella lets you know when rain or snow is in the forecast by illuminating its handle. Light patterns intuitively indicate rain, drizzle, snow, or thunderstorms based on automatically received local weather data from www.AccuWeather.com.

These are all examples of new Internet services as being embedded and blended into the objects, fabrics and the textures of our everyday surrounding.

Another trend of the "ubiquitous Internet" development is in terms of Internet being part of, and completely integrated in software applications installed on PCs, mobile phones, and on handheld devices. Here, the functionality and the access to online data are in focus. Instead of interacting with online websites these applica-

Figure 7. The Ambient Orb and the Ambient Umbrella (http://ambientdevices.com/)

tions are partly installed on the device to access peripherals and system resources (including e.g. computational power, memory, microphone, accelerometers, etc) but they also include Internet resources to make the interaction experience happen. So, instead of interacting with one single webpage the user have an interface capable of simultaneously interact with and trough several online resources.

One such example is the Midomi application which is a music search application for the iPhone 3G. In this application the user is asked to sing for 10 seconds into the iPhone mic. After that the application uses speech recognition to translate the song into an online query to an online music database. The database returns a list of search results related to the request and the user can then, by just clicking through the list listen to a few seconds from each song. Simultaneously the application sends another request to two additional online resources, i.e. the iTunes database and the YouTube database to check if the songs found can be bought from iTunes, and if there is a related music video to watch on www.youtube.com. As such, the Midomi application collects several different Internet resources and makes use of them in the creation of one new service for its user. In this way the application also saves a lot of work for the user compared to if he or she should have first run a speech recognition application to get the song into the computer. Then take the lyrics and use it in a more traditional Internet search to find a resource that provides a playable version of that particular song. Then, it would take separate actions to go into iTunes store to see if the song is there in case the user wants to buy it, and then log onto www.youtube.com and again search to see if there are any music videos related to this particular search. So, instead of going online to these different web sites the

Figure 8. The Midomi application running on an iPhone 3G

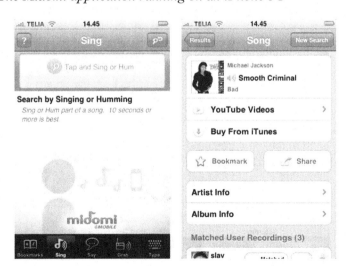

Midomi application is a good example of the "ubiquitous internet" in terms of how it gets blended into traditional applications. Figure 8 illustrate the interface of the Midomi application.

In this sense, these examples above illustrate that "ubiquitous internet" can refer to mobile Internet access, Internet services embedded in physical objects, or even Internet resources embedded in software applications.

In a similar way as in the Midomi example, the WeatherBug application (see Figure 9) collect weather information from the online website http://weather.weatherbug.com/ but present it in an interface with the same look and feel as any other iPhone application with only the most important information is presented including temperature, wind speed and wind direction and a three day forecast of the weather conditions. At the same time, the WeatherBug application collect images from different locations so that the user easily can tap the button labeled "Cameras" to get updated pictures of the weather conditions at different particular locations.

In this way the Internet becomes ubiquitous in several senses, it is integrated in several ways in the software application. But it is also a way of connecting to several different locations, and about bringing these different locations together in one single interface.

Still, "ubiquitous" can also refer to interactional issues beyond integration of dispersed resources. In fact, if we take a point of departure in the term "integration" and then move over to a concept like "transition" we can see that the term "ubiquitous" can also denote "being everywhere", and "being together from anywhere". As we integrate different resources into applications like the Midomi application or the WeatherBug we need to carefully think about the *composition* of the integration,

Figure 9. The WeatherBug application running on an iPhone 3G

i.e. the way that we bring together different information resources, and they way we implement functionality on top of these resources, as well as how we present the whole application as a whole is a really focal issue for any modern digital design. The integration of different internet resources in this sense can in fact completely redefine the use of a digital object, and redefine the whole meeting between a user and a piece of digital technology as we used to know it, i.e. a transition.

Another good example of *integration as transition* is the Ocarina application (see Figure 10 for two screenshots).

Ocarina is a software application, or actually a digital instrument that runs on the iPhone 3G. The Ocarina application uses the built in loudspeaker to play the tunes that is played on this instrument. However, and far more interesting is how the developers of ocarina used and integrated three of the other resources available on this machine, including the microphone, the multi-touch screen, and the wireless Internet connection.

Through a smart composition of these resources a new and novel instrument could be designed that completely changed the phone into a new musical instrument. To play on the Ocarina the user holds the "flute" with two hands like any traditional flute, and then blows into the microphone (see the yellow arrow indication for this in Figure 10, left) while at the same time taking different chords on the multi-touch screen. As the cords are played these tunes are then made available for others to access via their own Ocarina software as a real-time internet-based browser interface to the Ocarina players around the world (see Figure 10 for an example screenshot).

This unique integration of these different resources into a consistent whole changes the mobile phone into an "internet flute". However, the change is not about

Figure 10. The Ocarina application running on an iPhone 3G

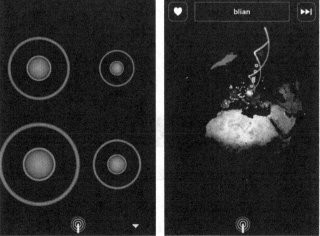

the device itself, but rather the way we interpret the interactional form associated with it. With this new form the device communicate a new *functional behavior,* and a new way of presenting itself to its user. At the same time, we can see how this device now demand a different *interactional commitment* from its user to get the interaction going, i.e. it builds upon the same interaction paradigm as a flute to play by blowing and pressing different parts of the instrument. Here, this is realized through the blowing into the microphone and through the touching of the instrument's interface (see Figure 11 for an illustration).

Finally, this new interactional form can then be represented online, and through doing that the Ocarina demonstrate a new kind of online social community, in which people can tap into, and listen to the playing of other Ocarina players in real-time, from any location in the world.

Further on, it is not only the interaction that is changed. In fact, the basic underlying technology has been redefined from being a mobile phone, to now being a flute. Also, our notion of what a flute is has been changed here. From a music instrument that is non-digital and used for local listeners to now being a digital instrument with a potential world-wide audience through being an internet flute based around an idea of an online music-sharing community.

If taking a step back and reflecting upon this device and software application we can see how it is in fact "ubiquitous" in several different ways. In one sense, the Ocarina application demonstrate another example of the ubiquitous internet, in the way internet technology is integrated and put to use to make this application work as described above. From another perspective, it is also a good example of a ubiquitous service, in the sense that it can be used everywhere, and finally, we can see it from the perspective of "ubiquitous interactional outcome", from the perspective that the music played locally can be listen to from any location in the world.

Figure 11. A user playing flute on the Ocarina application running on an iPhone 3G

From another strand of observations we can however make a far more interesting observation, and that is about how this application presents itself to the user. It is obvious that this application builds upon a different interaction paradigm, and that the user is expected to interact with the device in a completely different way than if using the device as a mobile phone. In fact, noting about the Ocarina application, or the way to interact with it remind of any interaction with a mobile phone. In a sense, the Ocarina application present the phone to its user as "a different phone", or in fact, not even a phone, but instead as a new device, or alternatively formulated, as a new everyday texture!

This small analysis might not be considered important just yet, but that has more to do with a matter of *scale* rather than whether or not it constitutes an important add to the elements that can define or even redefine the current interaction landscape.

If also extending our thinking about ubiquity and textures in another direction we can notice a strong development in the area of embedded computational power, or as it is sometimes labeled "embedded systems".

The embedded systems paradigm is guided by a strong vision about myriads of interlinked, networked computers that have been embedded in everyday objects, ranging from household equipment to the process industry. Today, a modern car comes with a huge number of computers, configured in different networks, and with an even larger number of sensors attached to these computers. In fact, the car is soon more about the digital than about the mechanical, and there is a whole field of research called "Telematics" looking into this development. The same goes for the process industry, for the development of remote diagnostics systems, and for the development of high-precision power–cranes, etc.

This development of "ubiquitous computing power" also include "embedded-ness" in our everyday lives and how computational power becomes completely blended with our everyday activities, and in fact leads to new everyday activities in themselves, to the extent that we do not think of them as being separated from the rest of what view as our surrounding, our activities, or our world.

From a birds-eye perspective we are witnessing an ongoing digitalization of our society, a development towards an interaction society (Wiberg, 2004) realized through powerful informatics, sometime labeled "ambient informatics (Greenfield, 2006), including the wide-spread adoption of mobile technologies, Internet use, and embeddedness of computational power.

From my perspective it is a development towards more and more digital, and digitalized services, a development that includes more and more digital devices, and more and more interfaces. In this sense, the interaction interfaces are themselves becoming ubiquitous.

As obvious from this description above it seems like the trend of ubiquity goes in all different directions to the extent that it might soon not be fruitful to use it as an analytical concept any more. So, if ubiquity is about "the way in which computational power finds its way into the fabrics of everyday life until it is indistinguishable from it" as formulated by Weiser (1991), then what concept might we use to address what is observable, and becoming apparent in this development? In this book I suggest that "textures" might just be that concept that can give us a conceptual tool to looks into the signs of how ambient informatics is forming today's interaction society.

I build this understanding on a basic assumption about the disappearing computer trend, and the raise of ambient information spaces. Further on, I build this on the current movement towards pervasive and ubiquitous computing, and on Weiser's (1991) idea about *"processing power so distributed throughout the environment that computers per se effectively disappear"*, and I reply to this statement about the current development arguing that we need concepts that not only address the disappearing aspects of computing, but also the appearing aspects, i.e. concepts capable of capturing the ways in which the appearing aspects of the interaction society might present itself to us as inhabitants of these digitalized environments.

So, in many ways we might say that there is a current movement towards a *ubiquitous computing paradigm*. It concerns the applications, the devices and the ways in which Internet and computational power gets blended into over everyday lives. In fact, in almost any aspect of our everyday lives. But on the other hand, this trend has a flip side, in that this development is also about a new *texture* taking form as part of our everyday world. Soon, we might be able to interact with almost anything, at anytime, from anywhere, and as a consequence interaction, and interaction design will thus be at the forefront of our concerns.

While both the ubiquitous computing paradigm, and the new textures might be somewhat abstract and hard to grasp there are some more visible signs of this development in our surrounding. Interactive architectures, which is a core object of study in this book is one such visible sign. And, the visual has always been important to us as humans. Through what we can observe we interpret and make sense of the world around us. The problem with the ubiquitous computing trend however is that most of it is invisible, and secondly, it is a fairly slow process which makes it even harder to spot. So, instead of trying to identify the underlying processes that drives this development, a more direct and more easy approach might be to just notice the instances in which this movement surface and then backtrack the development from these concrete examples. From my perspective, interactive architecture is one such visual sign or indicator.

So, given this development, how might we as humans relate to these new environments? Or, if formulated in another way, what might interaction with digital material look like and be about given this recent development?

To me, it is obvious that interaction will follow the same path of development as the general development of computing, Internet, and embedded computational power, i.e. interaction will also be ubiquitous or if re-formulated as a concept we might properly address human engagement with the digital as *"ubiquitous interaction"*. In terms of ubiquity, people now interact with anything, anyone, everywhere, and at anytime. In other words, interaction itself is becoming ubiquitous as the interaction landscape is growing and becoming instantly more widespread and complex.

So, it is quite important to notice that people are an important component here, and they engage themselves in this development, i.e. the development of ubiquitous interaction. If looking back say 20 years from now then we can clearly see the difference. 20 years ago synchronous remote interaction was basically achieved through one basic media, i.e. the telephone. While there were also a couple of broadcasting technologies around including TVs and radio, the basic two-way interactive session was typically short, seldom held, and typically isolated to this particular media.

Today, the situation is something altogether different. Media switches during active interactive sessions and *outeraction* activities to establish new interaction in between persons is becoming the normal state of interpersonal dialogues (Nardi, et. al., 2000). Soon, we might even leave the term sessions since we're right now multitasking within and in between different sessions and we create computational support that enable us to merge sessions, move sessions between devices, and we develop technologies for session awareness and session overviews (Wiberg, 2001). Currently people are not working with separated short-term sessions. Instead, we constantly deal with ongoing, multithreaded sessions and today we have the technologies developed to support this behavior including e.g. (wireless networks, usb-sticks, web accounts, security data traffic/encryption, authentication (who is who), and authorization (who is allowed to do what?) techniques.

In terms of frequency in use we can take one simple example. It is not uncommon nowadays that people check their email more than 60 times/day, or even constantly). Today, people have equipped themselves with digital technologies to make sure that they can have constant awareness of the email inbox activities, and when they are away from their PC they have a mobile email client running on their mobile phone, blackberry, or any other personal device.

In this emergent landscape of ubiquitous interaction we´re not isolated from each other. The model is not about individual work and isolated task or activities. Instead, the focus is on the landscape, and the inhabitants of this landscape, i.e. the persons around us. For this landscape we develop digital services that enable us to stay together although we're geographically apart and to share and co-create although we have different points of departures. Digital services like Twitter, facebook, linkedIn, myspace has enabled us to build and re-build our social networks and as such, these technologies has shaped a new interaction landscape for interpersonal communication, interaction and collaboration.

When sessions grow to session landscapes, when applications can move between devices, and when computation is separated from specific computers it will make less sense to focus on user interfaces, than to focus on the essence and character of interaction per se, i.e. to actually focus on the persons working and living in this landscape, and how we might be able to build digital solutions capable of contributing to this current trend. However, in order to make to shift from interfaces to interactions we also need to redefine how we model to human as part of this system or session landscape. In this redefinition I propose that we should leave the notion of a user, focus on persons and end up with an understanding of how to support the inhabitants of computationally scaffolded environments.

In the next two sections we therefore set out to argue for this shift of notion from user to inhabitant and from a focus on interfaces to interaction per se.

FROM COMPUTERS TO USERS TO PERSONS TO INHABITATS

If we look at computers and how these machines are currently changing from being distinctive physical and computational objects in the world, to becoming integrated, blended, ambient, disappearing, and "ubiquitous" computational materials, than that is still a perspective that is all about computers or computational power in different forms. This way of describing the current development is thus a highly technology oriented view.

On the other hand, when we talk about a human-centered perspective we sometime tend to forget about the technology in our efforts to describe the human, her needs, social situation, etc.

Thus, a challenge for anyone interested in understanding the current texturation of information and interaction technologies in our everyday world is to find a focus of analysis that is situated in between these two stereotypical worlds, i.e. to focus on the links or space in between rather than to focus on computers and humans as isolated entities. From my perspective, this "thing" in between computers and humans is interaction!

So, given the recent trend in which it is said that technology is disappearing, then one can at the same time ask the question of what it is that is "appearing" in this movement? If picking "interaction" as this thing that is emerging out of the meeting between computers and humans we can use "interaction" per se as a unit of analysis for understanding how technology is disappearing, and in fact, how the human is "appearing" more explicitly due to this current development.

In the 80s we had some focus on the user of computer systems in terms of a focus on e.g. ergonomics and human factors. In the 90s a big focus was on usability issues related to computer applications and a lot of new technologies, interface standards, etc were developed to make it more easy for persons to use a computer system. Today, however, the focus is less on aligning the computer and the user as it is about understanding us as humans from a much more rich perspective in which we take into consideration humans as creative, mobile, spontaneous, social and so on. Given one such enriched understanding of the person interacting with computers we have explored areas like "embodied interaction", "affective interaction", "tangible user interfaces", etc and we have explored new interaction modalities including e.g. gesture based interaction, mobile interaction and e.g. multi-touch displays.

Through this development we have not only fitted the computer to the human, but we have in fact explored new human activities, and capabilities for interacting with computational materials.

Over these years we have also shifted our perspective on the human *per se*. In the 80s and 90s it still made sense to talk about humans as "users" of computer systems. Basically, because "use" could be distinguished as a separated activity, in most cases taking place in front of a stationary computer, during a limited time, typically referred to as a session.

Today, it is however not equally easy to distinguish "use" from other everyday activities. Today we live with information technologies as a material, technique, tool and enabler and we do not make any hard distinction between everyday life and the one hand, and IT use on the other hand. Instead, these two are becoming one inseparable lifeworld. In this modern world we in fact have constant sessions running, and we tap into these streams of interactions now and then from our computers, mobiles, etc. People are still geographically bounded, but at the same time, they have access to information, friends and communication at anytime, and at almost any location. Through mobile email, twitter, facebooks and LinkedIn, just to mention a few digital services, we now have our conversations with others textured through digital channels, as a truly integrated part of our everyday lives. With mobile email a person can communicate asynchronously across any distance and across different time zones. Facebook and similar online social networking services brings geographically dispersed persons together over the net, and professional network services like LinkedIn connect our professional networks to enable new collaborations.

Computer infrastructures, communication networks, the internet and mobile devices co-creates a computational grid across our traditional landscape, and the next step probably includes a large scale digitalization of buildings, objects and public places as well. Together these resources form the basis for interactive environments with ubiquitous computational power accessible at anytime, digital services available throughout this landscape, and interaction modalities ranging from mobile interfaces to locationally situated interactive materials. This landscape might be best described as an interaction landscape, or a multitude of interconnected interactive environments similar to the description of P3-systems, i.e. People-to-people-to-places systems as described by (Jones et. al, 2004).

In these new interactive environments it might soon be appropriate to leave the notion of "user" behind. In everyday conversations people do not necessarily experience that they "use" their environment. We all know that we seldom talk about our homes as something we "use". Instead we live in our homes. We live, move, stay, and travel in cities and environments, we don't use them, except in extraordinary cases. An understanding of these new environments will probably have to shift the focus from use to being or living (Wiberg & Stolterman, 2008). As a result of this, we believe that the recent interest in experience in HCI research is highly appropriate when it comes to understanding this shift from "users to "inhabitants" and we can see promising attempts in this direction (McCarthy & Wright, 2003; Croon Fors, 2006).

When we inhabit these landscapes services will be constantly available, surrounding so physically and virtually, and it will be just a matter of how to find, "read" and tap into the sessions and services running as to actively engage ourselves in these new interactive environments.

To manage this "tapping in" activity we probably need to develop new interaction modalities since, in many cases this tapping will be in mobile settings, in public places, etc and it will not about single and simple sessions and services, but rather about service navigation and service selection in a complex of multiple ongoing and overlapping sessions. As such, the interaction landscape will probably appear in a similar complex structure as nature has revealed itself to us as humans as being highly complex although being structurally well organized if studied in detail.

However, while new interaction modalities, new devices and novel software and services are probably highly needed in order to cope with the increasing needs to effectively navigate and make use of this texture of services, devices, infrastructures and new materials, we believe that a far more challenging area is to develop a good understanding of this movement, and to develop a "language" for how to read these environments. I.e. there is a need to theorize, conceptualize and analyze this current movement, and to bring new conceptual notions into our everyday language as to be able to address and talk about this phenomenon as it is currently expanding across our society.

In this book we argue that "interaction through technologies" or in fact, "interaction through *textures*" might be one such conceptualization capable of faming at least one dimension of this current development. A focus on new textures will take into account the relation between computational materials, traditional materials, and the representational possible to create with these ingrediences. At the same time, this perspective in which these three aspects are conceptually separated, although they are fully integrated in practice, touches upon an understanding of a complex interplay between man/woman, the physical and the digital, and the virtual and the real in which we might pay more attention to the *effect* and *affect* associated with different forms of interaction in terms of active engagement with our surrounding interaction landscape rather than on humans, computers and their surrounding context as three different objects of study.

As we act with and through digital technologies we also engage ourselves as inhabitants in the modern interaction landscape. We access and use the digitalized textures around us, and at the same time our actions, and thus ourselves also becomes textured in the very act of doing this. Through this process, the interactive textures grow from its fundamental basis in various forms of computational materials into the social world of human interaction.

If thinking about interaction and the texturing of information and interaction technologies in terms of scale, we have already seen how the interaction landscape has scaled from the stationary computer, to laptops, handhelds and mobile devices, as well as it has scaled from local applications to database solutions, internet applications and services in "the could".

In architecture the notion of scale has always been an important concept, and in order to understand the next step in the digitalization of everyday environments, our built environment, and public places we might need to connect our thinking within the field of interaction research with the field of architecture, and to connect our understanding of digitalization with conceptual notions such as "scale".

So, what might future computational interfaces look like? Who will "use" these interfaces, and what could we call the "users" of these interfaces? To me, the only obvious answer is that if it is soon meaningless to separate use of computers from any other human activity, if computational power and computational materials are soon inseparable components of our modern world, then we should also switch from a notion of "users" to the notion of inhabitants as to truly acknowledge that information and interaction technologies today are a true integrated material element and activity in our everyday world.

In this world it might also be appropriate to exchange the notion of "user interface" or simply "interface" for the alternative notion of "interaction" for the very same reasons. If our whole surrounding becomes occupied with interfaces, if soon, the surrounding is a multitude of interfaces, then it would not make much sense to try to separate out interfaces from other textures in our surrounding. More about that in the coming section.

FROM INTERFACES TO INTERACTION

GUIs or Graphical User Interfaces was the main design paradigm of the 80s and 90s when it came down to finding solutions for man-machine interaction. Graphical user interfaces was the general label for screen-based solutions for human-computer interaction and it quickly became the leading interaction paradigm. Still, almost 30 years later graphical user interfaces are still the main design direction for traditional computers and digital devices (although some people still prefer commando prompt interaction).

If looking at graphical user interfaces on a very general level we can notice that the design typically concerns the *spatial layout* of graphical elements. This might be an obvious observation, but I would like to argue that this is an extremely important perspective since this also means that user interface designers have a 30 year long tradition of thinking about geography and places in terms of *spatial layout* although the spatial thinking in many cases, and in terms of scale, has been limited to a certain screen real estate and design for small displays.

However, we're now about to take the next step in computerization. People are taking about mobile systems, embedded systems, ambient intelligence, the GPS revolution, geo tagging, locative media, and not at least about ubiquitous computing and how new computational materials will be a challenge for architects (McCullough, 2004) and city planners (Greenfield, 2006). This implies that the screen real estate, as the typical canvas for interaction designers to work with, will grown from the standard 17 inches display to the environment as it will scale from the computer to the room, to the building, to the block, to public places, to the city and so on (Wiberg & Stolterman, 2008). In this sense the interfaces will grow to the scale of the surrounding, the surround will become an interfaces, or at least a mixture of interfaces sometimes interconnected, and sometimes synchronized. In one such environment in which we as people will live, i.e. to occupy as visitors, citizens or inhabitants we need to rethink our core focus as interaction designers. If interaction will be ubiquitous we first need to change perspective from a narrow first-person perspective on human-computer interaction, in which in focus on getting the man-machine loop to become well-functioning to a third person perspective in which we start a discussion about the very form of interaction per se, i.e. how we want interaction with and through digital materials to be situated in public places and in social settings. And in this thinking we might need to rethink interaction modalities for public interaction as to not only support efficient and natural interaction, but also to support meaningful behavior and think about how to develop graceful interaction modalities as will build interactive systems in which its user might be observed by others as they engage these computational materials in their activities.

When interaction technologies goes public at the same time as they get blended into the materials of our built environment and our social settings we might need to address the challenge of designing for "interaction in spaces" a challenge that I believe that interaction designers might be prepared to do due to their ability to carefully consider the *spatial* aspects of interaction design.

However, interaction is also very much about the *temporal dimension*. It is about how the interplay between the human and the machine unfolds over time and how computational power scaffolds interaction between people as they co-create their shared and personal interaction histories.

Some researchers (e.g. Maze, 2007) have argued that it is the *temporal form* of computational materials that should be the main focus for interaction designers. This, since the temporal dimensions of the digital is what makes it different from other materials as we know them. Any other material typically has a spatially defined form, a certain extension in space. Digital materials on the other hand, might also have a certain spatial form, but maybe more importantly, this form is dynamic and it can quickly change, or slowly change over time dependent on how its form is programmed to evolve over time, and dependent on our interactions with and through this material.

Over the years researchers and practitioners within the field of Human-Computer Interaction and Interaction Design have developed a large number of methods and techniques including e.g. Story boards, Use cases, Scenarios and Scenario-based design to address the temporal dimensions of interaction design. These efforts taken are all evidences of the importance of this temporal form and these methods developed serve as good examples of how interaction designers have struggled to find ways of capturing the temporal dimensions of how interaction unfolds over time. Although these methods and techniques has been developed to acknowledge this dimension of digital materials it should at the same time be noticed that so far we still lack good representation techniques describing the temporal aspects of interaction, or to describe the temporal character of an interactive product, application, service or environment.

Anyway, in my view, and according to the argumentation above it is my strong belief that Interaction designers has spatial and temporal thinking as two core competences which make them well prepared for the next wave of computerization of our society and our built environments.

With this point of departure taken we can now move over to a perspective that highlight *interaction* rather than *interfaces*, and towards a new perspective that extend the very notion of interaction from being about the kind of narrow line that in any simple model of human-computer interaction connects the human and the computer in a sense-and-respond feedback loop. Here, this extended perspective goes under the general level of *interaction per se* and it is about a perspective that thus focus on the understanding of interaction, on the modeling of interaction, and the form aspects of interaction as it constitute a whole space and material possible to tackle and address from a social point of departure as well as from a technology based design-oriented perspective.

To present this new perspective I will take a simple point of departure in maybe one of the most simple models of human-computer interaction that we can imagine, i.e. a model consisting of a human, a computer and some kind of interaction in between these two entities represented as a thin line that connect these two (for a schematic drawing of this see Figure 12).

In doing so, this first section of the book now continues to discuss the concept of interaction *per se*. In most textbooks in the area of HCI and interaction design the concept of interaction is combined with some additional concept to give it some meaning. Typical examples of this is e.g. "social" interaction, or "mobile" interaction. While this might make it easy for people to understand what interaction is really about, it does on the other hand in fact shift the perspective and our reflections away from the notion of interaction *per se*, and instead trick us into thinking about the other concept simultaneously introduced together with the concept of interaction. For the notion of "social interaction" our thoughts go in the direction of teamwork, coordination, roles, division of labor, turn-takings, etc. The similar is true for the notion of "mobile interaction" which might draw our attention to a line of thinking that might include e.g. the mobility of people, mobile professionals, and mobile devices. Clearly, the emphasis is on the added word while not much is said about interaction *per se*.

If looking into the literature in this direction of additional interaction concepts added we notice the coining of concepts such as "embodied" interaction (e.g., Klemmer et al. 2006), "tangible" interaction (e.g., Hornecker & Buur 2006) "social" interaction, and "seamless" interaction (e.g., Wiberg 2001) as well as a wide set of models of "mobile" interactions (e.g., Hinckley et al. 2000). However, while these models more specifically address various types of interaction and in doing so help to categorize different kinds of interaction, they fail to address interaction *per se*. In fact, the adding of another word before the word "interaction" in order to be more specific can be interpreted as a further sign of the lack of good ways to describe interaction *per se*.

The addition of a descriptive additional concept moves the focus away from the concept of interaction towards that descriptive. In adding a word like "embodied",

Figure 12. A basic schematic model of human-computer interaction

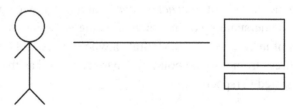

"mobile" or "social," the focus changes to the descriptive word, the added word, or the two words together, but avoids addressing how those added words change or add to our understanding of interaction *per se*. These additional words can help us learn more about a certain "use" context, or particular user need important for design, that should, however, not be confused with attempts made to formulate more detailed models about interaction *per se*.

In this chapter an attempt is made to address the concept of interaction as such. To do this the concept is first defined, followed by a discussion of the typical notion of HCI – Human-Computer Interaction in which I argue that we need to understand interaction in terms of *intersections* rather than *connections* in order to understand the creation, inclusion, attachment and sharing of places and objects as part of our everyday interaction with digital material.

So, if now going back to the typical model of human-computer interaction we can quite clearly see that it is a model that deals with a basic understanding of interaction as this *connection* between man and machine. In the most basic models this is typically framed in HCI as being about the three basic elements of humans, computers, and the interaction in between them in models like the one outlined in Figure 12. This connection-oriented view is the most typical view of Human-Computer Interaction in models that describe this as a loop between the user and the computer via input/output flows (e.g. Heim, 2007).

If carefully studying this model of interaction we can notice that it is really a computer-centered model. The computer is in focus. Interaction is just the thin line in the model that connects us as humans to this computational machine, and the very notion of human-computer interaction highlight that it is our interaction with computers or computing machinery that is the central aspect in focus for this basic model.

In reviewing the literature in this genre of HCI models from a graphical perspective it becomes obvious that most of the focus has been on humans and computers with very little focus on modeling the interaction *per se* (in these models, interaction is typically represented only as a thin line in between the human and the computer). This is also the case when reviewing the amount of academic literature published in the area of HCI, i.e. most literature on HCI is concerned with human factors or understanding humans interacting with computers, or about design of computer support to scaffold human activity.

According to Dubberly et al. (2009), these canonical models of human-computer interaction are structured along a basic archetypal structure – the feedback loop. In their description of this basic structure, they describe how information flows from a system through a person and back to the system again. It is argued that the driver of this loop is a person with a goal, and that he/she acts to achieve it (provides input to the system), measures the effect of the actions taken (interprets output from the system), and compares the results with the goal. The outcome of this comparison then directs the next action taken by that person. Dubberly et al. then describes Norman's "Gulf of execution – Gulf of evaluation" interaction model (Norman, 2002), as well as Norman's "Seven stages of action" model (Norman, 2002) then outlines three important additional questions in relation to these simple feedback-loop models of interaction: -"What is the nature of the dynamic system?"," What is the nature of the human?", "Do different types of dynamic systems enable different types of interaction?" While these questions might be focal given the traditional interaction model paradigm which focus on the human, or the dynamic technology, a shift towards a focus on interaction per se could lead to other models of interaction, and thus also raise other questions about interaction per se, i.e. questions more closely related to the character and dimensions of interaction rather than questions about system properties or human factors. As pinpointed by Dubberly et al. (2009), we still lack a good, shared understanding of what is meant when we talk about interaction.

Reviewing the current literature on models of interaction we might notice that there are several examples of input-output models for HCI (see Marchionini and Sibert, 1991; Boehner, 2005; Barnard, et al., 2000) this includes the human processor model (Card, et al., 1983), models describing standards for designing good consistent interaction, including the WIMP-standard and other GUI standards (e.g. Dam, 1997), as well as a number of other models describing different specific interaction modalities and interaction paradigms (e.g. Jacob 2006, Ishii and Ullmer 1997, Jacob et al. 1999, Abowd and Mynatt 2000, & Bellotti et al. 2002). Several recent models of users in relation to advances in the field of HCI including models of human perception in relation to HCI (e.g. Kweon et al. 2008, Dalsgaard & Hansen, 2008) can be found.

To summarize, there have been several good models developed that address and describe different ways of designing and evaluating computer support for interaction, several models developed to describe and analyze human needs, behaviors, motivations, activities and goals for engaging in interaction with computers, and models that can describe how humans might gain from interaction with computers in solving various tasks.

Still, there have been very few attempts made to address the basic dimensions and aspects of interaction *per se* and how it could be modeled. The exceptions to this include the theorizing of interaction in relation to systems (Barnard et al. 2000), the research and design driven approach to HCI (Zimmerman et al. 2007), and the need for new approaches to HCI including the identified need to integrate theory with HCI design work (Sutcliffe, 2000). In widening the scope of this literature review we can find good models for informing design based upon analysis of basic and frequent human activities including e.g. the task-artifact model (Carroll & Rosson, 1992), task analysis (e.g., Pinelle, et al., 2003), and the reference task model

(Whittaker, et al., 1997). It also takes into account the models developed in related areas of research, including relevant CSCW literature. The literature review also shows a number of workplace interaction models (e.g., Suchman 1995, Whittaker et al. 1997), computer supported group collaboration models (e.g., Ellis et al. 1991, Whittaker 1997, Hindmarsh et al. 2000), coordination models (e.g., Dourish & Bellotti 1992) and models describing other social aspects related to HCI. HCI social models include distributed cognition (e.g., Hollan et al. 2000) and situatedness of human activities (Suchman 1987). However, while these models have proven very valuable in understanding and describing computers in social contexts, they do not address nor model the dimensions of interaction per se.

From another perspective, the field of HCI has witnessed several valuable attempts to build theories of interaction through design. These include "Proof of concept" approaches (e.g., Toney et al. 2003) and the "Artifact as theory nexus" approach formulated around the idea that artifacts can manifest interaction theories through their design (Carroll & Kellogg 1989) and that special characters of a certain interaction model can be explored through the design of a prototype (Lim et al. 2008).

In this book, the concept of *Interaction per se* could be seen as both a valuable addition to the current body of research on interaction as well as for the profession of Interaction Design.

The lack of a shared fundamental understanding of interaction *per se,* has led to dramatic effects on our ability to discover new knowledge in the field of HCI systematically. Why is it that we have so effectively avoided addressing interaction *per se*? One interpretation is that we have been standing too close to this object of study, thus failed to see it. In other words, we have typically had a first person perspective on interaction in the interaction research that has been undertaken. In taking departure from the individual and his/her goals and activities and how technology helps or fails to support him or her in carrying out these tasks a more objective stance is suggested.

To tackle this issue, this book proposes a third person perspective on interaction so that we can look at interaction from the outside, i.e., interaction as understood and perceived by an observer of the person interacting with some digital technology. Thus we are able to look at interaction as a phenomenon "in the world" which can be studied and observed, including how people engage in interaction with digital devices in their everyday lives, and how parts of our everyday lives becomes part of digitalized interaction.

To summarize, there has been several good models developed that addresses and describes different ways of designing and evaluating computer support for interaction, and there has been several good models developed to describe and analyze human needs, behaviors, motivations, activities and goals for engaging in interaction with computers, and models that can describe how humans might gain from interaction with computers in solving various tasks. Still, we find very few attempts to address the basic dimensions and aspects of interaction *per se,* and how that could be modeled as an input to the current body of research on interaction and as a valuable input for the profession on doing interaction design.

If adapting this third person perspective we might notice that interaction is no longer an isolated activity in front of a stationary computer. Instead, and the other way around, interaction can now be observed as a phenomenon that surface through the embedding of technologies in our everyday lives.

Given one such perspective we might be able to identify interaction *per se* as an everyday phenomenon in which we frequently seek to involve digital technologies in our everyday lives, thus making this phenomenon surface and having impact for how it changes and form professional work settings to the reshaping of our everyday lives.

If starting out with a contextualization of interaction as an ingredient, or element of our everyday lives, we can easily see how we constantly adopt new technologies, e.g., notebook computers, netbooks, mobile phones, PDAs, etc, and how frequently we use these technologies, along with the wide range of specific applications that sits on these devices. Through this perspective, we can clearly see that interaction with computers is not a detached activity, separate from the rest of our lives, and instead is highly entwined with everything else in which we are constantly involved. To illustrate this we can use a simple user-centered model as outlined in Figure 13, which illustrates how we incorporate these technologies into the sphere of our everyday activities.

This inclusion of interaction technologies in our everyday lives raises a number of important questions about the ways in which we interact with digital technologies on a general level. In this research, the questions that have arisen have been categorized in terms of functionality, frequency, offload and access, and composition as follows:

Figure 13. Incorporation of interactions in our everyday lives

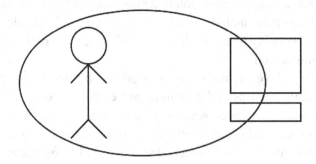

- **Functionality**: Interaction as an effective interplay to solve a specific task, i.e., "What task is to be solved through active engagement with digital technologies?"
- **Frequency**: How seldom or often does the interaction happen? Is it repetitive or a unique occasion?
- **Offload and Access**: Does the technology serve as a cognitive help, to offload the user? Is the technology a storage support to offload our memory and to make retrieval easier? Does it serve as a computational support to offload our cognitive capabilities, or does it provide access to data? The question is not about having these things implemented, rather it is about what the interplay looks like and how it is implemented in any digital technology.
- **Composition**: Which digital tools and services are used, and how these tools are assembled, combined or interlinked internally either for one specific purpose, or as part of an overall composition? (e.g., the way in which the iPhone is used today is a good example of how people build their own composition of services on an open technical platform). Expanding this category also covers questions like, "What is the set-up of technologies that people use in their everyday lives?"

The nature of these questions can be further summarized in Table 1, as they relate to each category identified.

In addressing questions, related to *functionality* and *frequency* of interaction, as well as interaction from the viewpoints of how interaction with computers might *offload* the user or allow *access* to digital material while considering the complete *composition* of different digital technologies embedded in our everyday lives we see are able to see that the nature of these questions is distinct. Questions regarding

Table 1. Dimensions of Interaction in everyday life

	Dimensions	**Aspects**	**Nature of questions raised**
1	Functionality	What a certain application can do for its user	Interactional purpose
2	Frequency	How often the application/digital device is used In which situations a specific application is used	Interaction contextualized
3	Offload & Access	- Offload to the environment (compare Norman) - Access resources - Read/write aspects	Interactional resources interplay
4	Composition	The combination of different technologies, OSs, applications, services, digital devices, networks, etc.	From self-contained interaction to an interactional palette

functionality refer to the purpose of the interaction *per se*; *frequency* must always be related to a specific context in order to know if it is high or low, i.e. there is a need for a reference point. *Offload and access* is about the interplay between the user and the computational resources available. The idea is to focus on *composition* leaving the simple loop model of interaction, and instead focusing on the entire interactional palette that a typical user constantly keeps running across with multiple digital devices and enabling technologies.

To further explore the notion and character of interaction we mighgt as well take a close look on the opposite dimension of this model, i.e. how computers engage us in the digital world and how we leave digital footprints, establish accounts and connections in the online world of interactions with computational materials and with others.

In examining how we, humans, are constantly present, mirrored, and in many other ways active in the digital world we can identify interaction through the existence of online communities, virtual worlds, social networking services, and even through the frequent use of email as an online tool for social interaction.

Online interaction should not be forgotten in any modeling of interaction *per se* on the contrary, and as pinpointed by e.g. Hollan (2000), the complex networked world of online interaction should be a focal aspect of our understanding of interaction.

"For human-computer interaction to advance in the new millennium we need to understand the emerging dynamic of interaction in which the focus task is no longer confined to the desktop but reaches into a complex networked world of information and computer-mediated interactions" (Hollan et al 2000, p. 192).

Figure 14. Inclusion of humans in the complex networked world of information and computer-mediated interactions

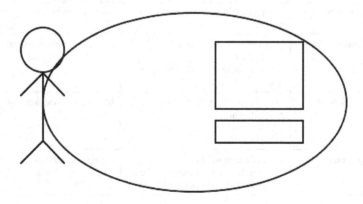

A simple technology-centered model illustrates how parts of us are frequently involved in online interactions, and how we are represented frequently and actively in this complex, networked, and digital world (see Figure 14).

The inclusion of humans in the networked world of interactions raises questions about the various interactions that we engage in when participating and using these online worlds. The number of different questions raised can also be cataloged into 4 broad categorizes: *representation, services, connections* and *sessions* as follows:

- **Representation:** How is the human represented in online services? (Including the whole range of solutions from the creation of simple, straightforward user accounts, to the design of complete online avatars.)
- **Services**: Which services are available to the user as represented in the online world? How does the user benefit from employing these services? What is expected, in terms of interactional engagement, from the use of these services?
- **Connections**: What are the established paths given a certain service? Moreover, how can the user configure or reconfigure the paths for different purposes? (Again including the whole range of connection configurations from basic online accounts to the set-up of buddy lists, social networks, etc.).
- **Sessions**: How does the user initiate, join or engage in sessions of interaction? How does the user keep an overview of ongoing and active sessions? How are these sessions related to the three aspects above?

The nature of these questions is further summarized in Table 2 as they relate to each category identified.

When looking at these categories as outlined in table x from a general perspective, it is easy to see how various online services, communities, virtual worlds, and social networking services could be analyzed via these questions. In essence, questions related to representation concern images of the user, or the user's actions, i.e.

Table 2. Dimensions of interaction as everyday life embedded in technology

	Dimensions	Aspects	Nature of questions raised
1	Representation	How the user is re-presented in the online world	Presentation or representation of the user
2	Services	Ensembles of resources for computational activities	Interactional tools
3	Connections	Established paths across the networked world	Interactional paths
4	Sessions	The number and types of various ongoing sessions	Interaction in action

the visible signs of the interaction performed by a user, as represented in an online space. The nature of the questions related to services deals with the tools available for interaction. The nature of questions about connections captures the paths that the interaction might take across the services and finally, questions concerning ongoing sessions are in fact questions about interaction as it is carried out via the connections and services available.

Given these two perspectives we might now consider the design space that these two areas form if considered simultaneously. In the exploration of interaction as a design space S. Heim's book "The Resonance Interface: HCI foundations for interaction design" (Heim, 2007), was inspiring. The title communicates an interesting aspect of interactive technologies, i.e. interaction is in a sense like resonance, it grows out of the interplay between our technologies and us. Resonance is as such a good metaphor for understanding Interaction as an emergent property with its own structure, form and appearance. Resonance surfaces as a temporal and ephemeral body between a musical instrument and the human ear in a similar way as interaction grows out of the interplay between the technology used and perceived by the human using the technology. Clearly, there is a temporal dimension in both resonance and interaction, both are only possible to observe as they happen, meaning that they are highly situational, temporal and volatile. At the same time, knowing about the preconditions for interaction allows them to be studied in detail before and after the interaction.

In the same way as *resonance* constitutes an interesting object of study in any music related area of research, it can be argued that so too does *interaction per se* constitute a similar unique object of study in the areas of HCI and Interaction Design. More specifically, this chapter takes a close look at the preconditions for interaction, i.e. the stable and "designable" aspects of interaction including the dimensions, aspects and design variables that form the design space of interaction.

Working from the two aspects of interaction as *1) technology embedded in everyday life* and, *2) everyday life embedded in technology* a model of the design space of interaction has been sketched out. The basis for this design space was outlined above through the categorization of various questions that have been raised about interaction as well as the nature of those questions. In the following tables, possible design variables of each dimension have been added to further sketch out this design space.

The intention is not to construct a complete model of the design variables of interaction. Nor is the aim for a complete identification of all the dimensions of interaction. Instead, the dimensions, aspects and variables outlined in Table 2 should serve the overall purpose of bring forth the perspective of interaction as an appearing form element or design space for human-computer interaction.

For any designer working with a certain material, being it wood, metal, plastics, concrete or glass it is important to understand the properties of that particular material, and to understand the design variables that constitute and frame the design space. Given a rich understanding of the design space and the properties of the materials brought into a certain design the designer can not only work with the specifics of a particular area, but also challenge our imagination of what a certain material can do for us in a particular design.

For HCI and Interaction Design, some fundamental knowledge about the dimensions that constitute and frame interaction *per se*, and the interaction design variables that follows upon these core dimensions allows a skilled designer to systematically work through this design space in the crafting of a particular software application, service, digital device or interactive space.

In the following two tables (Table 3 and Table 4) a first attempt to sketch out these design variables is presented.

If considering these four dimensions we can notice that in our everyday lives we use technologies to help us solve different tasks, or to engage technologies to enable us to do different things. Here, it is about the dimension of *functionality* in which we might consider the interaction design variables of affordancy, agency and application behavior as they relate to this particular dimension of this design space. We might also consider the *frequency* of use of these digital resources, and the ways in which the digital enable us to *offload & access* information to and from compu-

Table 3. Dimensions and interaction design variables given a perspective of interaction technologies embedded in everyday life

	Dimensions	Aspects	Interaction Design Variables
1	Functionality	What a certain application can do for its user	- Affordance - Agency - Design of application behavior
2	Frequency	How often the application/digital device is used In which situations the application is used	- Scale (design for frequent or non-frequent use) - Repetitions - Guidance (help)
3	Offload & Access	- Offload to the environment (compare Norman) - Access resources - Read/write aspects	- Computational support - Storage support - Information representations
4	Composition	The combination of different technologies, OSs, applications, services, digital devices, networks, etc.	- Borders & Interfaces, e.g. inter-application interfaces, (APIs), copy/paste/insert/export, import, user accounts, settings, etc. - Interoperability - Formats - Synchronization & data transfer

Table 4. Dimensions and interaction design variables given a perspective on Interaction as everyday life embedded in technology

	Dimensions	Aspects	Interaction Design Variables
1	Representation	How the user is represented in the online world (representations of the user)	- Gestalt & authentification - Media - Network (might be represented through its peers)
2	Services	Ensembles of resources for computational activities	- Compounds - Configurations
3	Connections	- Established paths across the networked world	- Accounts - Security - Spatiality
4	Sessions	The number and types of various ongoing sessions	- Access - Overview - Switches - Borders - Temporality

tational resources in our environment. Finally, this set of the design space leads us into a line of thinking that deals with the *composition* of different digital resources and the design variables related to the creation of an interactional wholeness based on different computational pieces

If we now shift our perspective and carefully pay attention to interaction as the ways in which our everyday lives are embedded in the world of the digital a number of additional dimensions and interaction design variables are emerging. In the table below we present a first sketch that outline a number of such dimensions.

In the same way as the embedding of computational power in our everyday lives adds to a new design space for interaction we can notice how the inclusion of the human in the digital world leads to an additional design space of representations, services, connections and sessions.

These two dimensions of interaction (i.e. interaction as technology embedded in everyday life as summarized in Table 1, and interaction as everyday life embedded in technology, as summarized in Table 2) form the basis for our exploration of interaction as the inner intersection of human-computer interaction. Having said this I would argue that in the intersection of these two dimensions we should be able to extract a number of variables, that taken together, constitutes a design space from the viewpoint of Interaction Design, and a conceptual contribution to the way we might model and understand interaction *per se*.

Specifically, examining these two tables in more detail in relation to the available literature in the areas of HCI and Interaction Design we can see from Table 3 how the dimension of *functionality* can be further elaborated through the design variables of *affordance* (Norman, 2002), *agency* (Suchman, 2006) and application *behavior* (e.g. Dirgahayu, 2008). Interaction *frequency* can be further addressed through the design variables of *scale*, *repetitions* and *guidance*. Furthermore, *offload & access* can be explored in design via the variables of *computational support*, *storage and information retrieval* solutions and *information representations* including the entire range from icon design to simulator environments; from simple tangible tags to complex intelligent systems. Finally, *composition* can be explored in the design space through the design variables of *borders & interfaces* (e.g. APIs), *interoperability* issues, *formats*, and ways of dealing with *synchronization & data transfer* across devices, services and networks.

In a similar way, Table 4 points at a set of design variables. The dimension of *representation* as an important aspect of online interaction might be explored through the design variables of *gestalt & authentification*, choice of *media* or *network model* (ranging from technical peer-to-peer solutions to social networking models) for the representation of the user. The interactive *service* design can be explored through the design dimensions of *compounds* design, i.e. to establish the necessary conditions for a certain digital service, and then design the range of *configurations* available for the user. Further, *connections* could be explored through the design variables of set-up and form of *user accounts*, implementation of *security* in relation to interaction, including everything from login routines to backbone network virus scanning. In addition, the dimension of *sessions* as a way of modeling interaction might be explored through the design dimensions of session *access* design (e.g. session management design), session *overview* solutions and ways of dealing with session *switches* and design of *borders* between ongoing sessions.

While we find good support in the literature for these design variables as outlined above, it is also possible to see many practical examples of how these dimensions surface in practice. If taking a step back from this theoretical approach and looking instead at interaction in everyday life and everyday life as interaction we can take on a third person view. When taking this third person perspective and looking at the complete interactional situation, rather than as a decontextualized event, discover that in our everyday lives we do in fact live with this design space and frequently also accept common design failures. We become accustomed to new ways of interacting as they surface in the interaction landscape. Below I intend to reflect a little bit upon this.

In our everyday lives we constantly live with design failures (Petroski, 1994), which we tend to accept, at least when it comes to computers. Perhaps it is just unreflected behavior or alternatively, because we have not treated interaction *per se* as a design space that could be as carefully carved out, and explicitly designed as any other consumer product. It might, for example, be interesting to know the total amount of minutes/week that people in any big city just sit and wait for their computer to wake up from hibernate mode, or even worse, if it needs to boot? Another example is that it usually takes any person that is about to show a slideshow presentation a couple of minutes just to get an ordinary projector to work with their computer (instead of spending that time talking to those present). As so elegantly formulated by Mazé (2007) interactions occupy time.

Furthermore, nowadays people seem to just accept the fact that their computers crash now and then or that their wireless keyboard loses its connection. Many people would never even try to pair a Bluetooth headset with their mobile phone, or upload their camera pictures to an online photo service. From the perspective of Interaction Design this has very little to do with the particular design of a button or a specific menu layout. Instead, I would say that it could be argued that people accept these things because the entire experience of the interaction is outrageous while at the same time, there is no language or interaction semantics developed (Krippendorf, 2005) to address what is wrong or how it could be repaired or improved upon. On the other hand, when people are presented with new ways of interacting with digital technologies that solve such basic problems they adopt such solutions quickly.

The forms for how we interact with and via the online digital world are constantly changing. New services are constantly developed and the legions of users move from one social online space to the next following the changing trends. How we present ourselves in these online worlds is also under constant development, from simple user profiles to the complex design of online avatars. Contrary to the lack of a language to talk specifically about interaction *per se* people have developed a quite detailed repertoar of concept that describe the activities they engage in through their interactions as the following section attempt to illustrate.

In this emergent interaction landscape people learn to *navigate, jump* between services, *combine* services in *mesh-ups* (Plewe, 2008), or *attach* information streams (e.g. RSS- or media streams) to themselves as they move along. They figure out how to *scrabble* between services, *chirp* on Twitter (Krishnamurthy et al., 2008) or *scrap* personal notes (Bernstein et al., 2007) and *lifehack* new paths across the interaction landscape, sometimes guided via some D.I.Y. – Do It Yourself – community. Additionally, people develop their ways of presenting themselves to others on the net, and some even develop their own set of online personalities. Through these online personalities, they comment upon the world around them, and new phenomena emerge out of these movements and activities, e.g. the rise of the "blogosphere" (Agarwal & Liu, 2008).

The tables presented in this chapter, together with the practical examples outlined above illustrate that interaction touches upon a wide set of dimensions possible to address from a design perspective. As such, it clearly sets the scene for Interaction Design in the architecting of the modern landscape. Nevertheless, given these insights, what does interaction look like when carried out? Interaction Design is sometimes described as being about the design of a temporal form (Mazé, 2007), but in which situations is this form present, and what does the interaction *per se* look like in these situations?

In this book, an alternative way of looking at human-computer interaction is presented in order to address these questions. This is presented as an intersection-oriented perspective on HCI through a Venn diagram approach to the modeling of interaction, as illustrated in Figure 15, thus moving away from the modeling of interaction as a thin line between a user and a computer.

In this Venn-diagram model of human-computer-interaction we can see how interaction might be modeled as a design space situated in between the user and the technology, thus constituting the inner intersection of this diagram in Figure 15. In more detail, this model can be explained as follows: In human-computer interaction, we have humans (1) interacting with digital technologies (2). From the wide range of digital technologies available, nowadays we incorporate some technologies into our lives (3) and create a composition of these technologies that works for us in our everyday life (see section 3). From the viewpoint of digital technologies, we also embed parts of our everyday lives in the digital world (4), as described in section 4 above. The part of us that is represented in the digital world (5) is sometimes described generally through e.g. Persona descriptions, or manifested as a representation of the individual in the form of anything from a simple user account (username and password) to a full-blown avatar (6). Similarly, the technologies that we incor-

Figure 15. Interaction as the inner intersection of human-computer interaction

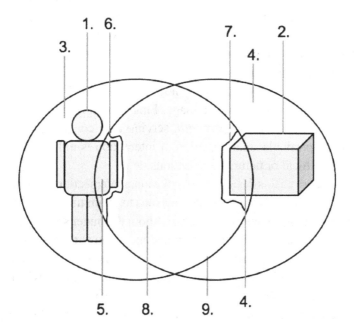

porate into our everyday lives are typically configured, integrated, and covered with some kind of user interface (sometimes graphical, but in other cases more physical, ranging from simple buttons to tangible user interfaces.) (7). But from the perspective proposed in this paper this also includes how the technology presents itself to the user. Given this description, we can now identify an interesting intersection between area 3 and 4 in this model, i.e. between the ways users incorporate digital technologies into their everyday world, and the ways in which humans engage themselves in interaction in the networked world. Therefore, if we also subtract 6 and 7 from this intersection we can see a new design space emerging with its own form and content, i.e. the design space of the inner intersection of human-computer interaction (8).

This identified design space (8) can be explored through the dimensions listed in Tables 3 and 4 above. At the same time an interesting design challenge might be to explore the border issues of this design space (9) in relation to people, available technologies, representations of us as users of these technologies, and the interfaces we create to scaffold interaction with any digital material. These border issues might include the *appearance* of the interaction as it is performed in any public space (e.g. what does it look like when a person is calling someone via voice-dial and then takes the call via a Bluetooth headset?) Another issue might concern *scale*. That is, for any particular solution for interaction that works for a small-scale implementation, a limited number of users, a limited number of information items, or similar, will the solution scale up when running the same configuration with thousands of users and thousands of information items? Will the solution work when scaling up the frequency of use at the individual level? As an example, we can take the "new WiFi identified" alert on an iPhone. This solution works well for the times when a user walks around and there might only be a few WiFi networks around. Nevertheless, what if the trend continues and we have a huge number of WiFi networks constantly available? Then the user would probably not view constant WiFi alerts as a feature, but rather as an annoying system message. Finally, a third concept related to the borders of interaction might be *strength*, serving as a concept that could denote whether or not a particular manifestation of interaction is in line with established social, cultural, ethical or natural conventions.

Having sketched out this design space as the inner intersection of human-computer interaction one might ask about the main reasons to claim this space. From our perspective, we argue that Interaction Design is about this inner space for two reasons. First, this space appears because of the mutual inclusion and adoption of (1) digital technologies into our everyday lives, and (2) how we include parts of our everyday lives in the digital world. This is a long-term, contextual perspective on interaction its importance, and its development. The second reason is more momentous and deals with the *mutual interactional commitment* in which people engage. In any situation in which we are to interact with digital technology, we commit ourselves to the interaction model and we expect the technology to do likewise. This engagement is about the building of a relationship with the digital technologies. We trust them to work in a certain way, and we count on being able to use the technologies in a certain way given a set-up of specific interaction models.

From a more philosophical viewpoint engagement and interactional commitment is about building relationships (See Buchanan's work from 1998), and these relationships are built over time. Having this said we should also consider the power that comes into play when designing interaction as a relationship to technology. As formulated by Greenfield (2006)*we engage ourselves in interaction*, or more importantly *the powerful informatics we are engaging* through our interactions with computers (Greenfield, 2006, p. 11).

Through this model as outlined above we're thus illustrating: (1) interaction as a form element manifested in between the user and the technology, (2) interaction as a mutual commitment between the user and the technology, and (3) interaction as an observable form from a third person perspective.

In this alternative view less emphasis is put on how, and for what activities, people use computers, in favor for a bigger emphasis on how people include computational power into their everyday lives (the circle around the human that partly also include the computer in the figure above), and how parts of us are inscribed in the digital world (the second circle that includes the computer and partly also the human. This alternative view enable us to focus on activities that have been made possible with the computer (and could hardly have been done without these machines, e.g. online social networking) and human activities that also becomes virtual foot prints in the digital world (e.g. logs) which in turn can be used to create new digital services (e.g. social navigation of books at Amazon.com, etc.).

Further on, in this book Interaction is also understood as the "inter actions", i.e. to interact is about a person engaging in the meeting with or through the computer, i.e. its about "becoming interaction", a phenomenological turn in which people and technologies becomes inseparable, and in which interaction becomes the focus of attention. As such, this line of thinking follows Donald Schön's (1984) idea about the tool as an extension of the body. Further on, we view interaction as a multitude of intersectional processes between humans and digital technologies that enables computer supported actions to be undertaken.

In each and every intersection between humans and computational materials we find a space of interactions. We find actions that people undertake to accomplish tasks, and we find information in many cases extracted from digital resources at use in these intersections. Here, we also find exchanges of information, communication, collaboration, expressions of ideas and the establishment of communication channels. In this interaction landscape we also notice links to other such intersections, crossovers between such intersections and the linkage and multitude of intersections available. If just studying IT use from the outside this will be to a large extend invisible. It is therefore important to engage oneself in this world of layered intersections of interactions as to discover the inner character of IT use, i.e. interaction.

Having introduced interaction as an act of, or perhaps the art of, creating meaningful intersections in between the human and the digital I now move on to theorize the concept of interaction even further as to address how digital objects and digitalized places are increasingly becoming part of our interaction rituals from the viewpoint of a model that first examine the notion of interaction in detail followed by an attempt to contextualize the notion of interaction in relation to the context in which interaction occur.

Interaction as the concept that sets out to describe the relation between the human and the computer in typical models of HCI – Human-Computer Interaction is an interesting concept in itself. As a binding concept between the two entities of humans and computers it might not be very much to say about it. However, if viewing interaction as 1) the interplay between people in the first sense, and 2) as an interplay between people and digital materials in the second sense, then interaction reveals itself as a whole area that can be studied from a multitude of viewpoints and perspectives.

Given a comparison between, on the one hand the areas of HCI and Interaction Design, and on the other hand the area of Architecture we might even introduce a third perspective here regarding the fundamental notion of interaction. In the area of Architecture the fundamental object of study, i.e. *architecture,* is sometimes described as: "1) the relations between materials in the first sense, and 2) as the relation between these materials and humans in the second sense" (Oosterhuist, 2007). In a similar way we could thus introduce this third perspective in which we address interaction as 3) a phenomena arising from the orchestration of computational resources in action, in which we're interested in this orchestration of different computational materials in the first sense as to understand how one such orchestration forms a basis for interaction.

In my elaboration on interaction as the inner intersection of HCI – Human Computer Interaction I was mainly focusing on the "in between" aspects of interaction. And I was interested in the "in between" aspects that dealt with the area between people scaffolded by computational materials. An area of actions in between people one might say. Thus, one way of understanding the concept of interaction is to take the word literary and examine it piece by piece. Interaction is thus a word that in fact consists of two words, i.e. the word "inter" and the word "action". Interaction is then about the actions in between – i.e. inter - actions. Further on, the notion of "action" points in a direction in which we can start to think about a "who" that is doing the actions undertaken, i.e. a human, a "user" or just people.

If interactions is about people, and if it is about what people do, i.e. the in between actions or "inter-actions", then we might also need to reflect upon with whom these interactions are played out. As soon as we initiate this line of thinking we should notice that interaction is not happening in a vacuum, without history, and without connections to other people. On the contrary, interaction is a social act and is thus part of the everyday social networking grid that makes us human in the first place. Given one such point of departure it becomes obvious that IT must be a perfect tool to take social interactions to the next level. From the simplest act of interactions taken by one single individual to fluid and frequent mass interactions is just a matter of scale in terms of social activities.

So, in the modeling of interaction we might see how the "inter" actions taken in fact scale to the level of social relations and relationships as we start to create shared interaction histories, shared channels for online interaction, etc., etc. Online social worlds, communities, social recommendation systems, home pages, etc. are just small evidences of this current development. So, in other words, the "inter" aspect of interaction is not situated in a vacuum. Instead, the "inter" aspects of interaction is a relational word that describes how interactions is related to persons in several different ways.

The same is true for the "actions" part of "inter-action". Of course, actions are not randomly undertaken by a random user. Instead, people typically strive to do meaningful things, and they act accordingly. We can therefore say that actions are typically formed in a certain social and cultural context. Another thing that is interesting with us as humans is that we're good at learning how to do things in a proper way, in a safe way, in an efficient way, or simply put… in a certain way. For us to really understand interaction I would therefore argue that we cannot look at specific isolated actions undertaken by a single user. Instead, we should pay close attention to how the single actions undertaken are part of larger action structures, action schemas and action scripts. Theories capable of addressing the structure and character of human activities has been actively developed in the field of interaction research over the last years. Among those theories it is worth mentioning e.g. Activity theory (ref, ref), Distributed cognition (e.g. ref), and Situated actions (ref) as a few examples of theoretical frameworks that deals with the structures of meaningful activities and actions undertaken by us as humans.

If looking at action scripts as the theoretical concept proposed in this chapter I suggest it as a framing concept for chains or sequences of trained human actions. In our everyday interactions we learn how to go about solving typical everyday problems. Such everyday issues are not something that we handle through an explicit and conscious act of structuring single actions into larger human activities. Instead, since we have experiences from similar cases, we apply our trained ways of going about doing the work, i.e. we apply our action scripts to the situation at hand. For interaction design it thus become important to understand such human action chains as to support routinized behaviors.

Interaction does not exist in a vacuum. Instead, our interactions with others are typically situated in a certain place, context or location. In my model of interaction as presented in Figure 15 I introduce the notion of "stages and places" as a concept borrowed from Goffman (1959) to talk about the locales where the interaction unfolds in the interplay between humans and computational materials.

Similar to how places and contexts clearly play an important role for the unfolding of interaction, then so does the objects that we surround ourselves with as we engage ourselves in interactions. Objects are part of the interactional games we engage ourselves in and they constitute the materials that we bring into the interaction. We use objects, we create objects and we relate to different objects in our interactions with others and in our interactions with and through computational materials. Some objects are especially important to us. Some objects are loaded with a history, memories and values. Sherry Turkle (2007) refers to these objects as evocative objects, and in a theory of interaction partly situated in our physical world I find it important to especially acknowledge those objects that has a deeper meaning and value for us as human beings. As evocative objects is about the things that holds some special meaning for us it becomes focal in any deeper discussion about human interaction. This, due to the fact the objects in many cases constitute the core object in focus for the interactions that we undertake.

The notion of evocative objects is also an interesting concept to introduce in a model of interaction since it adds a material dimension, and a material history to the conversation around the essence and character of interaction.

If speaking about action scripts and history, then any theory of interaction should also pay some specific attention to *interaction rituals*. If action scripts deals with routinized behaviors in terms of short chains of actions, then interaction rituals is about the large scale cultures created around our interactions with and through the digitals.

Interaction rituals is in this model of interaction a framing concept that describes the relation between single interactions undertaken and the context in which these occur. Interaction rituals are in themselves highly intertwined in the social and cultural context. As such, interaction rituals both connect to some established social and cultural values, at the same time as those values are communicated, strengthen and brought in action in the very act of interaction. Interaction rituals can further be understood as the culturally and socially embedded ways in which we interact with and through any everyday computational material.

In Figure 16 the concepts sketched out in this theory of interaction has been pulled together and schematically laid out in a model that describe interaction from the viewpoint of inter-actions as heavily connected to the persons involved in the interaction (relationships) and the meaningful objects they bring into the conversation (evocative objects). This model addresses the chains of actions taken (action scripts) and the places where the interaction occur (stages and places). Finally, the model describes the culture surrounding our interactions and how our meaningful objects situate themselves in the history and culture of interaction.

As the current form of this model illustrate some specific attention has been paid at constructing a model of interaction that both de-composes the very concept of interaction into smaller meaningful units of analysis while at the same time working as a contextualization of interaction per se. Through the in depth analysis of the core concept of interaction new concepts are brought into the picture which now enable us to situate interaction in a larger social and cultural context as well as it enable us to locate interaction as situated in the cross section of the physical, social and digital world.

The de-construction of interaction thus enables us to see the details of how interaction flows as series of actions, and through this model we can identify unique aspects of interaction *per se*. Further on, the conceptual exploration of this model enable us to see interaction in a larger context and how it related to the ways in which it integrate with our social world and sites where the interaction happens.

Figure 16. Interaction de-constructed and contextualization

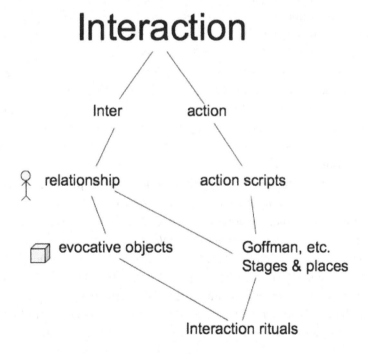

Having this said, I now move from an individual level of analysis to a societal level (similar to what I did in the book "The Interaction Society", Wiberg, 2004) for the purpose of discussing the emergence of interaction ecologies in which our built environment is part of the multiple intersections between humans and computational materials created as we interact. I then take one step back again as to address how the individual needs to develop an environment interaction repertoire to cope with this ongoing development.

In many cases, interaction technologies are embedded in everyday activities, and in everyday products, vehicles and environments. Computational power is in this sense becoming ubiquitous and part of everything, and everywhere. Through the adding of computational materials to the everyday we also engage computational power to the things we do, and we engage ourselves in our interactions with and through these computational materials. In this process we're engaging powerful informatics in our processes and, as Greenfield (2006) has acknowledged, we can now start to see the rise of ambient informatics as part of this development. Here, ambient informatics deals with the processing power of computational materials embedded in our physical, social and cultural surrounding and the processes through which we engage this ambient informatics in the activities and actions undertaken in our everyday lives. Ambient informatics might further on be described as the study of information and interaction technologies as completely interwoven in the textures of everyday life. Such computational textures scale from the texturing of information technology with other materials in the creation of new forms of representations to the ways in which modern interaction technologies scaffold, changes, enables or contributes to the ways in which we interact with other persons in our daily lives.

Textures are in a sense the patchworks of materials and social practices as they present themselves to us in our surrounding. Textures are thus heavily connected to the technologies and materials that constitute our built environment, at the same time as these textures also includes us in the jumble of physio-social interaction contexts. In other words, we're part of these textures, and in that sense also insepa-rable from the ways in which our social practices are stitched and interwoven with the built environment around us.

As a way forward to integrate the "interaction landscape" line of thinking as outlined above with an individual level of analysis we could use the notion of "in-teraction ecologies" as a conceptual bridge in between these two levels of analysis.

In quite similar ways as *information ecologies* in the context of an evolving information society has been described as a term that marks a connection between ecological ideas with the dynamics and properties of the increasingly dense, com-plex and important digital informational environment under the metaphor of an ecosystem, then *interaction ecologies* could be understood as a term that marks a connection between ecological ideas with the properties and character of interaction as the boundary object that dynamically connect people, places, materials and objects in highly distributed and highly dynamic processes of communication and collaboration.

Krippendorf (2005) describe the stages from compositions of resources into services, to compositions of services, to "ecologies of artifacts" i.e. the composition of technologies into wholeness from the individual's perspective. Such ecologies of artifacts might also connect to the interaction ecologies that groups of individuals co-create through their individual interactions.

In these interactions, and as we engage ourselves in interactions with others through the different ecologies of artifacts available we should be aware of the powerful informatics we're engaging (Greenfield, 2006, p. 11).

In the same sense as the laws of physics play a fundamental role in nature, we should be aware of how we're engaging informatics in our texturing and use of modern interaction technologies. More about this in the coming chapters.

FROM COMMUNITIES OF PRACTICE TO COMBINATIONS OF PROFESSIONS

The areas of HCI and Interaction Design has in many cases been quite isolated disciplines typically focused on small scale interface related problems with digital materials.

As the digital blends with the physical, as interfaces scale from the screen to the environment, and as we move from a focus on interfaces to interaction per se, there is a growing need to address this development from new perspectives.

In typical participatory design projects the idea of involving "communities of practice" (Wenger, 1998) has been a popular topic. Through close collaboration with the users, and through a better understanding of the users context the assumption is that interaction designers can build better systems to support their everyday activities.

However, as the digital scale from the device to the environment we also need to bring in more people, or at least several different competences at the development side of the process. Foremost, ambient informatics (through which IT weaves itself into the fabrics and practices of everyday life) calls for new approaches to advanced interaction design. I would therefore suggest the inclusion of "combinations of professions" as an important factor to address the design challenges of ambient informatics.

In other words, we need to extend our focus on "communities of practices" to include a focus on "mixtures of professions" to design new interactive environments, i.e. we need to "design the design teams" capable of addressing interactive architecture as a whole.

In this book a conceptual framework for understanding interaction through textures is presented. This framework deals with the new textures and materials facing todays designers, and it deals with the challenges these mixtures of professions will need to deal with in their everyday work of designing meaningful interactive environments. This theoretical framework builds upon previous research on P3-systems, current research on ambient informatics, and is guided by the practical examples that start to appear in the area of interactive architecture. In doing this we are especially inspired by the work by Sengers (2004), Greenfield (2006) and McCullough (2004) on possible integrations between the areas of architecture and interaction design.

Interactive architecture is a challenging area that calls for these mixtures of professions working together in the creation of new complex ecosystems of people, objects, built environments and social practices. In chapter 7 I present a case study of one such project in which we worked together in a multi-professional design team in the design of a public interactive environment for remote experiences of the far north.

In the creation of ecologies of artifacts, in the creation of ecologies of interactions, and through the construction of multi-professional design teams, another challenge is facing us. That is to also develop a language or semantics (Krippendorf, 2005) to enable 1) communication around the design of interactive environments across different design professions, and 2) to develop a language to specifically talk about the properties and dimensions of new computational materials and the character of interaction per se, and 3) to develop a language or vocabulary that speaks simultaneously to the structuring of atoms and bits in the creation of wholenesses across these ecologies and across the digital and the virtual. In this first chapter, some attempts to move in this direction have been presented.

It is now time to summarize the lessons learned from the first chapter of the book. From my perspective the main purpose with this chapter was to establish a conceptual platform for one of the core concepts for this book, i.e. "interaction". Since interaction is one critical concept, not only for this book, but for this emergent field of interactive architecture and the texturing of information technologies into our built environments it has been somewhat crucial to pay some extra attention to this concept.

In terms of the overall theme for this first section of the book, i.e. "think outside the box" then this chapter has contributed to this particular theme by presenting a view of interaction design that moves "out of the box" in terms of a major shift in focus from computers and user interface issues towards interaction as a design space situated in between humans and computational objects.

"Out of the box" has also been a guiding metaphor for the line of thinking presented in this chapter that has to do with other interaction technologies besides the stationary computer and the separation of the physical "box" or container for computational power, typically referred to as "computers" and the computational power *per se*, nowadays typically referred to as "ubiquitous computing". So, in a sense, the whole movement towards ubiquitous computing has demonstrated that "the box", i.e. our traditional understanding of the computer as framed through a screen and a keyboard, is now breaking down everywhere.

A POST-INTERACTION REFLECTION-THE RETURN OF BOXES

Having moved through a chapter focused on interaction from the viewpoint of "the breakdown of the box" as it starts to disappear into our surrounding it is now time to also spend some time on a "post-interaction reflection".

Similar to the current dissolving of the box we can now also start to see a simultaneous development going somewhat in the opposite direction, leading us into a time where we can also see "the return of boxes".

"The return of boxes" manifest itself frequently right now as everyday objects gets equipped with computational capabilities. However, it is not the return of the same kind of box. This time around it is less about the construction of the general-purpose machine. Instead, the new computational devices popping up everywhere are typically single use oriented artifacts that has for some time now been labeled digital artifacts, or "information appliances" (Bergman, 2000).

In this book, the issues of scale and scaling is one of the things that we need to pay specific attention to when addressing computation not only as an aspect of small objects, but also as city infrastructure and architectural element. As we re-introduce new computational boxes we should then also, given this scale perspective, ask ourselves whether this moves us in the direction towards clutter or in a direction in which the different pieces, or boxes, can come together under a general organizing principle, in this book thought of in terms of texture.

In the next section called "Towards Clutter or Texture?" I discuss appropriation of new technologies in relation to two approaches to structure our thinking around these new ecologies of computational boxes.

TOWARDS CLUTTER OR TEXTURE?

With "the return of boxes" follows a lot of questions. In our everyday practices we might hear people asking e.g. why they should have yet another device to carry around? Or why they no longer can fix their own car? (due to all the digital technology that is part of the design and functionality, and fundamental structure of any modern car).

These questions hint at the wider questions concerning if there is a guiding principle that we can follow when adapting new technologies, and questions related to if these boxes will be self-contained and hard to operate, or if these boxes will work in concert with the materials that surrounds us in our everyday lives.

Ultimately, this is a question of whether the return of boxes, in any form ranging from new transmaterials to physical information appliances leads us into clutter, or if we might be able to organize these into the textures of our everyday lives? That is, will technology evolve into self-contained objects of various kinds, or can we find ways of integrating them in relation to each other, and in relation to our physical and social world?

If we think about the direction towards clutter we think about disorder as the general principle and we might think about associated concepts like "fragments".

From Wikipedia we get an idea of how people view clutter and according to the masses, then "clutter" can refer to any of the following:

"It is the consumer exposure to hundreds of marketing messages per day, and most are tuned out."

It can also refer to "excessive physical disorder" including the following definitons:

- *Clutter (organizing): A confusing or disorderly state or collection; or the creation thereof. Excessive, unnecessary or uncontrolled clutter can be a symptom of compulsive hoarding.*
- *A type of light pollution*
- *Clutter (radar): Unwanted echoes in electronic systems.*
- *Clutter (marketing): The extreme amount of advertisements or products the average consumer comes into contact with. In TV and radio, commercials, upcoming show announcements and promotions, and any other broadcast material which does not belong to the actual program currently on.*

Thinking about "clutter" along the line of the return of computational boxes then this overload issue might be one of the most appearing dimensions. It might be some overload associate with the actual physical space that such new devices claim (similar to the question above about whether we actually need more computational devices to carry around), but more importantly we might face an issue of interaction overload. All these boxes might built upon different interaction modalities, different interaction models, having different user interfaces, and might need us as humans as the linkage in-between those (to update firmware, synchronize data, transfer data from one box to the next, etc.)

With new small devices introduced to the market followed by mega screens for public use, new tangible (digital) objects and new materials we need organizing principles that moves these issues to the background of our attention. Further on, as we scale this issue from the level of analysis on the individual to the level of the building and the city we might need to move from fragments to wholenesses in which we train ourselves to find patterns, sort, connect and organize our digital interaction landscapes. In this book we think of one such organizing principle that works across boxes, across the inside and outside of such boxes, and at the intersection between computational boxes and the world outside. That notion is an old but important one, i.e. texture.

Texture refers to the feel, appearance or consistency of a surface and it has to do with the quality created by the combination of different elements. Figure 17 below illustrate a good example of an everyday city texture that follows this simple idea.

Figure 17 illustrate the power of thinking along the line of "texture" when addressing material integration beyond simple clutter. With texture as an organizing principle the picture in Figure 17 shows us how this also works on several different levels. More specifically, we can see from Figure 17 how the old stones themselves communicate a certain texture. The surfaces of these stones are intimately related to the basic material from which each stone has been handcrafted, i.e. raw stone. The stones also work in relation to each other (creating a larger pattern) an this stone pattern stands perfectly in relation to one additional material in this composition, i.e. the old iron well cover. The concrete in between the stones make the pieces come together as a whole forming the larger texture of this old street.

What is obvious from this quick analysis is that texture enables us to move from a focus on how a certain material work in relation to a specific surface at the same

Figure 17. Several materials working in concert to form the texture of an old street in New York City

time as it allow us to move from that narrow focus towards larger assemblages of materials that form larger patterns or organized structures.

The notion of texture provides us with a perspective that enables us to simultaneously pay attention to details and wholenesses. As seen from the picture below (Figure 18), this is also an old street, but although being made of a similar stone material it communicates another texture (appearing to be more slippery, having different colors, and seems to have been used more).

The texturing of materials into larger compositions work not only at the level of the street, but also for larger constructions including buildings.

It is important to recognize that a texture does not need to be beautiful or elegant. The important thing is the composition and how the different materials work in relation top each other to form a larger appearance. Thus, as Figure 19 illustrate, the texture of a building facade in New York made up out of very old and rough materials can still work to form a coherent texture.

Moving from old buildings to the modern cityscape, and in doing so also initiate an exploration on how we might start to add digital technology to our built environ-

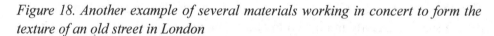

Figure 18. Another example of several materials working in concert to form the texture of an old street in London

Figure 19. Old materials working in concert to form the texture of an old building in New York City

ments we can also think about the integration of those in terms of how they work in concert with other old or new materials.

The picture in Figure 20 serves as one such good example. This picture shows a narrow street located in the Soho area of New York City. Here, LED lights have been installed in the ground and metal lines have been installed together with these lights to form a larger coherent texture working in composition with the street material. Taken together, these materials form a pattern similar to a circuit board.

An important lesson learned from the background research that I have conducted for this book is that no good texturation can be done if not carefully planned

Figure 20. LEDs mounted on the ground in a pattern that reminds about the form of a circuit board

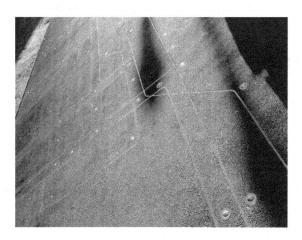

Figure 21. Air condition add-ons on a building façade as an example of poor integration of technology and building architecture

and executed from the beginning. Ones the fundamental structures are in place it is much harder to add something new to the composition and make it fully integrated.

In our modern cityscape we can see many examples today when pieces of technology has been added instead of being truly integrated. As add-ons to architectural systems including e.g. ventilation systems, door lock systems, electricity systems, lightening, and heating/cooling systems. Figure 21 provide one such example in which air condition has been added to this particular building like "boxes" mounted on the façade. If carefully planned from the beginning, those boxes could probably have been avoided and instead integrated in the walls of the building.

Obvious from this reflection on "the return of boxes" is that the notion of texture might serve as one fruitful concept to initiate a conversation about design of meaningful compositions across different materials. In the next chapter we take a closer look at this concept from the perspective that texture do matter!

REFERENCES

Aarts, E. (2005). Ambient intelligence drives open innovation. *Interaction*, *12*(4), 66–68. doi:10.1145/1070960.1070996

Abowd, G., & Mynatt, E. (2000). Charting past, present, and future research in ubiquitous computing. *Transactions on Computer-Human Interaction (TOCHI)*, *7*(1).

Agarwal, N., & Liu, H. (2008). Blogosphere: research issues, tools, and applications. *SIGKDD Explorations Newsletter*, *10*(1).

Barnard, P., May, J., Duke, D., & Duce, D. (2000). Systems, interactions, and macrotheory. *Transactions on Computer-Human Interaction (TOCHI), 7*(2).

Bellotti, V., Back, M., Edwards, W. K., Grinter, R., Henderson, A., & Lopes, C. (2002). Making sense of sensing systems: five questions for designers and researchers. In *Proceedings of the SIGCHI conference on Human factors in computing systems: Changing our world, changing ourselves (CHI '02)*. New York: ACM Press.

Bergman, E. (2000). *Information Appliances and Beyond*. UK: Elsevier Science & Technology.

Bernstein, M. S., Van Kleek, M., Schraefel, M. C., & Karger, D. R. (2007). Management of personal information scraps. In *CHI '07 Extended Abstracts on Human Factors in Computing Systems* (San Jose, CA, USA, April 28 - May 03, 2007). (pp. 2285-2290). New York: ACM.

Boehner, K., DePaula, R., Dourish, P., & Sengers, P. (2005). Affect: from information to interaction. In *Proceedings of the 4th Decennial Conference on Critical Computing: Between Sense and Sensibility (CC '05)*. New York: ACM Press.

Brownell, B. (2005). *Transmaterial: A Catalog of Materials That Redefine our Physical Environment*. Princeton Architectural Press.

Card, S. K., Moran, T. P., & Newall, A. (1983). *The psychology of human-computer interaction*. Mahwah, NJ: Lawrence Erlbaum Associates.

Carroll, J. M., & Kellogg, W. A. (1989). Artifact as theory-nexus: hermeneutics meets theory-based design. In *Proceedings of the SIGCHI conference on Human factors in computing systems: Wings for the mind (CHI '89)* (Vol. 20).

Carroll, J. M., & Rosson, M. B. (1992). Getting around the task-artifact cycle: how to make claims and design by scenario. [TOIS]. *ACM Transactions on Information Systems, 10*(2). doi:10.1145/146802.146834

Croon Fors, A. *(2006)*. Being-with Information Technology: Critical explorations beyond Use and Design. *Umeå University: Department of Informatics. (PhD thesis)*

Dalsgaard, P., & Koefoed Hansen, L. (2008). Performing perception—staging aesthetics of interaction [TOCHI]. *ACM Transactions on Computer-Human Interaction, 15*(3), 1–33. doi:10.1145/1453152.1453156

Dam, A. (1997). Post-WIMP user interfaces. *Communications of the ACM, 40*(2).

Das, S., & Cook, D. (2006). Designing and Modeling Smart Environments. In *Proceedings of the 2006 International Symposium on World of Wireless, Mobile and Multimedia Networks WOWMOM '06*. IEEE Computer Society.

Dirgahayu, T., Quartel, D., & Sinderen, M. (2008). Designing interaction behaviour in service-oriented enterprise application integration. In *Proceedings of the 2008 ACM symposium on Applied computing (SAC '08)*. New York: ACM Press.

Dourish, P., & Bellotti, V. (1992). Awareness and coordination in shared workspaces. In *Proceedings of the 1992 ACM Conference on Computer-Supported Cooperative Work (CSCW '92)*.

Dubberly, H., Pangaro, P., & Haque, U. (2009). What is interaction? Are there different types? *Interaction, 16*(1).

Gárate, A., Herrasti, N., & López, A. (2005). GENIO: An ambient intelligence application in home automation and entertainment environment . In *Proceedings of sOc-EUSAI '05*. ACM Press.

Goffman, E. (1959). *The Presentation of Self in Everyday Life*. GardenCity, NY: Doubleday.

Greenfield, A. (2006). *Everyware – The dawning age of ubiquitous computing*. Berkeley, CA: New Riders.

Grudin, J. (1990). The Computer Reaches Out. In *Proceedings of CHI'90* (Seattle, WA). ACM Press.

Heim, S. (2007). *The Resonant Interface – HCI Foundations for interaction design*. Reading, MA: Addison-Wesley.

Heim, S. (2007). *The Resonant Interface – HCI Foundations for interaction design*. Reading, MA: Addison-Wesley.

Hinckley, K., Pierce, J., Sinclair, M., & Horvitz, E. (2000). Sensing techniques for mobile interaction. In *Proceedings of the 13th annual ACM symposium on User interface software and technology (UIST '00)*. New York: ACM Press.

Hindmarsh, J., Fraser, M., Heath, C., Benford, S., & Greenhalgh, C. (2000). Object-focused interaction in collaborative virtual environments. *Transactions on Computer-Human Interaction (TOCHI), 7*(4).

Hollan, J., Hutchins, E., & Kirsh, D. (2000). Distributed cognition: toward a new foundation for human-computer interaction research. *Transactions on Computer-Human Interaction (TOCHI), 7*(2).

Hornecker, E., & Buur, J. (2006). Getting a grip on tangible interaction: a framework on physical space and social interaction. In *Proceedings of the SIGCHI conference on Human Factors in computing systems (CHI '06)*. New York: ACM Press.

Ishii, H., & Ullmer, B. (1997) Tangible bits: Towards seamless integration interfaces between people, atoms, and bits. In *Proc. CHI 1997* (pp. 234-241). ACM Press.

Jacob, R. (2006). What is the next generation of human-computer interaction? In *Proceedings of the extended abstracts on Human factors in computing systems (CHI '06)*. New York: ACM Press.

Jacob, R., Deligiannidis, L., & Morrison, S. (1999). A software model and specification language for non-WIMP user interfaces. *Transactions on Computer-Human Interaction (TOCHI), 6*(1).

Jones, Q. (2004). People-to-People-to-Geographical-Places: The P3 Framework for Location-Based Community Systems. In *J. Computer Supported Cooperative Work, 13*(3-4), 202–211. doi:10.1007/s10606-004-2803-7

Krippendorff, K. (2005). *The semantic turn: A new foundation for design*. CRC Press.

Krishnamurthy, B., Gill, P., & Arlitt, M. (2008). A few chirps about twitter. In *Proceedings of the first workshop on Online social networks (WOSP '08)*. New York: ACM Press.

Kweon, S., Cho, E., & Kim, E. (2008). Interactivity dimension: media, contents, and user perception. In *Proceedings of the 3rd international conference on Digital Interactive Media in Entertainment and Arts (DIMEA '08)*. New York: ACM Press.

Lim, Y-K., Stolterman, E., & Tenenberg, J. (2008). The anatomy of prototypes: Prototypes as filters, prototypes as manifestations of design ideas. *Transactions on Computer-Human Interaction (TOCHI), 15*(2).

Lindwer, M., Marculescu, D., Basten, T., & Zimmennann, R. Marculescu, R., Jung, S., & Cantatore, E. (2003). *Ambient intelligence visions and achievements: linking abstract ideas to real-world concepts*. IEEE Xplore, IEEE.

Marchionini, G., & Sibert, J. (1991). An agenda for human-computer interaction: science and engineering serving human needs. *SIGCHI Bulletin, 23*(4).

Mazé, R. (2007). *Occupying Time: Design, Technology and the Form of Interaction*. PhD Thesis, Malmö University, Sweden.

McCarthy, J., & Wright, P. (2003). *Technology as Experience*. Cambridge, MA: MIT Press.

McCullough, M. (2004). *Digital Ground – Architecture, Pervasive Computing, and Environmental Knowing*. Cambridge, MA: MIT Press.

Nardi, B., Whittaker, S., & Bradner, E. (2000). Interaction and Outeraction: Instant Messaging in Action. In *ACM Conference on Computer Supported Cooperative Work (CSCW2000)* (pp. 79-88).

Norman, D. A. (1993). *Things that make us smart*. Reading, MA: Addison Wesley.

Norman, D. A. (2002). *The Design of Everyday Things*. New York: Basic Books.

Oosterhuist, K. (2007). *iA #1 Interactive Architecture*. Rotterdam: Episode Publishers.

Petroski, H. (1994). *The Evolution of Useful Things: How Everyday Artifacts-From Forks and Pins to Paper Clips and Zippers-Came to be as they are*. New York: Vintage Books.

Pinelle, D., Gutwin, C., & Greenberg, S. (2003). Task analysis for groupware usability evaluation: Modeling shared-workspace tasks with the mechanics of collaboration. *Transactions on Computer-Human Interaction (TOCHI), 10*(4).

Pinhanez, C., & Bobick, A. (2003) Interval scripts: a programming paradigm for interactive environments and agents. *Personal and Ubiquitous Computing, 7*(1), Springer-Verlag.

Plewe, D. (2008). Transactional arts: interaction as transaction. In *Proceeding of the 16th ACM international conference on Multimedia (MM '08)*. New York: ACM Press.

Preece, J., Rogers, Y., & Sharp, H. (Eds.). (2002). *Interaction Design: Beyond Human-Computer Interaction*. John Wiley.

Sengers, P., et al (2004). Culturally Embedded Computing. *Pervasive Computing, 3*(1).

Siegemund, F., Floerkemeier, C., & Vogt, H. (2005). The value of handhelds in smart environments. *Personal and Ubiquitous Computing, 9*(2). doi:10.1007/s00779-004-0311-x

Suchman, L. (1987). *Plans and Situated Actions: The Problem of Human-Machine Communication (Learning in Doing: Social, Cognitive and Computational Perspectives)*. New York: Cambridge University Press.

Suchman, L. (1995). Making work visible. *Communications of the ACM, 38*(9). doi:10.1145/223248.223263

Suchman, L. A. (2006). *Human–machine reconfigurations: Plans and situated actions*. Cambridge, UK: Cambridge University Press.

Turkle, S. (Ed.). (2007). *Evocative Objects: Things We Think With*. Cambridge, MA: MIT Press.

Weiser, M. (1991). The computer of the 21st century. *Scientific American, 265*(3), 66–75. doi:10.1038/scientificamerican0991-94

Wenger, E. (1998). *Communities of Practice – Learning, Meaning, and Identity*. Cambridge, UK: Cambridge University Press.

Whittaker, S., Swanson, J., Kucan, J., & Sidner, C. (1997). TeleNotes: managing lightweight interactions in the desktop. *Transactions on Computer-Human Interaction (TOCHI), 4*(2).

Wiberg, M. (2001). *In between Mobile Meetings: Exploring seamless ongoing interaction support for mobile CSCW*. Umeå: Department of Informatics, Umeå University (PhD thesis).

Wiberg, M. (Ed.). (2004). *The Interaction Society: Practice, Theories, and Supportive Technologies*. Hershey, PA: Information Science Publishing.

Wiberg, M., & Stolterman, E. (2008). Environment interaction: Character, Challenges & Implications for Design. In *Proceedings of the SigMobile and ACM conference "MUM 2008 the 7th international conference on Mobile and Ubiquitous Multimedia."* ACM Press.

Zellner, P. (1999). *Hybrid Space – New forms in digital architechture*. Thames & Hudson.

Zimmerman, J., Forlizzi, J., & Evenson, S. (2007). Research through design as a method for interaction design research in HCI. In *Proceedings of the SIGCHI conference on Human factors in computing systems (CHI '07)*. New York: ACM Press.

ENDNOTE

[1] By November 2007, the total number of mobile phone subscriptions in the world had reached 3.3 billion, or half of the human population (although some users have multiple subscriptions, or inactive subscriptions), which also makes the mobile phone the most widely spread technology and the most common electronic device in the world. (http://investing.reuters.co.uk/ news/articlein-vesting.aspx? type=media&storyID=nL29172095).

Chapter 2
Textures Matters!

We live our lives with textures. We see them, feel them, interact with them, and we are constantly aware of them. Textures are in many ways the "skins" (Lupton, 2002) of our everyday world. This chapter discusses the importance of textures in general terms as this surface or "skin" of our built environment, how texture help us to navigate in built environments, and how the notion of texture has previously been defined in the literature of material science and architecture.

In its most basic form, textures are about surfaces, i.e. it is about the visual qualities of our surrounding, or the "skin" (Lupton, 2007) of the world around us. From an architectural viewpoint this "skin" is very important to us as humans since we are constantly reading our environment to interpret it and to make sense of it, and to formulate theories about the things we see around us (Weick, 1979). Throughout this sense-making act we are constantly looking for aspects in our surrounding that make sense to us, and in doing so we are looking for patterns in our environment as to understand it as a whole.

However, while Lupton (2007) takes on a biologically grounded approach to address the development of new surfaces through the concept of "skin", this chapter argues for the architecturally grounded notion of "textures" to address the current blending process of our built environment with our digital world, constituted through new innovative materials with digital properties typically referred to as *transmaterials* (Brownell, 2005; 2008).

DOI: 10.4018/978-1-61520-653-7.ch002

In this book the theoretical notion of "textures" to some extent works as a guiding concept on both a literary and metaphorical level. Literary speaking new digitalized textures is the most obvious sign of an ongoing digitalization of our built environment, and metaphorically the notion of textures extends flat surfaces into new materials and fabrics and adds another layer onto our reality at the same time as the notion of textures allow us to connect the "surface" or skin" of a material to be fully connected to the material properties of that particular material or composition of materials.

As the following example will show, this sense making process around the textures that surrounds us in our every lives are so important that sometimes we are even creating representations of textures as to keep the appearance of a working wholeness in our physical surrounding intact.

If looking at the two pictures below from the train station in Amsterdam in the Netherlands we can notice how the building has been covered with a tarp that has the exterior of that same building printed on it. This, not only to cover the construction site and to protect the fasade during some repair work, but obviously also in order to keep the exterior, or the "texture" of this old building intact throughout the process of restoring this old train station.

As these two pictures above illustrate (Figure 22), the importance of textures for us as humans are clear, and the importance of *articulation* of textures (i.e. the level of details in a certain texture) also comes into focus here. Further on, and as the two pictures above illustrate, we are as humans very dependent on the appearance of our surrounding, and sometimes we intentionally articulate the textures as to create meaningful and aesthetically pleasing surroundings.

On the contrary, this might also be one reason why we immediately react when we see the orange tarp used at the left side of the train station building instead of yet another tarp with the original facade printed on it.

Figure 22. A textile-based texture that represents the underlying wall-based texture of an old building during some re-construction work of the facade

A critical challenge though for any texture design is to choose what material to work with. As in the case above it is critical that the visual appearance of the façade is good in terms of a flat surface. Here, the visual qualities of the facade are important and it is designed to be observed from a distance. In other cases the *feel* of the texture might be of focal concern. Therefore, any texture based design needs to be properly connected to the purpose of the texture as the texture will not only communicate a message or representation, but will also communicate some properties of the materials from which it is constructed. As to exemplify, the tarp with the printed facade do not only communicate a picture of the exterior of that building, but if standing close to the tarp it is also possible to see what kind of materials that has been used to create this texture including e.g. the textile or plastic material used, the printing technique, the resolution of the pictures used, the color correction schema applied, etc.

To create meaningful textures it is thus equally important to pay specific attention to the intended *appearance* of the texture as to pay attention to the materials chosen for a particular texture design, and the combination of different materials into a *coherent* structure. If a good mapping between these two aspects can be achieved it is likely that the texture will appear as a surface of high quality. If this mapping is however not achieved it is likely that the texture will communicate poor quality or a feeling of kitsch. Texture as the connection between a certain form and the underlying material properties is thus of critical importance in the design of representations, and in the creation of meaningful environments.

Another example of the way in which texture matter, and as an example of current efforts made to work with texture as to create wholeness in terms of appearance of different materials working together is the new Cool Art inverter from LG. This advanced piece of technology has been wrapped into the form of a traditional art frame as to blend itself into almost any indoor environment (see Figure 24). As illustrated by the following picture (see Figure 23) the content displayed in the frame can easily be altered as to work in any composition.

Figure 23. Content alteration procedure for the LG Cool Art Inverter as to adjust the texture of this piece of technology as to work in composition with other elements in the design of an indoor environment

Figure 24. Digital technology as painting textured in a living room

Through this ability to adjust the appearance of the technology it can be fully integrated in the wholeness of the space in which it is installed – i.e. it can be "texturized" in relation to the overall composition of the space. In Figure 24 and 25 that is further illustrated in which the inverter displays A) a piece of modern art (Figure 24), and B) a photo of the couple living in that particular house (Figure 25).

In a similar way, the electronics manufacturer Sony has designed one of their TVs as an art frame as to make the TV part of, or more easily texturized, in any hone environment. As an example of this see Figure 26.

In an attempt to define textures we can from the area of e.g. material science (e.g. Randle & Engles, 2000) and the architectural strand of literature (e.g. Ching,

Figure 25. Texturized technology in elegant interior design in the form of the LG Cool Art Inverter which has been designed as an art frame as to blend itself into any indoor environment composition

Figure 26. A TV set texturized as an art frame as to work in composition with the total appearance of the wall as a "gallery" or art collection

2007) notice that "texture" is typically defined as *"the feel, appearance, or consistency of a surface"* (a definition also used by Oxford dictionary).

As the above reasoning illustrate, this definition is quite useful for talking about textures in practical contexts as each of these concepts highlight different conceptual aspects of materials as they are used in larger assemblies of designed wholes.

Further on, if going into the literature within the field of material science we can see that:

"In most materials there is a pattern in the [crystallographic] orientations which are present and a propensity for the occurrence of certain orientations caused firstly during crystallization from a melt or amorphous solid state and subsequently by further termomechanical processes. This tendency is known as preferred orientation or, more concisely, texture" (Randle & Engler, 2000, p.3).

Here, we should notice that while texture might refer o the structures of designed wholes, they do at the same time refer to qualities fundamentally situated in the properties of a specific material at hand.

In this chapter I present a number of different examples of textures (see e.g. Figure 27 for an example) in order to demonstrate the importance of textures and how we can use textures to e.g. express artistic ideals, create whole-part consistency, and draw attention to different areas of our surrounding.

The pictures below show three such examples of (physical) textures (Figure 27).

The first example shows a concrete wall in which round empty spaces of air are working together with the hard, intense concrete material in the creation of a wall structure that is not only functional to separate this space from the rest of the

Figure 27. Three different examples of textures in physical environments

building to form a room, but it is also a piece of art that immediately draws some attention to it from any visitor to this public lecture hall in Sweden.

The second example is from the ICEHOTEL in Jukkasjärvi in the far north part of Sweden. Here, the architects and designers have worked with the ice, the light and the darkness as raw materials in the creation of an entire ice hotel. The texture of this environment is both welcoming and mystique at the same time. A texture capable of communicating the spirit of raw natural materials through careful design and architecture of a space created out of exactly those basic elements in nature. The wholeness of this space forms a wholeness or texture in which the different parts scaffold each other in a material orchestration of the far north and the exotic wilderness in Sweden.

Finally, the third texture used as an illustration of textures here is also a picture from ICEHOTEL in Jukkasjärvi, Sweden. Here, it is not the interplay of the wholeness that creates the texture, but rather the concistency of the rectangular squares of ice forming the wall structure of the interior at ICEHOTEL.

"Textures" is an interesting notion since it deals with surface and raw material at the same time. It is in a sense simultaneously about the appearance and the essence of a material. In a broad sense, this book is about these new textures and how they occupy, constitute and enable our everyday lives. I see these new textures, which partly are created through the adding of computational power, as visible signs of an emerging interaction society (Wiberg, 2004), or if formulated in another way, as an "Interaction grid" laid out across our society, geography, our built environments and our social rooms.

Computational materials are not only the physical hardware or the logical software, but also the services that these fundamental cornerstones of computers enable. As such, digital services adds an interesting philosophical dimension to the creation of new textures in that such textures can be made from physical and digital raw materials, but also partly realized through the adding of a digital service to the texture. In those cases, the texture might not be equally easy to discover visually as in the case with the train station construction site. Still, a skilled person in the area of interaction design or interactive architecture should be able to "read" the details of such new textures in which e.g. devices, services and physical representations are heavily intertwined. From my perspective, these are the building blocks of the modern textures that any designer, architect or artist will deal with in a nearby future. And from my perspective I like to think about the enabling character of these new textures as a wholeness in terms of an interaction grid. This interaction grid might be physically manifested in physical objects but a huge part of this grid is about digital materials including e.g. online resources, storage, processing power, information flows (including the whole range of solutions from e.g. secure data transactions to open RSS-streams), communication sessions, functions, algorithms, and various representation techniques.

Skilled programmers, interaction designers, human-computer interaction specialists, and others have recently started to play around with this interaction grid through the combining of different computational resources into new digital textures. This phenomenon has recently been labeled "mash-ups" (e.g. Murthy, et. al., 2006) and currently several companies are developing tools to make mesh-up design more easy to do. This includes online services like Yahoo pipes, Above All Studio, Dapper, JackBuilder, RSSBus and DataMeshups.com.

During the last few years researcher have also explored the creation of such digital textures in combination with physical materials through the design of various tangible user interfaces or simply "TUIs". These TUIs enable the texturing of digital and physical material into consistent structures that appears as a whole. Examples from this area include e.g. interactive textiles, interactive art pieces, and interactive lightening (e.g. Edmonds, et. al., 2004). Here, traditional raw materials of textiles, canvases and light bulbs are combined with some computational material including e.g. processing power, information sources and sensors in representations that sits in between the physical and the digital world.

Interactive architecture is now one empirical indicator of the next step in this development. Both in terms of scale (from the small device to the size of the building), but also in terms of the people involved in the process of design. From being an issue for information architects, programmers and interaction designers this phenomenon is now hitting the masses. Designers, architects and artists will come together and work with the people that will inhabit these new spaces.

While the notion of textures is specifically introduced in this book to shed some light on the development towards digitalized environments the fundamental value of textures is a more widespread concept and it can be found in a wide range of areas including e.g. conversation analysis, art, architecture and material science.

So, if now relying on the definition of textures found in material science (e.g. Kocks, et. al., 1998, Randle & Engles, 2000; and Rollett, 2008) and the architectural strand of literature (e.g. Ching, 2007) we might also notice that this definition of textures as being about "the feel, appearance, or consistency of a surface" is quite similar to modern definitions of user interfaces in interaction design and HCI literature. I.e. "the feel" of a surface map quite well onto the ways in which we describe "look and feel" aspects of user interfaces including immaterial, emotional and perception related aspects of digital user interfaces. "Appearance" is also similar to the notion of "representation" as it is being used in the computer science literature, and "consistency" is yet again a concept with clear anchorage in the Human-Computer Interaction literature, which includes similar concepts including "consistency", and "coherency" which again points at our needs to be able to "read" the environment as a meaningful wholeness.

Given this way of translating the notion of texture from the area of architecture and material science to the area of human-computer interaction and interaction design, then I also find it necessary to go into details about the computational as a material and de-construct the user interface for the purpose of discovering the "raw material" of the computational, unhidden behind any surface, but instead use this notion of texture to rediscover this modern dynamic material. In the next section I will therefore set out to start this exploration.

DECONSTRUCTING THE USER INTERFACE

Given the recent development in ubiquitous computing, ambient intelligence, embedded computing, and interactive architecture it is becoming increasingly hard to push the traditional "graphical user interface" metaphor as the leading concept for interaction design any much longer. Instead, as computational power gets blended with our surroundings we need theories and concepts capable of addressing how the physical, the social and the digital is now becoming one. In this chapter I propose "texture" and "texturation" as two interlinked concepts capable of describing the new "surfaces" of our reality and the process through which this integration happens.

According to *Wikipedia (*www.wikipedia.org*)* the notion of "texture" refers to:

"The properties held and sensations caused by the external surface of objects received through the sense of touch. Texture is sometimes used to describe the feel of non-tactile sensations. Texture can also be termed as a pattern that has been scaled down (especially in case of two dimensional non-tactile textures) where the individual elements that go on to make the pattern not distinguishable." Wikipedia (08-10-19)

The physical environment is in many ways very rich. We can see patterns in the physical environment on many levels of details ranging form macro-structures to patterns hardly observable with microscopes. Today, this is very different from the limited input/output facilities of modern computers. Typically, a keyboard and a mouse are used for input, and an ordinary screen for output. The surface, or the "texture" of this material is flat, dead and very limited compared to the raw materials in nature. However, this stereotypic way of interacting with computational materials in terms of processing power, storage, networking and input/output is now rapidly changing due to the development into tangible interaction, interactive architecture, ambient intelligence, etc. In all these subfields a lot of initiatives are taken to explore material blending of physical materials with the digital.

If looking into "texturation" as the process of "material blending" from a wide range of different directions in which digital technologies are getting totally blended into the fabrics of everyday life we can at least distinguish three such directions, including a *literary, logical* and *philosophical* direction.

From a *literary* point of view we can notice how digital technology gets "blended" into our physical surround in the creation of so called "ambient information spaces" (e.g. Pousman & Stasko, 2006). Here, the ultimate goal is to create physical spaces in which computational power is ready at hand in the environment, but still visually hidden as to make the processing power of the computational present while getting rid of the intrusive packaging of the computational in the traditional form of a computer (e.g. a stationary computer or a laptop).

From a *logical* point of view the current development and widespread adoption of new mobile services, technologies and networking capabilities are creating a digital "layer" or "interaction grid" across our physical geography thus enabling computing virtually everywhere (Greenfield, 2006). An understanding of how this logical interaction grid can be accessed, used, and blended with our built environments is crucial in order to understand the current streams of development in terms of texturation of information and interaction technologies in our everyday world.

Finally, from a *philosophical* viewpoint Dourish (2006) has acknowledged the recent "re-spacing of place" as an important movement from virtual online worlds towards mobile interaction including new phenomena like e.g. "smartmobs" (Reingold, 2002), mobile twittering, and mobile email. This direction is fundamental on a philosophical level, at the same time as it is heavily connected to the other two levels of texturation operating in this current development.

If looking at these three directions we might also notice that besides being different and complementary perspectives they all bear with them a fundamental change. The *literary* direction moves computational resources into the built environment thus enabling new materials that can constitute our built environments. The *logical* direction is not as hands-on as the literary direction, but ubiquitous access to computational power will have an equally important impact on the built environments. Finally, the development pointing in the direction of a philosophical turn from the "re-place-ing of space (Harrison & Dourish, 1996) towards the "re-space-ing of place" (Dourish, 2006) describes a movement from the creation of virtual worlds towards the true integration of the virtual in the physical world. This is an important ontological shift that means that the worlds of the virtual and the digital in becoming one, and not only co-exist, or become overlapping, but they will be fully integrated and we thus need a design thinking that takes these dimensions of our world into serious consideration.

Serious design thinking in this area forces us to de-construct the user interface of computers as we know it today, and instead direct our attention towards interaction *per se* and what kind of interactional commitments people what to engage themselves in, computational materials instead o computers, and textures of physical-digital materials rather than flat surfaces. Such design thinking can lead us in the direction of resolving how we should go about texturing information and interaction technologies in our everyday world, from social contexts to the physicality of our built environment.

DISCOVERING TEXTURES

New textures in the form of e.g. new innovative display techniques, digital facades, interactive sculptures, etc. are now finding their ways into the built environment and the public space. In one sense, it is an obvious sign of an ongoing digitalization of our society which might be easier to "see" than e.g. the current widespread and large scale adoption of computers in our homes or the rapid increase in the adoption and use of mobile phones across the whole population at least in the western world. Still, as with most changes in our society development in the areas of interactive architecture, new materials and new textures is happening gradually and slowly.

To understand this development we should probably view it as an iceberg in which most of the development happens through a slow transition towards digitalized environments, and in which the extreme buildings including art museums and concert halls covered with e.g. led pixels are manifestations and concrete signs of a much more fundamental development. Our job as professional designers, architects and interaction specialists is to keep track of these manifestations of change since they serve as important hallmarks of the current development, and as important points of departure for evoking conversations about these slow change innovation processes that is forming and re-forming our society and our built environment.

Not only due to the process of slow changing movements in the digitalization of our society, but also due to the very character of textures *per se*, it is hard to distinguish the textures around us without a particular analytical lens and a certain perspective on the world around us.

Textures are hard to "see" and discover due to the very nature of textures. This might be complex to understand, but it is hard to separate an object or a material from the rest of the world without understanding it through its texture. Equally, it is hard to discover the texture of the material in terms of how it is connected to the raw materials from which it is made without just focusing on the surface, or the "skin" of a product or an object. What makes it difficult is that textures sits in between materials and this "skin". To discover textures is not about discovering "surfaces". Nor is it about seeing the raw materials from which things are built. Instead, textures are about seeing the structures in between. It is about seeing how material properties are communicated through the form that a certain material, or collection of materials have been given through the process of design. Here, it becomes obvious that in order to discover textures we need as a good understanding of what textures are, and we need a good repertoire of examples that illustrate how we might identify, work with and understand different textures as to also learn how to discover them given different circumstances and areas of application. In the following section an attempt is therefore made to elaborate upon various application areas of textures as to enrich our understanding of how it is integrated in areas like music, physics and computer science, and how we might use this analytical "lens" to read our world in new ways.

The notion of "texture" has illustrated its value and bearing for several different areas including e.g. geology, in which it describes the physical appearance or character of a rock, in food, then concerning the way food feels in a person's mouth, in cosmology, as a type of theoretical topological defect in the structure of space-time, and so on.

Generally speaking the notion of textures brings together appearance, feel and consistency of a material. The concept has certainly been employed in a more metaphorical register as well, often used to describe the "feel" of non-tactile sensations. E.g. in painting it has been applied to describe the feel of the canvas based on the paint used and its method of application, i.e. as a way of addressing an Effect or Consequence of the material. Further on, in music, the notion of texture has been introduced as a way to describe the overall sound created by the interaction of aspects of a piece of music, thus functioning as a descriptive model of interaction a certain type of interaction. From a historical and social perspective we can also find examples of the application of the notion of texture to describe character structure, including various life experiences resulting in the "texture" of one's character.

Texture can also be termed as a pattern that has been scaled down (especially in case of two dimensional non-tactile textures) where the individual elements that goes on to make the pattern not distinguishable.

More closely related to the area of computer science the notion of texture has been mostly applied to describe e.g. a bitmap image applied to a surface in computer graphics, or as e.g. well-known software programs to typeset TeX and LaTeX.

If now taking one step back, and if we look into questions related to how the notion of texture is addressed in the area of painting we notice that here "texture" typically refers to the feel of the canvas based on the paint used and its method of application. In other words, then texture refers to an *effect* or *consequence* of the material in focus. Similarly, if looking in the area of music, then texture typically refers to a way to describe the overall sound created by the interaction of aspects of a piece of music. Thus meaning that here the notion of texture function as a *descriptive model of interaction*, or *model of a composition*. In other words, texture might refer both to material properties and how these properties are communicated through a given texture, as it has to do with compositions of materials and the methods of carving out a certain texture.

In my own research I am using the term "texture" to refer to the negotiation, interface or transition between surface and structural form. In doing this I strive to articulate both the ways in which this term speaks to both a gap in the current literature and I demonstrate how the term organizes thinking across material, digital space, or physical and symbolic representations in a manner useful to new materials

ARTICULATION OF TEXTURES

When going into details about textures we should also think hard about how we describe the structure of the very concept of texture, i.e. "the textures of texture". That is, we should challenge ourselves and think about whether the notion of textures is just a word or label, or if it is in fact a gateway to a larger theoretical framework in which we strive to interlink the physical with the social through social and architectural thinking on places. I think that we're aiming for this second perspective. In doing so we should think about how textures not only relate to materials, but also adds to the formulation of architectural elements as well as how textures add to, or affect our understanding of these built environments.

In my research I am addressing the notion of textures through the following diagram (see Figure 28). In this diagram I outline the basic aspects of textures in relation to the physical surrounding from an architectural point of view, and then we integrate that perspective with a description of how we see these textures as being interlinked with digital technologies from the viewpoint of interaction design in an attempt to outline this "texture of textures".

In this model I chose to view the notion of textures from two basic perspectives. I view textures as the surface aspects of design materials, or architectural elements, i.e. how a certain material might appear ones installed in a physical space, and how it might work together with other materials in that particular space. I think about this in terms of textures as the surfaces of the "real", i.e. as surfaces of materials. On the other hand, I am equally interested in understanding how textures are perceived and brought into use in people's everyday lives.

Figure 28. Schematic model illustrating the "texture of textures"

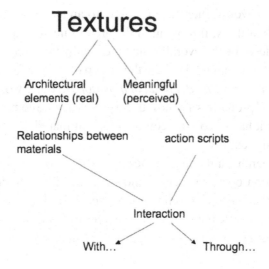

As illustrated in Figure 28 a plausible understanding of textures can be given from 1) an architectural perspective in which we pay close attention to "the real" or materials as they form new structures and elements that taken together gives us full scale built environments and 2) as a concept which deals with the way we perceive and experience our surrounding as a meaningful whole. Following the architectural line of thinking then these architectural elements come together as textures as we start to understand and read the relationships between different materials that compose a built environment. At the same time the textures that we perceive and understand also gives us the tools to act upon the things we perceive, thus enabling us to develop certain scripts of actions possible to execute in any familiar environment. Finally, the architectural perspective together with our interpretation of the world around us enable us to start working with the materials, i.e. to interact with and through the materials at hand, digitalized or not.

MEANINGFUL ENVIRONMENTS

Given a perspective in which textures are heavily related to architecture and to the creation of meaningful environments we should also spend some extra time to reflect upon the relation between "textures" and the notion of "meaningfulness" as another important concept in relation to architecture. In its most basic form, meaningfulness is achieved when we understand what we experience, i.e. when we're confronted with something and it make sense to us, we can connect meaning to it, and we can label it "meaningful".

This notion of "meaningfulness" might also be achieved if the design of a certain texture is made in relation to an identified human need, or if the texture also corresponds well to a certain form that enable a solution to a problem, or a function that enable us to do things that might be hard, or even impossible without that certain element at hand.

On a deeper level, meaningfulness might also need to be connected to our ability to describe the purposefulness of an object, environment or action. Alternatively, if the "meaning" of it is connected to some fundamental values grounds in our lives which might range from aesthetic values to more fundamental ethical, political or religious values.

In the end, what makes a certain texture work or not in terms of meaningfulness is in fact embedded in the very concept of textures. Texture is simultaneously about surface and the underlying material. Texturing is about creating this relation between the surface expression and the properties of the material at hand. Thus, if a certain material isn't textured properly, it will be obvious that it does not relate or fit with the other co-present textures and materials thus failing to work as a texture in a certain context.

A texture gives access to a material by making the material more abstract, but simultaneously making its representation more clear. In the creation of meaningful environments we should carefully consider this fact. Raw materials are simply materials without a designed texture. A raw material typically has a certain texture, but it has not been purposefully formed through the process of design. Through design a raw material can be refined and adjusted in relation to other materials as to make it work in composition with other materials. In this process, the raw material is becoming something different from its basic character as it gets tweaked into a new form. This is what I mean when saying that materials are becoming more abstract through the design process of texturization. Further on, the statement that a texture makes a material's representation more clear might also need some clarifications. If texturation is about the design process of carefully considering the unique properties of a material and how it can be used to express a certain material more clearly then the representation of the material will become clearer. E.g. a diamond in the ruff is one thing, but if cut properly, i.e. in relation to the specific character of that particular piece of material its value and appearance can be much more clear. That is, even though it is still the same raw material its representation is enhanced through a design process that has paid specific and detailed attention to the properties of the material at hand.

In the area of craftsmanship we have a long tradition of working with the details of material in a process of bring forward the uniqueness of a piece of material in which the texture plays an important role. We see it in the craft of wood, in glass design, and in the handling of iron. Thus, it is not unlikely that we in a nearby future might pay equal attention to the fundamental properties of computational materials as to explore how it texturize it in various physical and social contexts.

Speaking about different contexts, we should also acknowledge the wide range of textures, and modes of approaches to textures in our society. An understanding of these different modes is crucial to design meaningful textures. In more concrete terms, then texture in its most basic form is about the surfaces that connect the appearance of a material to the material properties from which the texture is realized. In that sense we can say that textures communicate properties of a material. This communication is crucial for any meaningful texturation.

Further on, textures also communicate arranged materials. Here, the term "arranged" refers to a purposely designed composition of materials that make them appear as a coherent and meaningful surface to an observer.

Texture might also be understood not only as a character of an object or a surface, but as a verb. Then texture, or texturization, becomes a process that is interesting to observe and analyze from a design perspective on how to create meaningful designs. In this process, adjustments are made to materials as to make them work together as a whole. As such, texture appears as a method or technique of adjusting parts in relation to a theory of the whole as to make the composition of these materials meaningful.

Textures might also work as media or a channel. Either a channel capable of connecting remote persons in real time (a plausible scenario if networked IT is part of the materials that form a certain texture), or as a stage for face-to-face interaction. Such media textures might also work as an historical bridge (e.g. the Egypt hieroglyphs might be one such texture). Still, if these textures make sense to us, we can also say that they contribute to the meaningfulness of a certain place, location or object in how it speaks to us, or connects us across times in terms of history, and across places in terms of geography.

Some materials might come in small pieces, but it might be the case that the materials at hand are big chunks of materials (like mountain rocks, or large IT-infrastructures). Here, textures can thus also be about how we see these large structures. That is, textures offer us a lens through which we can perceive and interpret the world around us. And, such textures can present us with some signs on how these large structures might be accessible, manageable, configurable and used. The relation between textures and infrastructures could therefore be described as the *enabling* (i.e. the structure or infrastructure) and the *enabler* (i.e. the texture). Without the proper gateways or methods of access (i.e. textures) the potential of an established infrastructure cannot be put to use or even explored.

There is however a paradox hidden in this argumentation. On the one hand, we can see this clear relation between texture and material. On the other hand however, a well-implemented texture can also hide the underlying infrastructure. We can see this happening in a wide range of fields ranging from e.g. design of ambient information spaces to how politics work in the society. Through elegant texturing of IT in a physical space the computer itself can disappear and only leave the computational power traceable in the room. Similarly, a political agenda can be elegantly texturized in the societal debate so that the rhetoric of the agenda is hard to distinguish from the raw facts underlying a certain question. Ultimately however, this is a question about intertwining materials and appearance, i.e. it is about designing meaningful, or apparently meaningful textures.

Given this reasoning a four leveled design challenge for anyone interested in designing meaningful IT-enabled environments based on this notion of texture is now possible to outline.

First of all, if IT is part of the overall design, it is a material that needs some specific concerns. IT is normally treated as already texturized in a very specific form. When someone says "IT" or "computer" then most people think about a stationary computer or maybe a laptop computer. These forms are heavily connected to the essence of what a computer is in the minds of people. To some extent, it is almost the case that the form has substituted the properties of computational materials. Sometimes I have challenged friends and colleagues by picking up my mobile phone and say that them that I will make a call from my computer. This statement is typically viewed as kind of odd. Probably due to this fundamentally rooted view that a computer also have a certain physical form. This can of course also be extended to all cases in our society in which we have embedded microprocessors, including e.g. street signals, refrigerators, cars, etc. To me, it is extremely important that we constantly challenge this stereotypic view of the computer as to keep our perception and imagination open for how computational materials could be part of our everyday textures.

Secondly, if we manage to separate IT from traditional thinking around its form we're then facing the next design challenge. This challenge is then of course about shaping this material and to give it a new form. Following the line of reasoning as put toward in this chapter this will be an act of texturization in which basic questions about the properties of the computational and how these properties of the material can be brought forward into the design of a meaningful surface needs to be addressed. Through a proper texturization process the computational will be intertwined with other materials thus making it totally integrated in its new form.

A third challenge is then about connecting it as part of any underlying infrastructure, being it IT networks, standards, or electricity issues, or more social issues related to policies, routines, social behavior, organization, division of labor, or other social structures.

Having the technology texturized both physically and socially, then the fourth challenge is about the texturing of a new technology in peoples everyday lives. That is, how to present this new texture as a canvas that people can "read" or understand, as well as "write" in terms of use and alignment to their everyday activities. More about that in the coming section.

READING AND REWRITING TEXTURES

It might be part of human nature that we always want to adjust everything in the process of adopting new objects into our lives. If we're buying a house we might want to re-decorate it. If we get a new computer we might want to "personalize" it with our own wallpaper, personal settings, etc. In some general words, we do not only want to "use" an object, understand it, and in that way "read" it into our lives. But we're typically interested in also "rewriting" these objects in terms of changing its purpose, reframing it, adjusting it, etc as to fit our everyday needs and lives.

This section above illustrates these two aspects of reading and rewriting textures quite well. The textures around us give us some "clues" or signs about how to interpret the different materials that we see, as well as it gives us some clues about *how to* read these textures. Through the act of reading textures we learn about the surrounding. On the other hand, the re-writing of textures gives us the opportunity to not only observe, but in fact have an impact on, and change the things around us, i.e. to re-write the textures that form our physical surrounding.

We can "read" and "write" the physical in a wide range of ways, i.e. through various actions taken we can "read" or "see" different aspects of the physical, and the ways we can "write" or affect the physical also ranges from small scale and simple interventions to advanced actions that might even redefine the fundamental properties of a certain material (compare e.g. the simple action of cutting wood to advanced gene-manipulation of plants).

With these two approaches to textures ready at hand we might now be ready to think about our surrounding in terms of textures (i.e. the ability to "read" textures), and we might be ready to both structurally plan for changes in the current textures of our built environment (i.e. the re-writing texturation approach typically labeled "architecture").

Still, in order to understand and work with the so-called "new architecture" including e.g. the area of IA – interactive architecture we need to apply this thinking to modern information technology as a design material possible to texturize, read, and re-write.

REFERENCES

Brownell, B. (2005). *Transmaterial: A Catalog of Materials That Redefine our Physical Environment*. Princeton Architectural Press.

Brownell, B. (2008). *Transmaterial 2: A Catalog of Materials That Redefine our Physical Environment*. Princeton Architectural Press.

Ching, F. (2007). *Architecture: Form, Space, and Order*. New York: John Wiley & Sons, Inc.

Dourish, P. (2006). Re-space-ing place: "place" and "space" ten years on. In *Proceedings of the 2006 20th Anniversary Conference on Computer Supported Cooperative Work* (Banff, Alberta, Canada, November 04-08, 2006), CSCW '06 (pp. 299-308). New York: ACM.

Edmonds, E., Turner, G., & Candy, L. (2004). Approaches to interactive art systems. In S.N. Spencer (Ed.), *Proceedings of the 2nd international Conference on Computer Graphics and interactive Techniques in Australasia and South East Asia* (Singapore, June 15-18, 2004). GRAPHITE '04 (pp. 113-117). New York: ACM.

Greenfield, A. (2006). *Everyware – The dawning age of ubiquitous computing*. Berkeley, CA: New Riders.

Harrison, S., & Dourish, P. (1996). Re-place-ing space: the roles of place and space in collaborative systems. In M.S. Ackerman (Ed.), *Proceedings of the 1996 ACM Conference on Computer Supported Cooperative Work* (Boston, Massachusetts, United States, November 16 - 20, 1996) (pp. 67-76). CSCW '96. New York: ACM.

Lupton, E. (2007). *Skin*. Princeton Architectural Press.

Pousman, Z., & Stasko, J. (2006) A taxonomy of ambient information systems: Four patterns of design. In *Proceedings of AVI '06 - the working conference on Advanced visual interfaces*. ACM Press.

Randle, V., & Engler, O. (2000). *Introduction to Texture Analysis: Macrotexture, Microtexture, and Orientation Mapping*. Singapore: Gordon and Breach Science Publishers.

Rheingold, H. (2002). *Smart Mobs: The Next Social Revolution*. Cambridge, MA: Perseus Book Group.

Weick, K. E. (1979). *The Social Psychology of Organizing* (2nd ed.). Reading, MA: Addison-Wesley.

Chapter 3
A New Architecture?

There are several indicators pointing in one interesting direction, i.e. the rise of a new paradigm for architecture. Or, if formulated slightly different, then it is about the rise of a new architecture.

As indicated in chapter 1 and 2 we're formulating new life worlds right now in which computational power is an essential element. Sometimes these life worlds are purely digitally based in that e.g. new social networks are formed on the Internet in online forums like Facebook and Linked, or across online communication services like Twitter. In other cases, computational power is used as one design material intertwined with other materials in real world physical installations. It is in this second sense that interactive architecture comes into the picture, and it is here we might say that we can start to see a new architecture arising.

In this chapter we first take a look at traditional architecture from the perspective of what fundamental building blocks this area is made off. Thus, we're not going into history of architecture. Neither are we reviewing the different genres of architecture as they have been developed in different countries over different ages. Instead, we look at the fundamental concepts that form the area of architecture *per se*.

Having reviewed the area of architecture from this conceptual perspective we then take a look at some indications pointing in the direction of a new architecture. Finally, this chapter discusses the potential of this new architecture in relation to the notion of the "sciences of the artificial" as proposed by Herbert Simon (1969).

DOI: 10.4018/978-1-61520-653-7.ch003

TRADITIONAL ARCHITECTURE

So, how might we frame architecture? What is architecture all about? Or formulated slightly different, then what are the fundamental concepts or primary elements on which any architecture rests? If we are to talk about interactive architecture, or if we are to speak generally about a new architecture then we first need a good understanding of architecture *per se*.

If first looking at traditional architecture we can say that it is about the built environment, and typical architectural systems deals with the architecture of *space, structure,* or *enclosure*. This includes questions about organizational pattern, relationships, clarity and hierarchy. Formal image and spatial definition, qualities of shape, color, texture, scale and proportion, as well as qualities of surfaces, edges and openings. Here, a *spatial system* refers to the three dimensional integration of program elements and spaces that accommodates the multiple functions and relationships of a building. Further on, a *structural system* might be a grid of columns supporting horizontal beams and slabs, thus being about the fundamentals to enable and keep the physical form intact. Finally, an *enclosure system* can be defined as the use of elements to frame a specific piece of architecture, e.g. four exterior wall planes defines a rectangular volume that contains the program elements and spaces (Ching, 2007).

To these basic systems we can then add e.g. circular systems that deals with movement through the built environment, and we might add context as an important perspective for understanding how different architectural solutions could be brought together in the creation of functioning wholes, both in terms of physical realization as well as how it correspond to a certain accommodated program.

When saying that a built environment is accommodating a *program* this includes an understanding of the use of that built environment in terms of e.g. user requirements, needs and aspiration, as well as the acknowledging of socio-cultural factors, economic factors, legal constraints, and historical tradition and precedents (Ching, 2007).

In terms of architectural systems and orders we can in traditional architecture identify at least three different levels. These three levels include the *physical level* that deals with questions related to solids and voids as well as questions related to interior and exterior.

Further on, the *perceptual level* deals with questions related to sensory perception and recognition of the physical elements by experiencing them sequentially in time. Some typical areas of architectural systems and organizations on this level include e.g. approach and departure, entry and egress, movement through the order of spaces, functioning of and activities within spaces, and qualities of light, color, texture, view, and sound.

Finally, in architecture the *conceptual level* deals with questions related to comprehension of the ordered or disordered relationships among a building's elements and systems, and how we respond to the meanings they evoke. This level frames architectural systems and organizations dealing with e.g. images, patterns, signs, symbols, and context. In architecture, this notion of context can be described as the relationships between functions, space, form and techniques. Here, technique refers to the theory, principles, or study of an art or a process. (Ching, 2007).

Traditional architecture is about the built environment and it can be viewed or understood as being designed as 1) a coherent structure (internal state), and 2) a relational surface (correspondence). In order to "read" one certain architecture it is important to take these two dimensions into account. In this book, the notion of texture has been introduced to make this transition between the internal state and the surface as smooth as possible. In fact, as presented in this book, then texture is this concept that unifies the internal state with the surface of a material, an element, a facade, or even a whole architectural installation (ranging from the public sculpture or a single building to large scale architectural structures, blocks or systems). In other words, if any architecture is to make sense for its observer or inhabitant it needs to communicate not only its form and use, but also make sense in terms of how these two are interlinked in the built environment.

To systematically work in this direction a basic understanding of the conceptual primary elements in architecture is needed. In this next section I therefore present the most basic concepts underlying any architecture situated in the physical world.

THE BASICS OF ARCHITECTURE

There are at least four fundamental primary elements working together in any architecture. These four include the concepts of *point, line, plane,* and *volume*.

A point indicates a position in space. Conceptually, a point has no length, width, or depth, and is therefore static, centralized and directionless. According to Ching (2007) as the prime element in the vocabulary of form, a point can serve to mark e.g. the two ends of a line, the intersection of two lines, the meeting of lines at the corner of a plane or volume, or even the center of a field. As highlighted by Ching (2007), an interesting aspect of a point is that although it has neither shape, nor form, it begins to make its presence felt when places within a visual field.

"At the center of its environment, a point is stable and at rest, organizing surrounding elements about itself and dominating its field. When the point is moved off-center, however, its field becomes more aggressive and begins to compete for visual supremacy. Visual tension is created between the point and its field" (Ching, 2007, p. 4).

As this quote illustrate, the basic concepts in architecture is not only functional concepts that describe certain aspects of the built environment. Instead, these concepts are very much about the ways in which we perceive the built environment, and potentially about how we might interact with or through it. These basic concepts can be used to draw our attention to some specific parts of the built environment, thus guiding us to "see" how we potentially could interact with a space, or how we could make use of it in several different ways.

If moving on to the next basic concept in architecture and, if following an order of increased complexity, the next concept is the *line*. A line can be defined as an extended point that holds the dimensions of length, direction and position. Another way of defining a line is to say that it is the connection between two points separated in space. This definition gives a line a finite length. However, a line can also be considered a segment of an infinitely longer path. If talking about direction, then as formulated by Ching (2007) two points also suggest an axis perpendicular to the line they describe and about which they are symmetrical.

Following this scale of complexity now direct us towards the third concept, which is the notion of *plane* in architecture. A plane can be defined as an extended line (if extended along this perpendicular axis as described above). A plane extends the line with bearing properties of not only length, but also width, as well as having properties of shape, surface orientation, and position. If looking at different ways to realize a plane we can start off with a simple model in which two parallel lines visually form a plane. As described by Ching (2007) a transparent spatial membrane can be stretched between them to acknowledge their visual relationship. The closer these lines are to each other, the stronger will be the sense of plane they convey. If taking this example one step further, then a series of parallel lines, through their repetitiveness, reinforces our perception of the plane they describe. This series will not be perceived as several separated planes, but instead, these planes will be understood as a wholeness in which each plane links together with the others to form one coherent structure.

Finally, the forth concept of *volume* can be defined as an extended plane with the properties of not only length, and width, but also depth. These three dimensions of length, width and depth form the basic conceptual essence of a volume. A volume also holds the properties of form and space, surface, orientation and position Ching (2007). Form is also the primary identifying characteristics of a volume. This is especially interesting in relation to the notion of texture as being especially highlighted in this book. As it can be noticed here, it is at this level of complexity we can start to see structures in materials, materials formed into surfaces beyond flat 2D-planes, and thus where material choices really comes into the picture in the area of architecture, and architecturally situated texture design. In relation to this we should also acknowledge that a volume can be either a solid, i.e. space displaced by mass, or a void, i.e. a space contained or enclosed by planes. This is also of particular interest in relation to texture since the appearance of a texture is on the one hand about the ways in which the material is carved out to a certain from, but equally out the ways in which voids has been used to mark out a certain texture. Thus, equal attention needs to be paid at material-based design and void-based design when focusing on the creation of new architectural textures.

If taken together, then these four concepts give us a basic theory, or at least a conceptual framework that describes the primary elements of architecture. In doing so, it provide us with a foundation for analyzing built environments, as well as it functions as a simple guide in the design and realization of new environments. These four concepts also provide us with a conceptual framework for positioning the notion of textures in relation to architecture. Both, in terms of the level of complexity this concept of texture coverers, but also in terms of how the concept include both aspects related to solids and voids as fundamental aspects of any material, surface, or built structure.

Still, there are many more concepts that can be brought into the picture as to enrich our understanding of architecture from a conceptual viewpoint. Following Ching (2007) one such extension might include e.g. basic concepts like *edges, corners,* and *circles,* as well as more complicated architectural terms including *interlocked spaces, adjacent spaces, clusters* and *grids,* followed by some advanced architectural principles for the structuring of space including e.g. the notions of *hierarchy, datum, rhythm, repetition* and *transformation.*

All these concepts also have their definitions, properties and techniques for application. Taken together, these concepts forms a language or semantics (Krippendorf, 2005) for addressing specific details, dimensions and perspectives in relation to architecture as an area of study, as well as a practice.

On a strategic level, this language gives us a tool to talk about the composition of elements and materials into meaningful spaces. Also, on a literary level, these concepts given us some valuable tools for articulating various dimensions of textures as an important aspect of architecture.

ARCHITECTURE AND THE BUILT ENVIRONMENT

Architecture as a field has a special relation to our built environment. It is not purely a theoretical field, but in fact a very practical approach to large scale designs in our society. In fact, architecture might be considered as a design approach to our modern world. Of course, architectural thinking, and concepts rooted in the literature of architecture could be used purely to analyze different aspects of the built environment. Still, however, it is a field that is highly design-oriented and future-oriented. It is a normative field situated in between theory and practice that strives to inform us on how to build socially-, and technically sound spaces. Thus, architecture is not only interested in the *built* world, but also heavily focused on the process of *building* as an active social and material intervention approach to our society.

Architecture is also a plan-driven field. It is a proactive approach filled with methods and techniques for planning for the built environment to be. Thus, architecture is not only focused on this process of actually building spaces. That might be the result of a successful process in architecture. Instead, architecture as a field and approach to the built environment covers the whole process from ideation to sketches, model makings, drawings, blueprints, situation plans, etc. as well as the processes surrounding building and constructing new spaces.

In metaphorical terms architecture can be thought of in many terms including e.g. model, plan, structure, philosophy, history, and message. In terms of model architecture has always been about modeling the built environment, and to make models of alternative future built environments. Following this future-orientation in architecture then the notion of plans comes into the picture. Architecture is also about making these plans and about using models, sketches and blueprints to visualize what the built environment could be about in relation to the different architectural systems as outlined in the beginning of this chapter. When talking about these systems then it also becomes natural to think about architecture in terms of design of structures. When looking into any architecture we can notice that any built environment in fact consist of several systems working together in parallel. Still, architecture is not only about the presence and the concrete aspects of building new spaces. On the contrary, architecture is very much about the past, or at least about traditions and history in which new designs can be situated in terms of building genre, trends, époques, etc. Thus, history is a very important concept to bring along any description of what architecture is about. Having these two dimensions of "right here, right now" construction of built environments in combination with historical anchoring activities in architecture also invites philosophy as a natural part of architectural thinking. And, given that we think hard about the meaning of architecture and how meaning gets inscribed in architecture I am sure we also need to consider how architecture also function as a media, and how architecture can be thought of as a carrier, or container of messages.

TOWARDS A NEW ARCHITECTURE

There is an ongoing digitalization in and of our society. Related to the field of architecture we now have a wide set of digital *tools* available in support of various architectural processes (including e.g. CAD tools – Computer Aided Design tools,

3D tools, animation tools, etc). We are also experiencing a fast growing interest and development in creation of new *digital places* including virtual cities and online social communities.

From another perspective, and as highlighted in this book, digital technology is starting to have a direct effect on the built environment itself as computers gets *attached*, or *embedded* in our physical environment.

Up until now architecture and interaction design has been two separated instances for design thinking[1]. However, there are some growing obvious signs of a development in which these two trends are merging. This includes e.g. practical cases in which these two fields meet in installations ranging from e.g. the attaching of digital displays onto existing façade textures (see the picture below for one such example) as well as exteriors covered with novel display technologies. These signs of a merger between architecture and interaction design is also evident in the current literature including the recent work by McCullough, 2004; Bullivant, 2005; Spiller, 2002; and e.g. Sparacino, 2008. As these technologies develop they will be more interactive and more embedded in the textures of the built environment.

Following this line of development in which we texturize digital technologies as part of our built environments it becomes obvious that we're facing a new line of development in architecture. Digital technologies will constitute a new design material for architects and with the capabilities that follow with this technology, including the possibilities of making built spaces dynamically informative, reactive, responsive, and interactive, we might even want to think about this line of development more in terms of a shift, i.e. as a fundamental shift in architecture – towards a new architecture?

Probably this development is not happening dramatically over night. Instead, this will probably be a slow process in which building owners might work together with technology providers, interaction designers, media producers, architects, etc with small scale installations that over time will build up more complex partly digitalized spaces. Figure 29 is a good example of this slow change development. In the beginning this was a typical building with no digital elements being part of its exterior design. Over the years, however, and in line with the technical developments, the corner facade of this building has been equipped with some new digital elements. In terms of the form factor of these elements they are clearly not embedded as part of the exterior. That is, at least not yet. Contrary to this simple observation, however, we might also notice that the display elements have been given a curved form as to make them follow the exterior texture of this building, as a way of adjusting these elements somewhat to the physical form of the building. One could easily image that given more advanced technologies that would make it easier to adjust the displays to the physical texture of this building then the digital

Figure 29. Added digital technologies to an existing physical texture

elements would probably end up being much more integrated in the overall exterior design of this particular building.

As these elements are added to the facade they do not only challenge the physical form of this building, and its exterior texture. The adding of the digital elements also challenges the purpose of the exterior and what it communicates.

The rounded corner of this building indicates an opening or entrance to the building, and the corner also creates a void outside that work as an open space safe from traffic outside the entrance. The corner design also increases visibility for the traffic in this crossroad. With the added digital technology, this simple architecture is challenged. The digital elements could on the one hand be used as to increase the "message" behind the architecture of this particular building. Typically, though, these kinds of digital signage are placed rather random on many buildings in cities in which the content and intended use of the displays draws the attention away from the architecture of the building, challenge the architecture, or make the architecture blurrier.

Thus, a central challenge for this new architecture must be to strive to align physical and digital materials into textures capable of communicating the built environment as a whole, or formulated through the terms introduced earlier in this chapter, as one coherent appearance and architectonic message.

Today, there is a lot of experimenting with new digital materials going on in architecture and interior design. In different ways the digital is introduced into physical spaces as to enrich, challenge and re-think a physical space. The following pictures from a shopping mall in Dubai serves as a good and typical example of how digital technology is integrated in an experiment on how to create new digitalized architectural textures at the scale of a public meeting spot (see Figure 30).

Figure 30. Digital texture in a shopping mall in Dubai[2]

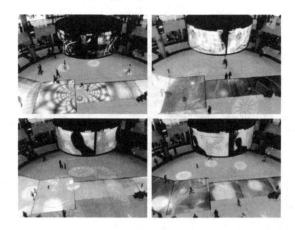

PHYSICAL AND DIGITAL MATERIALS

Throughout this book the physical and the digital has been discussed as two rather different strands of materials. While the next chapter is focused on describing the new materials available for a new architecture, there are also some needs for a more general discussion about the physical and the digital in relation to architecture as a general approach to the creation of meaningful environments.

In architecture we need to deal with materials on a scale ranging from pure material properties, to the architectonic elements that we use in the creation of new spaces.

In terms of new materials we need not only to understand their properties and the ways they can be programmed, but we also need to understand the enabling character of these new materials.

If taking one step back to review the new digital materials, sometimes referred to as "transmaterials" (Brownell, 2005; 2008), we notice that these materials will *enable* a complete blend of our physical and digital surrounding. In terms of properties we can think about these materials through the concepts of e.g. level of embeddedness, visibility and access forms (preferably from the viewpoint of "interaction modalities" as a concept borrowed from the interaction design literature).

We can also think about these new materials in terms of how we label or conceptually describe them. Here, we might borrow concepts rooted in the tangible interaction design literature (e.g. Ishii & Ullmer, 1997) when we talk about e.g. computational fluids, transmaterials and smart textiles.

Moving along this scale from material properties via concepts that illustrate how we describe and view the character of these materials towards the materials in use we should also have an active discussion on how these new forms of the digital will enable new kinds of places, new social rooms, and new environments.

NEW ENVIRONMENTS

Having looked into the recent development of new transmaterials, and having had a discussion about the possibilities of a new architecture we now direct our attention to the new environments that might come out of this development.

Here, I present and discuss a few very basic examples of digitalized environments. In this discussion I seek to relate these efforts taken both to the area of architecture, but also to the area of interaction design for the purpose of enriching our understanding of these new architecturally situated interactive textures that are slowly being introduced in our built environment.

The examples of new interactive textures as presented here ranges from quite separated technologies placed in our surrounding to really integrated solutions where the technology is indistinguishable from both the appearance and functionality of a place.

The first example is illustrated in Figure 31. Here, the wall to the left of the escalator has been covered with a grid of light diodes all connected to a computer. Through this installation the light patterns on the wall can change dynamically in several different colors. As illustrated in Figure 31, at that moment when this picture was taken the light close to the camera were almost white, whereas the light upstairs was pink.

In terms of new textures this example illustrate one of the most basic aspects that digital materials might add to architecture, i.e. the possibility of having more dynamic elements in an otherwise quite static environment. If thinking about different levels of complexity in new textures this could be seen as a low-tech example that illustrate a *"dynamic texture"*.

Figure 31. An ordinary escalator and a wall covered with digital light diodes

Even though this installation might be pleasant to look at, or something that might add a feeling of "life" in this environment, it is still far from working as an interactive texture.

In other cases there have been successful meetings between digital technologies and escalator installations. For instance, there are examples of escalators that move very slowly if no one is nearby or on the escalator. The slow movement then actually serves the two purposes of both saving energy, but also in communicating, though its slow movement, that it is actually in use and not out of order (which could be a reasonable interpretation if the escalator was not moving at all). Instead, through the slow movement the escalator invites people to ride with it, and as soon as someone approaches the escalator it picks up its normal transportation speed again. Here, one such installation could be thought of as *"responsive texture"* that reacts in relation to the presence of persons within nearby proximity of the escalator. From the field of interaction design we might say that this installation gives its user some cues about its *affordance* (Norman, 1993; 2002) as well as its functionality (the slow movement also indicate direction of its service, i.e. if the escalator is moving upstairs or downstairs).

In terms of interactive textures, then a huge challenge for architects and interaction designers will be to think about meaningful installations in which the environment not only provide us with a dynamic texture, or respond to our physical actions taken, including e.g. basic bodily movement (like in the escalator example, or as in the case with any shopping mall entrance with automatic door openers), but in fact takes the potential of digital materials to the next level, i.e. the level of interactive textures.

Moving forward to some additional examples we can easily find several installations of public *"informative textures"* in just about any city. As illustrated in Figure 32 we find these building size displays with advertisements in any bigger city. One problem with these displays is that they easily take over, any almost replaces the physical architecture as they tend to cover not only building elements, but in fact whole facades. Most of these displays are also designed for solely one-way communication, typically design to broadcast information to just about anyone present at specific site.

Very related to these informative textures, although more directly designed as navigational aids and support for decision making and action taking are the large public displays typically mounted on walls at every airport (see Figure 33). These displays are specifically designed as textures that should draw our attention to e.g. "final boarding calls", "cancelled flights", "changed departure gates", etc. and these changes are typically marked with a sharp red color as in Figure 33 as to draw our attention to those important information slots.

Large public displays are also in use for other purposes. Figure 34 shows one such example from a bank office in New York City. Here, the ever-changing figures

Figure 32. Building-size public displays

Figure 33. Departure hall with several large public displays

from the stock market are constantly moving from the floor to the sealing in combination with a circle display showing the latest news from around the world.

In terms of "interactive textures" these public displays give us guidance and information for informed decision making at airports and are in that sense more interactive than the wall-mounted light diodes next to the escalator as exemplified in Figure 31. Still, even though the information is useful for the recipient it is not much interaction going on with the information at hand.

Also, from an architectural viewpoint most of these public displays are not even close to being integrated with the other materials that form the physical space of the airport. Instead, most of these kinds of solutions are more guided by the screen resolution available on a particular screen than guided by some true architectural thinking on how to architecturally embed information in physical space.

In the area of *digital signage* (e.g. Muller & Kruger, 2007; Muller, et. al., 2007) the question of where to put what information in a physical location has been frequently debated. Also, questions about how to display information, and how to make

Figure 34. Digital screens as architectural textures showing animations of financial data at a bank in New York City

information available for interaction in public places has been a widely discussed topic (see e.g. Vogel & Balakrishnan, 2004). However, it is not only obvious in the literature that people have struggled to understand how information could be made present, available and attractive for active use in public places, and there are many examples of e.g. information kiosk design projects that have ended up as the information kiosks in Figure 35. I.e. as putted aside, without even a power cable, as monuments of technology-driven hopes about interaction with information in public places. To me, this is no surprise. Instead, it is good evidences that if we want to introduce interaction technologies in public spaces, then we also need to think about how to closely, and elegantly, integrate the functionality and appearance of a piece of digital material in relation to the form of the rest of the physical space, i.e. to texturize the digital technology in the physical space, and to deeply consider how the whole composition of physical and digital materials can appear as one consistent texture for anyone present in the spaces we're creating.

Figure 35. Non-active public interactive information kiosks

There are of course other everyday installations that illustrate a successful com-position of physical and digital elements into coherent structures. The next picture for instance (see Figure 36) shows an ordinary set of buttons in a modern elevator. For many persons, this is just a product. However, from the perspective of interac-tive textures, this is in fact an interesting example. In this installation a successful meeting between the physical and the digital has been achieved in which the logical layout of the buttons (i.e. the digital interface) map onto the physical layout of the floor of the building. It is a simple installation. Yet, it serves its purpose of moving people up and down in the building, and it tells the people waiting on different floor not only the current location of the elevator, but also its direction of movement (up or down). Further on, it is capable of handling a series of commands so that it re-members the different floors people want to get off at, but still manage to sort these commands as to let people off in the order of the floors in the physical building (instead of moving the elevator up and down according to the order of commands given by its passengers). The interface is simple, and as already said, structured in relation to the floors of the physical building. Beyond that, the interface also contains a few symbols to open and close the elevator doors as well as an alarm button in case of an emergency (see Figure 36).

As this example illustrate, in the design of a modern elevator the architecture of the building has been taken into serious consideration. Also, the designers have looked into typical use scenarios, and worked out a design that correspond to some typical and frequent user needs.

In terms of texturized technology, there is no standard container of a computer visible in this case. Instead, the interface buttons has been smoothly integrated with the overall aluminum design profile of the elevator as to make the computer visu-ally "disappear" in this space. Yet, we should not be fooled thinking that this is a mechanical elevator. Instead, this is a highly advanced product, not only capable of

Figure 36. A typical elevator interface elegantly textured in the aluminum design

transporting people up and down in a building, but also to make that as efficient as possible. This computational capability of modern elevators are possible to observe especially in large buildings in which a set of elevators might work in concert to serve the people moving around across the different floors of the building.

To summarize, in this case the interactive texture is clear from many different perspectives. It is a concrete, easily noticed, standardized interface that clearly illustrates how to operate the physical elevator. Even the buttons have been formed as to make them easy to push, and the emergency button has been given a red "warning circle" as to make it clear that it is a special function in this elevator. As already said, the interface is elegantly textured with the aluminum material used for the interior of this elevator thus also functioning as a smooth transition between the digital service of the elevator and its physical form and physical manifestation of this service. Also, the concrete mapping between the elevator interface and the physical floors of the building adds to the lowering of the learning barrier for understanding this simple interactive texture.

Contrary to this concrete and everyday example of interactive textures we can now shift our perspectives and look into current research projects on design of ambient information spaces. Here we find e.g. the Hello-wall project (Prante, 2003) as illustrated in Figure 37. Here, the design thinking rely less on concrete functional mapping between the digital and the physical. Instead, the focus is on the "calm" aspects of technology (Weiser & Brown, 1997) and on architectonic thinking in which digital information is dynamically inscribed in the physical texture of the architectural elements including e.g. the interior walls. In this case, no obvious user interface is visible. Instead, the designers rely on abstract representations of information and abstract coding of messages to the persons present in the environment. Here, the focal idea is that the digital materials should remain in the background of our attention in the same extension as the rest of the physical materials that form this particular space. Hence, in order to "read" this texture the inhabitant of this space need to know about how to read the texture as to also understand information and messages as textured in the very texture of these walls.

In terms of technical realization this project could be described as a project in which a public display has been realized through a novel representation technique that makes the output appear as actually being part of the wall texture. Far more interesting, however, is the idea to have these kind of digital services working, and visible in public spaces, highly integrated in the overall architecture of the built environment, but still being heavily texturized into the background of our attention as to actually make the digital technology disappear, leaving room for more interesting face-to-face encounters and social interaction in this public space.

So, in different ways, the texturing of information and interaction technologies in our built environments is already happening. Still, and as these simple examples have illustrated there are several ways, and several different approaches that can be considered as to align architectural thinking with interaction design projects. In doing so, we can release a great potential in design of service-enhanced environments,

Figure 37. The Hello-wall project. A public display and novel representation technique that makes the output appear as part of the wall texture

in the design of smart spaces, in the design of digital agency in physical space, and in the design of new textures.

REFLECTION: INTERACTIVE TEXTURES AND THE SCIENCES OF THE ARTIFICIAL

In a sense, interactive textures and interactive architecture present us with not only an interesting design account situated in the borderland between architecture and interaction design, but also with an interesting case in relation to the basic foundations of design research.

If we situate design research as an applied approach that follows Herbert Simon's (1969) basic outline of the sciences of the artificial, then this growing area present us with a highly interesting case for several different reasons.

When looking at the ground-breaking ideas formulated and presented by Simon (1969) we find that his theory view our world as an artificial world, i.e. a world which is to a large extend built by us as humans, or in other ways affected by human actions. Following Simon's line of thinking, then most of the things around us, including ordinary products, cars, houses, etc. are not given by nature. Instead, we have deliberately designed these things. As researchers in any subfield of the sciences of the artificial we should therefore not only aim to describe or predict changes in nature. Nor should we merely describe changes in our society. Instead, given the artificial nature of our object of study we should also be design-oriented in our approach. That is, if the world around us is designed by us as humans, we should of course not only study and aim for descriptions it, but we should also actively explore it through the process of design, and as we go along we should also strive to learn about this process of design as an approach of our modern world, i.e. to conduct design research. As formulated by Simon (1969) we should take on a design account and not only explore the existing world, but also preferable future worlds.

Here, we can see how this theory of our world presents us with an interesting design challenge. On the one hand we should strive for research that gives us new, and hopefully better, knowledge about the world around us. Through this process our understanding of the world will be better. On the other hand, we should strive for new knowledge on how to change the current world into a better one. This is a change-driven, design-oriented approach which evokes thinking on sustainability. Or, if formulated in different terms, this extends the perspectives of research from being about the *true* (traditional research), to the *real,* i.e. design (Nelson & Stolterman, 2003), as well as the *good*.

As an overall design challenge for the area of design research we therefore need to integrate the perspectives of the true, the real and the good in the change projects we engage ourselves in.

In relation to the area of interactive textures this issue is now putted in the spotlight. In traditional architecture a key word is stability. This is given from the fact that most materials are quite static. As such, traditional architecture, and traditional materials are hard to change. However, new materials, in this book referred to as transmaterials are fundamentally different from many traditional materials in that the materials properties of computational can be easily reconfigured, transformed and re-articulated. In fact, these materials are so dynamic that they can be set to easily change even when installed in a physical space in direct correspondence with actions taken by any person occupying this space.

As we move from stable architectures to more dynamic structures we need to consider the dynamics of these installations in relation to what people might do in their interaction with and through them. This raises questions about interactional access to architecture, e.g. who is allowed to do what in and with an environment?, and ultimately this might relate to legal and ethical concerns as well as privacy matters, policies and rules.

Again, this is about sustainability and how to approach this area from the perspective of the creation of not only technically- and socially sound environments, but also sustainable environments in terms of interaction with and through the new textures these environments provide.

With new transmaterials at hand, and through the realization of interactive textures we can see how such technological developments accelerate the need for good models capable of guiding our design thinking in this area, i.e. we need design research in the area of interactive textures.

If looking closely at so called new materials from the perspective of the sciences of the artificial we might notice that it is not only about new surfaces, but in fact about new textures that fundamentally changes the character of our built environments. In a sense, these new textures do not only redefine physical spaces, but far more interesting, if the modern artificial world is about these new textures, then we might argue that these new textures are actually redefining nature.

In terms of the redefinition of nature we can see how new textures not only move computational power into our physical environment. But, also how this blending of the digital into our everyday worlds in fact challenges the old restrictions of places, i.e. the fundamental definition of a place along the dimensions of time and place might not be applicable in these new environments. Just to give a few examples. New technologies enable geographically remote persons to be simultaneously co-present at other places, and traditionally geographically bounded conversations are now possible to tap into from virtually any location. Further on, ephemeral conversations are pro-longed in virtual rooms, and messages from the past are now constantly and seamlessly blended with our opportunistic interactions with others. Things have changed and computational power is one important element in his transition.

As our conversations with other are incorporated in the textures of our built environments we can also see how interactive textures that constitute spaces extend themselves to other places. In this transition the textures also becomes media capable of broadcasting information as well as serve as platforms for social interaction.

It is indeed an interesting development, but it calls for a thoughtful approach (Löwgren & Stolterman, 2007), and there is a need for a design research agenda to address and tackle this development. One such agenda needs to be based on fundamental values of sustainable development, and it should be capable of addressing e.g. the texturing of information and interaction technologies in our built environments, the creation of new interactive textures, the texturing of social messages, rituals, cultures and norms in physical space from an holistic perspective, and explorations of new materials from a particularity perspective.

Through one such undertaking we should be able to arrive at better or richer theories about the modern artificial world, at least from the viewpoint of interactive architecture. And, in doing so we might be able to start an important job in the formulation of a texturation theory, i.e. a theory about new textures, the texturation of digital materials in physical settings, and about the process of texturing physical an digital materials into meaningful compositions.

REFERENCES

Brownell, B. (2005). *Transmaterial: A Catalog of Materials That Redefine our Physical Environment*. Princeton Architectural Press.

Brownell, B. (2008). *Transmaterial 2: A Catalog of Materials That Redefine our Physical Environment*. Princeton Architectural Press.

Bullivant, L. (2005). *4dspace: Interactive Architecture, Architectural Design*. Wiley-Academy.

Ching, F. (2007). *Architecture: Form, Space, and Order*. New York: John Wiley & Sons, Inc.

Hello. Wall - Beyond Ambient Displays. *Video and Adjunct Proceedings of UBI-COMP Conference*.

Ishii, H., & Ullmer, B. (1997) Tangible bits: Towards seamless integration interfaces between people, atoms, and bits. In *Proc. CHI 1997* (pp. 234-241). ACM Press.

Krippendorff, K. (2005). *The semantic turn: A new foundation for design.* CRC Press.

Löwgren, J., & Stolterman, E. (2007). *Thoughtful interaction design: A design perspective on information technology.* Cambridge, MA: MIT Press.

McCullough, M. (2004). *Digital Ground – Architecture, Pervasive Computing, and Environmental Knowing.* Cambridge, MA: MIT Press.

Muller, H. J., & Kruger, A. (2007). How much to bid in digital signage advertising auctions? In *Adjunct Proceedings of Pervasive 2007.*

Muller, J., Paczkowski, O., & Kruger, A. (2007). Situated public news and reminder displays. In *Proc. European Conference on Ambient Intelligence* (pp. 248–265).

Nelson, H., & Stolterman, E. (2003). *The Design Way: intentional change in an unpredictable world.* Educational Technology Publications.

Norman, D. A. (1993). *Things that make us smart.* Reading, MA: Addison Wesley.

Norman, D. A. (2002). *The Design of Everyday Things.* New York: Basic Books.

PranteT.RöckerC.StreitzN.StenzelR.MagerkurthC.AlphenD.v.PleweD. (2003).

Simon, H. A. (1969). *The Sciences of the Artificial.* Cambridge, MA: MIT Press.

Simon, H. A. (1969). *The Sciences of the Artificial.* Cambridge, MA: MIT Press.

Sparacino, F. (2008). Natural interaction in intelligent spaces: designing for architecture and entertainment. *Multimedia Tools and Applications, 38,* 307–335. doi:10.1007/s11042-007-0193-9

Spiller, N. (2002). *Reflexive architecture, Architectural Design.* Wiley-Academy.

Vogel, D., & Balakrishnan, R. (2004). Interactive public ambient displays: transitioning from implicit to explicit, public to personal, interaction with multiple users. In *UIST '04: Proceedings of the 17th annual ACM symposium on User interface software and technology* (pp. 137-146). New York: ACM.

Weiser, M., & Brown, J. S. (1997). The coming age of calm technology . In Denning, P. J., & Metcalfe, R. M. (Eds.), *Beyond Calculation: The Next Fifty Years of Computing.* New York: Springer Verlag.

ENDNOTES

[1] Except for a few examples including e.g. the book "Digital Ground" by Malcolm McCollough (2004).

[2] Photos taken by Ulf Wiberg

Section 2
Foundations:
Elements, Textures and Architecture

Beyond Boxes:
Basics That Matter

In section 1 of this book I outlined the breakdown of the box and the importance to start considering interaction *per se* as a design space to explore. Further on, the importance of texture was introduced as to establish a connection between the surfaces we potentially interact with and through with the underlying enabling materials.

In this section of the book the foundations for interactive textures are outlined and reflected upon. Here, we move beyond the framing of the computational as boxes and instead we return to the basics that matters, i.e. the computational materials that enable new computational compositions to be manifested in the world. In doing so, this section of the book provide three chapters devoted to 1) enabling technologies including new materials and elements, 2) an outline of the basic and fundamental building blocks for a theory capable of defining and addressing interactive textures including issues of how these relate to representations and how we might interact with and trough these textures, and finally 3) some thoughts on how these enabling materials work across the scale from small objects to large scale architecture.

Given a new point of departure in which we have left the boxes behind, this section of the book establishes a new ground for thinking about the computational along new forms. These forms build on digital elements as part of new interactive textures. Further on, these textures are part of larger architectural installations, which in turn are part of larger design matters including e.g. city planning, and ultimately the design of our environment. The basics that matter do not only operate at the level of material properties but are in fact focal building blocks of the new landscapes we're creating.

Chapter 4
Enabling Technologies

In this chapter I take one step back and look more closely at the enabling technologies that contribute to the development of new interactive textures for architecture and landscaping.

Before going into the area of enabling technologies, however, we first need to go into details about materials and elements. That is, in order to talk specifically about these two concept in any precise way we need some working definitions and ways of separating these two concepts from each other, as well as a conceptual ground for integrating them in our thinking on new spaces.

NEW MATERIALS AND ELEMENTS

Materials

Materials are substances or components with certain physical properties which are used as inputs to production or manufacturing (Randle & Engler, 2000). Basically materials are the pieces required to make something else. From buildings and art to cars, stars and computers.

A material can be virtually anything: a finished product in its own right or an unprocessed raw material. Raw materials are first extracted or harvested from the

DOI: 10.4018/978-1-61520-653-7.ch004

earth and divided into a form that can be easily transported and stored, then processed to produce semi-finished materials. These can be input into a new cycle of production and finishing processes to create finished materials, ready for distribution, construction, and consumption.

Materials can also be thought of as the basic building blocks from which we can produce other stuff, being it products, architectural elements, or full-scale buildings.

Elements

In close relation to the notion of "materials" we find the notion of "elements" (e.g. Ching, 2007). However, in order to really understand the complex relation between the concepts of materials and elements we might need to go back in history and review the background of the term "elements" in order to fully understand that concept.

As we know, many ancient philosophies used a set of archetypal classical elements to explain *patterns* in nature. In this context, the word "element" referred to a substance that was either a chemical compound or a mixture of chemical compounds, rather than a chemical element of modern physical science.

Further on, the notion of elements has throughout history had deep philosophical and cultural meanings. For instance, the Greek classical elements (Earth, Water, Air, Fire, and Aether) date from pre-Socratic times and persisted throughout the Middle Ages and into the Renaissance, deeply influencing European thought and culture.

A focus on "elements" as an approach to see and describe "patterns" is an interesting conceptualization in relation to the theory of textures and texturation processes as pushed forward in this book. As described in chapter 3 we might think about architecture as a complex system of several overlayed patterns or structures. Since architecture can be understood in terms of systems and structures, then this linkage to elements as patterns is a valuable perspective since it unifies architectural elements with the notion of textures.

If we now take a point of departure in some philosophical quotes like the following two we might start to see how new digital technologies, as materials might become important cornerstones in the new elements or patterns we design into the textures of modern architecture.

Starting off with a first quote from Greenfield (2006) we notice how computational materials will seamlessly integrate itself with the materials and products of our everyday lives:

"computation would flourish, becoming intimate intertwined with the stuff of everyday life". (Greenfield, 2006, p. 11)

Further on, a second quote by Greenfield (2006) pinpoints that this blending of the physical and digital will not only be about having access to computational power and digital content from any geographical location, but in fact, computational material (Vallgårda & Redström, 2007) will actually blend itself and be part of "everything" and probably then also an equally integrated part of the elements we use in the creation of new textures.

"ubiquitous" meant not merely "in every place", but also "in everything" (Greenfield, 2006, p. 11)

As such, computational power will not only work as a new material for architecture and landscaping but will in fact be part of the structures and textures of the built environment. As such, computational power will blend itself into the new elements that will enable the creation of new environments.

Through this blending process of computational power into the materials and elements in our everyday lives there will be an increasing need for skills related to how to "read" any surface as a potentially interactive texture.

If now reviewing these enabling technologies we can distinguish as least two different dimensions of its enabling character, i.e. new enabling *fabrics* and new enabling interaction *modalities*.

In terms of *enabling fabrics* we can further distinguish between "real" materials and "virtual" materials. Here, "real" refers to tangible, observable materials, including new transmaterials and novel display techniques (e.g. water displays, pixel walls, etc.) as well as more traditional computational materials like e.g. mobile phones. Similarly, "virtual" materials are the computational materials that are not equally visible, but equally present in any location, and in any object. These materials include e.g. mobile services, WiFi/3G/Bluetooth, and other access forms, so called "Hot spots", and protocols, middleware, technology interfaces, etc.

In terms of *enabling interaction modalities* we can in a similar way acknowledge this dimension as an enabler of new interactive textures through the new ways of engaging ourselves with and through materials that these modalities enable. This includes e.g. techniques for motion-tracking, gesture-based interfaces, and multi-touch techniques, as well as new ways of accessing and distributing information across the digital landscape. Here, some recent examples include RSS-streams, and other information push services, and integration capabilities between services, typically labeled mesh-ups or web 2.0.

ARCHITECTURAL THINKING ON ELEMENTS

As we scale our thinking from basic raw materials to architecture, and even landscaping we should in this process also situate the notion of elements in the context of architectural thinking. If materials are seen as fundamental structures, systems and patterns, then these elements are, in a sense, important cornerstones for architecture, and should work as a good point of departure for architectural thinking.

Following the line of thinking as outlined by Oosterhuist (2007) in his book "#IA1 interactive architecture" in which he states that "*interactive architecture is not about communication between people, it is defined as the art of building relationships between built components in the first place, and building relations between people and the built components in the second place*" we might think of these relations between materials as structures or patterns. In this way, these relations describe the *composition* of materials into architectonic elements.

In these compositions materials form elements (including patterns, structures, and systems), and these elements forms and constitutes spaces, places and our built environments. In this thinking we might as well think about whole environments in terms of compositions. That is, we could think about the meaningful ordering of objects, things, materials, systems and elements.

When applying an architecturally situated approach to thinking on new elements there are two different approaches in this undertaking worth considering in detail. One the one hand we might think about "elements" as architectural "building blocks" or architectural parts. This perspective gives us the advantage of thinking visually about how different parts or building blocks might appear if assembled, combined or separated in one way or another.

An alternative perspective on compositions of elements in architecture might be to think about these elements as patterns, systems and structures. This might not give us the same visual understanding of a composition. However, this alternative perspective provides us with an understanding of how an architectural composition might be understood as a meaningful wholeness from a conceptual viewpoint as well as from a functional perspective.

COMPOSITIONS

Throughout this chapter, the notion of compositions has been a returning concept in the discussion of new materials and architectural elements. In this section I therefore go into some detail about this concept of compositions as a way to enrich our thinking on how we might compose materials into elements, and how we might work with these elements in larger architectonic structures.

To some extent, architecture can be seen as a profession and a process focused on the "design of meaningful wholes". This designed wholeness can be described as a composition. This composition is simultaneously both a state (being it stable or dynamic) and a process, or, as formulated by Nelson & Stolterman (2003):

"A design is always a composition. To design is to be creative and innovative, but more importantly, design is to cause things and/or people to stand together as a unified whole – a composition. Creating such a system of unification means bringing parts, pieces, functions, structures, processes and forms together in such a way that they have a **presence** *and make an* **appearance,** *particularly of unity, in the world. Composing is an integration of several strategies of unification. These strategies use rules of relationships (protocols), in the creation of compounds, functional assemblies, patterns, systems and wholes." (Nelson & Stolterman, 2003, p. 207).*

In this quote we also notice how working compositions have a presence and make an appearance in the world. In this sense, the notion of compositions also fills an important conceptual role in the theorizing made about textures in this book. A working interactive texture is a material blend between physical and digital materials in which the composition of these two basic elements appears as one meaningful interactive texture.

Here, we should also highlight how compositions might work at different levels in design, from composite computational materials (Vallagårda & Redström, 2007) to compositions and orchestrations of interactive environments. As we start to play around with physical/digital compositions, physical computing, sketching in hardware activities and service compositions we can see a whole palette growing of materials, elements, and compositions in the making.

In our understanding of built environments as compositions, and if following the quote from Nelson & Stolterman (2003), we might also want to consider us as humans as part of the compositions we're creating. The inclusion of us as humans in the design loop relate questions of meaningfulness to user needs a requirements and questions about appearance to issues of human experiences in the environments we're creating. This, in turn, leads us in the direction of a human-oriented approach to architectural thinking and new interactive textures.

INTERACTIVE TEXTURES

So, how might we define interactive textures? Apparently some definitions are needed if we are to formulate any theories about this area, and if we want to use this notion with some precision in practice. If looking at this concept from the viewpoint of "interactive textures" then surely the dimension of interactional engagement and involvement as described in chapter 1 is of crucial importance in one such definition. On the other hand, if understood from the perspective of "interactive textures", then we should acknowledge the ways in which these textures create not only new surfaces, but also new ways of using materials and new ways of expressing material properties through the appearance of that particular material in use. In other words, this part of one such definition needs to acknowledge dimensions of the physical world as both surfaces and materials at the same time. Here, it is likely that the notion of both materials and elements come into the picture. Further on, when highlighting the texture aspect of interactive textures then we should pay specific attention of the different dimensions of textures including a discussion of textures in terms of appearance, attention, representation of signs, meanings, feelings and messages. In a definition of interactive textures we might also want it to relate to the basic definition of textures as being about *"the feel, appearance, or consistency of a surface"*.

Given these points of departures I would propose that interactive textures could be defined as: *"meaningful compositions of physical and digital materials that together appear as one consistent surface that enables interaction with and possible through it, while at the same time communicating the material properties from which the surface of the texture is made."*

One obvious aspect of this definition of interactive textures is that it highlights the articulation of these new textures. This is important for any definition of textures, but also of crucial importance in a definition of working interactive textures since one of the main challenges for any designer of new interactive textures is about designing these textures as to make them readable for any potential person that should be able to interact with and through these new materials.

On the other hand, there are some sci-fi authors, e.g. William Gibson who have highlighted that in a nearby future it might be meaningless to even talk about the digital and the physical as two different materials:

"One of the things our grandchildren will find quaintest about us is that we distinguish the digital from the real, the virtual from the real. In the future, that will become literally impossible." - William Gibson

Still, however, as long as we use these words in our everyday language when talking about the physical and the digital I find it useful in a working definition of interactive textures. From another perspective though, we could also interpret the quote by Gibson as yet another indicator of these two components coming together in design of new interactive textures.

TEXTURES IN DETAILS: THE MAKING OF THE NEW

In the end of chapter 1 I highlighted how the notion of texture enable us to pay attention to certain details and to pay attention to the interplay between visual appearance and the materials from which a certain form is created. In this section this focus on details is further highlighted.

As already described, the reading of textures requires a close up look and to pay attention to details. Since the typical PC has not yet paid to much attention to texture, but has rather been occupied with the notion of surface, and since today's tangible interfaces are much in their first stages of development this section take us one step back towards old textures created from old materials. The important message here is that this perspective might in fact tell us a lot about which qualities in textures to search for as it enable us to see close up textures of high quality. For this section I direct a special thanks to the photographer Maria Juhlin for the beautiful pictures she has taken for this book. Thank you!

In this section I start out with some basic textures that illustrate the interplay between numerical information and the material composition from which the texture is made. Following from that I then move into digital materials and look into how new interactive textures are created within the area of interactive textiles. This is done because of two basic reasons. First, these interactive textiles are beautiful, just like the numerical textures in the following pictures, but secondly also due to the fact that when it comes to interactive textiles the designers have actually managed to perfectly integrate digital and non-digital materials into compositions that form textures that communicate unification beyond the simple raw materials. As such, these interactive textures also serve as an important proof-of-concept for how alignments can be made across digital and non-digital materials. Having provided some examples of these new textures I then present a couple of pictures from the making of such textures as to give a feeling of hot new interactive textures are created, followed by an image that illustrate how these integrated materials not only form a texture possible to feel, see and grasp, but also appear to us as a composition that stands out almost like a piece of art.

Starting off with the picture in Figure 38 we can see an example of a simple interplay between two basic materials, i.e. the brick wall and the black color used to paint the numbers on the wall.

These numbers are not just painted "on" the wall (in the sense of covering the wall). Instead, these numbers work in concert with the brick wall. The bricks themselves are rectangular, sharp and edgy, and so are the painted numbers on the wall. The organization of the bricks forming the wall creates horizontal lines that also guide the horizontal placement of the numbers on the wall. Further on, the lines are visible across the numbers and at two occasions (for the first number 3 and for

Figure 38. The painted numbers on the brick wall forms an interesting texture based on two basic materials

number 8) there are in fact no paint on one of the lines going straight across these numbers).

Working in concert these materials form an interesting texture from two basic materials. In other words, it is an interesting interplay between different elements together forming a texture.

The next figure (see Figure 39) presents a similar picture illustrating interplay between two basic materials (iron and paint). Here, the numbers have been aligned in relation to the iron bolts creating an interesting collage.

As a reference case we can also study the next figure (see Figure 40) in which the composition is not equally clear in the sense that here it appears as if there has been an attempt made to make something new on a very old surface resulting in a competition between the material rather than a composition.

Texture as composition is also fascinating even if there are only old materials involved. As in this following case, see Figure 41, in which we can see the combination of old paint on a piece of old wood. Of special notice here is the interplay between the materials that together create this compositional appearance.

Moving from old materials like crackled paint and old wood towards new modern digital technology and electronics we might not only consider these new materials from a use perspective in which ask questions about these materials at the level of its application, but we might also ask questions related to how these new technologies might work in composition with other materials.

While it was not particularly hard to apply an artistic eye in the reading of the composition of old paint and old wood as a coherent texture we should in an equal way train ourselves to view compositions including digital materials in the same way.

In the next figure (see Figure 42) a deliberate choice has been made to take a photo of some simple light diodes from an artistic perspective to move us in a direction where we leave perspectives focused on the use qualities of digital technologies towards a perspective where we pay close attention to the aesthetic dimensions of

Figure 39. Another example of two basic materials forming an interesting texture through the interplay between the iron and the painted numbers

Figure 40. The painted number on this picture looks "new" in relation to the very old looking background

Figure 41. Old paint and old wood working in composition

the electronics per se and how these qualities might work in concert with other materials to form larger interactive textures.

While electronic components can be aesthetically pleasing to look at in its raw form it is far more interesting to start to also look at digital materials in composition with other non-digital materials.

In Figure 43 a picture of an interactive textile is shown where these small LED diodes has been woven into the textile together with a conductive thread that enable a microprocessor to communicate with these lights.

The LEDs are easily discovered in Figure 43 and in the sense that they appear as if they have been "attached" to this piece of fabric although the conductive threads that link these diodes together has been seamlessly integrated in the textile.

This is not equally obvious in the following picture (see Figure 44). Here, conductive thread has been used together with normal stitching threads in different colors to create a woven fabric with computational capabilities.

In Figure 45 another example of integrated conductive threads is shown.

The integration of different materials into a larger structure with a certain texture is very much about the crafting out of a composition.

In this particular case this act of composing is about weaving together similar, although slightly different, materials (see Figure 45).

Figure 42. Focusing on the aesthetic dimensions of electronics

Figure 43. LEDs woven into a piece of fabric to create a textile based interactive texture

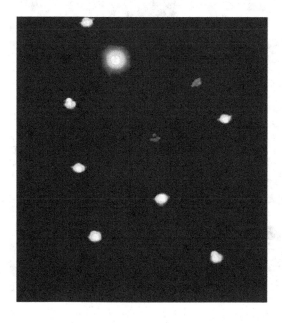

Figure 44. Soft textile with integrated conductive threads

Figure 45. Another example of a soft textile with integrated conductive threads

In the following sections I will provide some close-up pictures to illustrate how close to the materials that one actually need to be to acknowledge the qualities of a certain material that can be used to create a certain texture. In other words, it is about saying close to the materials, almost at the level of material properties.

The picture in Figure 46 illustrates a close up photo of one material used in the creation of conductive threads. From this close up photo, we can see the very fine lines that when twinned together form a thread that can be used for stitching.

To be good at linking this level of details to what it will appear as when working in composition with other materials and at another scale is about training and an aesthetic eye. For a person with less experience it might be hard to really understand and see where material properties transform into material appearances. That is the texture aspect of the material composition. Figure 47 below provide another example of this kind of close-up perspective necessary for making good material compositions.

While the close-up perspective is important to get a feel for the material properties there is also a need for a perspective that works compositional.

The compositional perspective is about seeing different raw materials in relation to each other and developing an idea of which materials to selected for the crafting out of a new texture. Figure 48 work as one illustration of this compositional per-

Figure 46. Close-up photo taken of a conductive thread

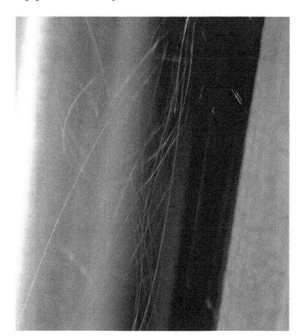

Figure 47. Close-up photo of one material used in the stitching of new textiles

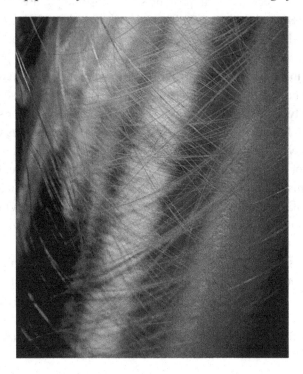

Figure 48. A set of threads selected for the machine stitcher

spective where a selection of different threads has been made for a machine stitcher that weaves these threads together.

The next step in the creation of a new texture is to integrate the different material selected. This can be a handmade process or an automated one.

For this process several materials come together to form a new material (with borrowed properties from the materials it is built from). This is a critical process that demands a lot of planning as to ensure that the materials work in concert to form a larger assemblage (and not just clutter). The following picture serves as an illustration of this weaving together process (see Figure 49).

As the integration process continues the materials blend into a composition that starts to form a new texture (see Figure 50).

Finally, the weaving process is done and we have a new texture that works compositionally across the materials from which it has been designed (see Figure 51). In a sense, and after a thoughtful and deliberate process of choosing and bringing together different materials, the composition stands out as en emergent property from the interplay in-between the materials.

It is important here to understand that these examples from the process of creating new interactive textiles only serves just as an example of the more general process of working compositionally in the creation of new textures. For any process concerned with the creation of new textures this is a process that needs special attention at the different levels of focus as described in this chapter. From the perspec-

Figure 49. Integration of different materials into a working composition with a certain texture

Figure 50. Materials coming together to form a new texture

Figure 51. Composition as an emerging aspect of the interplay between digital and non-digital materials woven together into an interactive textile

tive of this book, this process is general and it is actually just a matter of scale (from the scale of the texturing of small objects to the scale of architecture and the cityscape).

In more general terms, this last section has illustrated the practical process of staying close to the material, acknowledging the material properties, and selecting which materials that should be integrated into a meaningful composition. Further on, this section has intended to show that this process is about the careful crafting of relations between materials to work compositionally forming larger patterns and structures.

Now we have seen the creation of new textures in practice, but how might we organize out thinking around these compositions? What are the more general frameworks that we can use to guide our thinking along these lines? In the next chapter we move from this practical perspective on materials, textures and compositions towards the theorizing of interactive textures for this purpose of exploring the underlying principles guiding material integration as textures.

REFERENCES

Ching, F. (2007). *Architecture: Form, Space, and Order*. New York: John Wiley & Sons, Inc.

Greenfield, A. (2006). *Everyware – The dawning age of ubiquitous computing*. Berkeley, CA: New Riders.

Nelson, H., & Stolterman, E. (2003). *The Design Way: intentional change in an unpredictable world*. Educational Technology Publications.

Oosterhuist, K. (2007). *iA #1 Interactive Architecture*. Rotterdam: Episode Publishers.

Randle, V., & Engler, O. (2000). *Introduction to Texture Analysis: Macrotexture, Microtexture, and Orientation Mapping*. Singapore: Gordon and Breach Science Publishers.

Vallgårda, A., & Redström, J. (2007). Computational composites. In *Proceedings of CHI '07 - the SIGCHI conference on Human factors in computing systems*. ACM Press.

Chapter 5
Theorizing Interactive Textures

BLENDING ARCHITECTURE AND INTERACTION DESIGN

In this section of the book I move from an example-driven approach to interactive textures to a more theoretical strand in which I will set out to discuss interaction with and through interactive textures, as well as discuss interactive textures in terms of representations, navigational aids, and user interfaces.

In doing so, I first start with a discussion of the role of architecture in our society and in our everyday lives followed by a discussion on textures in relation to representations as to establish a link between architecture and the area of interaction design. Here, I will specifically review the efforts made so far on bridging these two areas and mark out the conceptual "state-of-the-art" when it comes to theorizing in this area. Further on, a discussion on textures as navigational aids are initiated in which architectural thinking meets some conceptual notions from the area of interaction design. Finally, the chapter ends with some theorizing around interaction with and through textures as to fully explore a true blending of architectural thinking with interaction design reasoning.

According to Tietz (1998) architecture is a ubiquitous and a quite focal aspect of our everyday lives:

DOI: 10.4018/978-1-61520-653-7.ch005

"The architecture that surround us defines a crucial part of our everyday lives. It shapes and defines the frames for our lifes, the rooms in which we live, work, socialize, do our shopping, and spent our leisure time" (Tietz, 1998, p.6).

So, the ubiquitous co-presence of both architecture and digital technologies and services in our everyday lives is obvious. Still, although there has been several voices raised for a closer relation between interaction design and architecture (see e.g. Streitz, et.al., 2002, p. 555; Jones, et al., 2004 and Sengers, et al 2004) there are still very little work that has explicitly set out to adapt an architecturally informed approach to the areas of interaction design and ubiquitous computing. As formulated by Sengers, 2004:

"Imagine a world without architects, where only engineers construct buildings. With a keen eye towards functionality, these engineers would make sure buildings were sound, but something would be lacking. People would miss the richness of architecture – the designed connection to their lives, history, and culture. The designed experience of these buildings would be irrelevant to their social and personal concept of buildings. Yet this is the world researchers are inadvertently creating with ubiquitous computing" Sengers, et al (2004, p. 14).

This, despite the fact that several of the most recent attempts made in these areas of research focuses on design of various digital augmentations of our physical surrounding as to enable new novel place- and location-based services in support of social interaction "in the wild", and in public places.

In this book I specifically aim at addressing these new practices and this relatively new phenomenon, i.e. the current blending of building materials with interactive components which challenges us as artists, architects, designers, theorists, and geographers, to develop our language and designs towards the "use" of these environments, articulating both what it means to interact in these new modes of place, and framing interaction with and through so called "interactive architecture". In doing so, I take as an important point of departure current literature which describes, analyses and theorize the ongoing integration of digital technologies in our built environment (e.g. Greenfield, 2006).

Further on, my theoretical work on interactive textures builds upon a conceptualized understanding of the integration of architecture and digital technologies as "Media spaces" to address how digital technologies enable us to spatially stretch places, connect places, connect to other human beings across geographical distances in the creation of so called "Media districts" (Indergaard, 2004).

As to further create a theoretical foundation for interactive textures I take an explicit point of departure in current research that has addressed the integration of architecture and digital technologies from the viewpoint of "interactive architecture" (e.g. Oosterhuist, 2007; Bullivant, 2005; 2006; 2007). Interactive architecture can be described as an emerging field of research in the borderland of architecture, art installations, public performance, and novel use of digital technologies. Some researchers have used alternative terms such as "responsive environments", or "responsive architecture" (e.g. Bullivant 2006), while other have labeled the integration of digital technologies in built environments as "hybrid spaces" (e.g. Zellner, 1999) to address a development towards a complete blend of our physical and digital world, and to address a development in which the traditional physical and social public domain is being supplemented by zones, places and subcultures that transcend the local to interlink with the translocal and the global (Rheingold, et.al., 2007).

In this chapter I will, with a point of departure taken in this theories of new places, present and discuss the following theoretical models including a model of 1) Textures as navigational aids and as interfaces for interaction with and through textures, a model of 2) Textures as architectural elements and as perceived elements of our surround and how that is linked to what we can do with modern interaction textures (i.e. interaction with and through textures), and finally, model 3) the relationship between interaction modalities, textures and structures in the context of interaction with and through textures.

TEXTURES AND REPRESENTATIONS

The notion of texture is, as outlined in chapter 2 a concept rooted in the areas of material science and architecture and can, if somewhat simplified, function as a word that describes the surface of an object. In similar terms, the notion of representation is a concept with its roots in the areas of computer science, informatics and interaction design, which similarly can be described as a concept dealing with what is visible, i.e. a concept highly related to surfaces.

With a basis in a given material different textures can be created, or crafted out of the material which in turn can give a certain material quite different appearances. Similarly, we can easily change the representation of a given set of information in the area of interaction design.

Here, we can see that there is a similar relation between materials and textures as it is between information and representations. If we were asked to quickly review the areas of architecture and interaction design we could say that the two areas are highly different as architecture focuses on the physical world, whereas interaction design focuses on the digital world. Still, however, that might be one to oversimplified description of these two fields. On the contrary, if carefully considering these two design practices we should notice that they share not only this relation between raw materials and designed appearance, but are in many ways related both when it comes to the outcomes of the design processes as well as the methods through which the end results are achieved.

If looking at this example about the relation between material and texture on the one hand, and information and representation on the other hand from the theoretical grounds of interaction design we find e.g. the theoretical work on information architectures and information spaces by Benyon (2004) of particular interest.

According to Benyon's model on information architectures and design of information spaces (2004) we can, given one basic set of information (e.g. hours, minutes and seconds) in many cases represent this in several different ways (the typical analogue clock vs. a typical digital clock is a good example of this difference).

This is also true when it comes to the relation between materials and textures. Very many different textures can be carved out from the same kind of material. However, each of these textures will be dependent on the properties of the material, similar to how any representation of information will be dependent upon the sets of information available.

If there is not a good match between a given material and the texture of the material (e.g. if a piece of painted plastics is supposed to look like aluminum) then there is a big risk of failing to have an adequate mapping between the (intended) material texture and actual (perceived) texture. In such a case, there is a big chance that the texture appears as "kitsch" rather than as sound good quality.

Further on, we can clearly see here that the question of material choice becomes an important issue for any designer in this area due to this relation between texture and materials.

If thinking about these concepts above, and how materials related to textures as information relates to representations, then another striking connection between the area of architecture and the area of interaction design is on a conceptual level. In interaction design these notions of "information architecture" and "information spaces" are typically used as metaphors. Still, the metaphors are not randomly chosen. Instead, it is obvious that some architectural thinking on information design has been applied as to understand how to design these systems as part of our built environment.

TOWARDS A THEORY OF TEXTURES

When moving beyond the common distinction between the physical and the digital as to reach a position in which these two are becoming one (as in the case with e.g. tangible computing), and when moving away from the notion of computational surfaces (e.g. displays) towards computational textures some interesting observations can be made while following this line of thinking. When introducing the notion of texture some modeling can be done in which a new design space emerges around textures – or design textures – especially when applying this model of textures to integration of physical and digital materials.

The following model aims to describe compositions of different materials and how these materials relate to the notions of surface, texture, and appearance of wholeness, and in relation to fundamentals or values.

In this model (see Figure 52) we have two basic materials (A and B) used in a composition (A+B). Each material (A & B) has its own texture (represented as the thin lines above each square of A and B) and each texture has a certain relation to the material from which it is crafted (arrow 1 and 2). In any design the integration (3) of different materials and textures is crucial for the overall appearance of the design as a wholeness (C). The choice of different materials can further on build on a common value base or foundation (D). And the choices of different materials, the closeness or distance between material and texture (representation of material) and whether there are strong or weak links between materials and textures in the creation of wholeness and in relation to basic values is a question about design (E).

If now exemplifying this model we might think about the design of an object based on e.g. "eco-friendly" materials only (e.g. the value ground, D). We can think about how different textures work together as to communicate wholeness (C). We can also think about how the different textures used communicate material properties, and how the integration is made between different textures (either through integration, or through the use of emptiness, (a common technique e.g. in graphics and layout design professions).

Figure 52. Modeling of material integration as texture

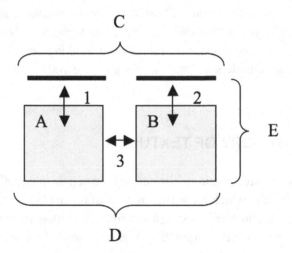

If there is a close connection between value ground (D) and choice of materials (A and B) we might talk about the design (E) in terms of quality. If the texture or appearance of the material is not connected to the material properties we might talk about "kitsch", e.g. laminated surfaces that try to imitate wood although it is in fact made of plastics. On the other hand, the blending of computational materials with physical materials also enables us to expand the distinction between physical material and its appearance (i.e. to expand the distances of arrow 1 and 2). Thus the designing of the textures (E) and their compositions when it comes to these new digitalized materials will also be about design that link overall appearance of the composition (C) to the fundamental values or value ground on which the design is built (D).

If now briefly exemplifying this model we might imagine the design of an object based solely on e.g. "eco-friendly" materials (e.g. the fundamental value ground, D). Here, we might think about how different textures work together as to communicate wholeness (C). We can think about how the different textures used communicate material properties, and how the integration is made between different textures (either through integration, or through the use of emptiness, (a common technique e.g. in graphics and layout design professions). If there is a close connection between value ground (D) and choice of materials (A and B) we might talk about the design (E) in terms of quality. If the texture or appearance of the material is not connected to the material properties we might talk about "kitsch", e.g. laminated surfaces that try to imitate wood although it is in fact made of plastics. On the other hand, the blending of computational materials with physical materials also enables us to expand the distinction between physical material and its appearance (i.e. to expand the distances of arrow 1 and 2). Thus the designing of the textures (E) and their compositions when it comes to these new digitalized materials will also be about design that link overall appearance of the composition (C) to the fundamental values or value ground on which the design is built (D).

In more general terms, we[1] see a vocabulary growing out from the fundamental notion of texture forming a relational language that further scaffolds our thinking - from materials typically framed trough the concepts of *properties* and *appearances* towards larger assemblages of materialities constituted by its *connections, complexities, compromises,* and *compositions.*

From an understanding of 'aesthetics' as being about our senses and our responses to an object, then one might ask not only how we might best describe the character of our senses, or our relations to objects, but also how we might best describe these objects or materialities that transcends into our social world, in fact in many cases working as the constituting basis for the social. In the vocabulary of Orlokowski and Scott (2008) we might ask for a vocabulary that enable us to speak fluently about "assemblages" of materiality, or talk specifically about new computational composites (Vallagård & Redström, 2007).

In this book I suggest the following foundational vocabulary grounded in the notion of *texture* that enable us to relate material appearance to material properties, providing us with a conceptual ground and point of departure for developing a whole set of concepts that might sharpen our language for addressing the material turn and the physical-digital integrations that follows one such aesthetics.

Through the following sections I present the C6-principles of *Connections, Complexities, Compositions, Competition, Compromises*, and *Coherence*. The development of these principles are guided by established design theory on material compositions (e.g. Nelson & Stolterman, 2003) and these developed principles work as conceptual cornerstones for a relational language that should enable us to address and talk specifically about computational materials working in a relational concert with other materials, i.e. as an interactive texture.

1. Connections

The notion of "Connections" is the first concept in this relational vocabulary. Connections refer to the ways in which pieces of a design is assembled into a larger structure. The notion of connections deals with the ways in which atoms and bits are interrelated, referring to one another, or scaffolding each other as part of a design. From this perspective, we view connections as a concept that enable us to describe and organize relationships between surface and structure, and across different substrates, scales, layers, and situations, and ultimately between the physical and the digital, and around the digital as a material – a computational materiality.

In this vocabulary we notice two types of connections including 1) *vertical connections*, and 2) *horizontal connections*. Vertical connections connect appearance to material properties whereas horizontal connections connect different materials into larger chunks or assemblages of materials. Together, the vertical and horizontal connections give a design its ultimate appearance with its presenting features:

"The most immediate form of appearance has to do with its presenting features – the qualities that inform the senses most directly." (Nelson & Stolterman, 2003, p.2 219).

For the creation of new interactive textures this implies that it is a design decision to be made about how to craft these connections to let some aspects work as presenting features whereas other materials are connected to scaffold one such particular appearance. As for any computational materiality the aspect of dynamic appearance is also focal to attend to in this aspect, meaning that these crafted connections made might also change over time making materials switch position between presenting feature adding to the appearance, and structure, working for the material scaffolding of appearance. This is an important aspect of the crafting out of new interactive textures that moves us into the notion of – complexities.

2. Complexities

The notion of *complexities* enables us to address the dynamics of crafted connections in-between and within materials as a fundamental aspect of new interactive textures.

This notion of complexities enables us to talk about emergent properties and emergent appearances of material assemblages (similar to how the gestalt laws of perception in psychology tells us that the human brain is capable of reading out complex and multiple patterns from simple visual elements working in composition). According to Nelson & Stolterman's (2003) theory of design, then complexity describes this dynamics of connections and complexity itself as the consequence of this dynamics:

"Complexity, a distinctive attribute arising as a consequence of the dynamic interactivity of relationships" (Nelson & Stolterman, 2003, p.73).

Interestingly enough complexity deals with a broad range of issues, from structural issues, via presentation, to human factors of "perception" an in terms of a distinctive attribute of the aesthetics of connections as dynamics – i.e. as an important aspect of the aesthetics of these new interactive textures.

3. Compositions

Working through these concepts we also realize how connections and its dynamics forming complexities into structures and appearances calls for organizing principles capable of arranging chunks of materials into working assemblages, making unifications of materials work in concert instead of collapsing into clutters. In the previous chapters we have denoted this as "compositions" and following the reasoning of Nelson & Stolterman's (2003) then:

"Composing is an activity where judgments are made, using aesthetic principles like balance and symmetry, about relationships between details and the whole" (Nelson & Stolterman, 2003, p. 209).

In such terms, *composition* is related to the notion of *connections* working to relate vertical and horizontal connections into meaningful wholes.

In working with composition, through the planning, placement and arrangement of elements, one might risk logical fallacy, in which one assumes that a whole has a property solely because its various parts have that property. As such, composition works outside the scope of linear relations between material properties and appearance, working more directed towards the crafting out of wholeness from details, i.e. aesthetics of presented wholeness beyond functional connections or assembled pieces thus dealing not only with totality of materials used, but in fact the emergent character arising form the dynamic interplay in-between these materials.

In computer science, the notion of composition typically refers to the act or mechanism to combine simple functions to build more complicated ones. As such, the notion of composition not only relates back to the issue of connections, but it is also heavily related to the issue of complexities as outlined above.

4. Competition and Compromises

In many cases there is an unbalance in a composition. This imbalance can be further elaborated and for this particular framework we provide the two concepts of *competition* and *compromises* to speak specifically about overbalanced and underbalanced compositions.

In this context, the notion of *competition* refers to a contest uphold between materials being part of the texture of a computational composition where a single material might compete for the goal of a design, or compete with another material for a design goal that cannot be shared. In this framing, competition might not only surface at the level of materiality appearance, but might also work at the level of material properties or arranged structure of materials. In this case, the design is overbalanced in relation to the overall design.

On the other hand, the notion of *compromises* tells us that in a composition some materials might not come to their full use, but might in fact be underused in relation to the overall design. In general terms a material compromise might be to use another material to work, or appear as the material actually needed as part of a particular composition. It might also be that of a material having to give up part of, or all of its properties or functions in a larger composition. As for a third perspective, a compromise might also arise at the level of composition as a consequence of lack of proper materials, or inabilities to unify these into a meaningful whole, i.e. to have the materials working in – *coherence*.

5. Coherence

Coherence is the final cornerstone of this proposed theory of texture as a relational structure across different materials. As this section will illustrate this concept not only deals with a fundamental aspect of texture, but it also relates back through all of the concepts described above, making its way back to the initial concept of connections.

As for a start, *texture* does not only concern the relations between material properties, structure and appearance, but also, texture is about consistency, i.e. about the ways in which a composition holds together, presenting itself through the performance of its form. In our vocabulary we view this form-related performance in terms of its semantically meaningful unification i.e. – *coherence*.

In the presentation of the notion of *composition* we used the description of "working assemblages". But what is that? One straight-forward answer to this question is that it is something that is working as a composition not only at a functional level, but also on the level of the aesthetics of a materiality, i.e. a something that we need a better vocabulary for. Here, this concept of aesthetics dealing with meaning and legitimacy of a composition is referred to as *coherence*. When something is presented as meaningful and legit we can think of one such composition not only as "real", but also in terms of "true", where a "true" composition is what distinguish one such compositions from kitsch, making the composition stand out as a bearer of true qualities rather than upholding only a sense of quality in appearance (this relates back to aesthetics of the simulated vs. an aesthetics of the real, i.e. back to a possible aesthetics of the computational per se). If comparing this to similar ideas within the field of architecture it can be noticed how e.g. Farrelly (2009) describe "the truth to materials in similar terms":

"The idea of "truth to materials" is an essential consideration when understanding architecture. In architectural terms, to be "true" is to be honest. A building that uses brick to construct a wall, which in turn supports a roof, is using materials honestly. A steel-framed building that incorporates a brick wall is not necessarily true to its materials because there is a sense of "hiding" the building's real structure and creating an illusion of another sort of architecture" (Farrelly, 2009).

In a similar way Nelson & Stolterman (2003) discusses how a design can be true or not in relation to its ultimate appearance and character:

"A design's ultimate appearance can hide or reveal its true nature, its character and its soul. The most immediate form of appearance has to do with its presenting features – the qualities that inform the senses most directly." (Nelson & Stolterman, 2003, p.2 219).

As seen from this quote this relates back to the concept of "connections", adding to this the issues of meaningfulness, truth, and legitimacy. In fact, Nelson & Stolterman (2003) continues in this direction, reaching back to the fundamental question on significance in relation to meaningful compositions, at the same time again, re-connecting to the issue of texture through their notion of "meaning making elements" as affordance, representation, association and information:

"The nature of a design can be both trivial and significant. Designs gain significance by carrying meaning through such meaning making elements as affordance, representation, association and information." (Nelson & Stolterman, 2003, p.2 219).

As for a summary, this proposed framework view design as the process of bringing together material compositions and the crafting out of new relations between materials, i.e. as the making of textures. It is our strong belief that the relational vocabulary as presented in this section might work to address computational compositions from the viewpoint of computational aesthetics and as a guiding framework for the crafting out of new interactive textures.

In the next section I move from this relational language that can guide the compositional activity of creating new interactive textures towards the next aspect of texture that has to do with how these also work as navigational aids in our everyday lives.

TEXTURES AS NAVIGATIONAL AIDS

Textures connect the surface of an object, an architectural element, or even a whole environment to the raw materials from which it is made from. As such, textures relate to materials as representations relation to any given set of information.

Textures are also about these surfaces that surrounds us. In doing so, they do not simply "cover" the raw materials, or express certain qualities of them, but in fact, they function as visual, tactile, and sometimes audio cues for us in our daily lives. As we interact with the textures around us, we do not only use the textures, but we also "read" the textures as navigational cues. E.g. the texture of an object can tell us how to hold it, use it, throw it, etc. The texture of a building might tell us where the entrance is, where to go, where different rooms are located, etc. As such, we do not only read the texture per se, but we also read these textures as to extract some navigational information from them.

Here we might notice two different levels of representations when it comes to textures. One the one hand, textures are representations which function as a "skin", "surface" or interface to a certain material. This view allows people to use or access a material, or it might give them the opportunity of taking advantage to certain material properties. On the other hand, textures work as "referral" representations meaning that they do not only function as a gateway to the material from which they are made, but in fact, they work as a pointer to something else. Most typical, a texture might tell its user how it is supposed to be used. E.g. a screwdriver might for instance have a formed soft rubber cover as a texture indication of how to properly hold or operate the screwdriver.

Here, a related and very important notion is the concept of consistency, and as already pinpointed it is also a focal part of any definition of textures. Given one common texture for one particular use it is important to follow such conventions in new designs as well as to benefit from the experience a user might have from other similar textures. That is, if following social conventions, and (socially) trained ways of reading textures in use (experience) we can guide a potential user on how to "read" a texture in the way it was intended to be read and understood.

This line of reasoning can be further illustrated in the following model in which textures might work as a representation both in terms of a surface, as well as a navigational aid. Here, we can think about textures on three different levels. First, it is about the textures per se and how they related to the materials from which they are made as outlined in chapter 2. Second, we can understand textures in terms of the different models of representations possible to connect to a certain texture. This is about how the texture is presented and "read". Finally, we might want to think about how a certain texture is used through the notion of "interaction", not only with a texture, but also interactions through textures. In Figure 53 these three levels are schematically outlined as follows:

Signs, patterns, structures, and cues. These are all examples of words that we connect with the notion of textures. These notions are all about directions and about guidance. As humans we are trained to read these navigational cues in textures and we fill these signs and cues with meaning. The reason why we do this is ultimately because we believe in meaningful designs. However, as also outlined in the model above new materials do not only allow for interaction with these materials, but do in fact allow for interaction through these materials. More about that in the next section.

Figure 53. Schematic model of the notion of texture as it relates to the notions of representation and interaction

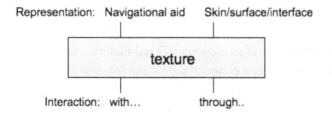

INTERACTION WITH AND THROUGH TEXTURES

New so-called *transmaterials* (Brownell 2005; 2008) can be thought of as physical instances of "everywares". As formulated by Greenfield:

"Everyware is information processing embedded in the objects and surfaces of everyday life" (Greenfield, 2006)

This is an obvious line of development and we can see this through new computational textures being developed. We can also experience interaction with these new textures through the development of new interaction modalities that allow for hands-on interaction with objects situated in between the physical world and the digital world. Some recent examples here include interaction modalities for tangible interaction, gesture-controlled interaction modalities and e.g. multi-touch interaction.

As we introduce computational capabilities to new materials and as we equip these with proper interaction modalities we might soon start to think about how these computational materials, objects and elements are not only physically combined and assembled, but also how they are logically connected. That is, what are the underlying structures, systems and infrastructures that allow for these new materials to communicate, exchange information, logically connect, sync and interact in concert?

When formulating and raising these questions about new textures we might not only focus at the texture at hand, or in front of us, but in fact, we ask traditional questions concerning the computational, although being fully embedded in the world of physical materials.

And, as we add computational power to the physical world we do not only add the capabilities of calculation, storage, processing, transaction power, and networking, but we also add media capabilities to the physical materials of our built environments. By doing so, we add a rich media dimension that allow for new forms of interpersonal interaction through these new textures in which remote persons can act in concert with co-located ones, and though which new forms of information flows, communication, collaboration and coordination might evolve as we develop these new materials.

In Figure 54 a schematic model of this media dimension of new textures is outlined. As illustrated in this figure we might think about these new textures in relation to new interaction modalities and underlying enabling structures. When it comes to new interaction modalities we can think about those as the designed gateways to access the material as a computational material, and as a media. Through these modalities people can connect, communicate, share materials and information and potentially even add to the material composition of the object or element at hand. In the same sense as textures related to materials it is also true that these

Figure 54. Schematic model of the notion of texture as it relates to the notions of interaction modalities and underlying (infra) structures

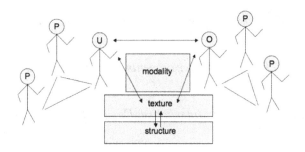

new materials relate to the textures. If the interaction with or through the texture is to be understood and experienced as being meaningful it is important that an appropriate interaction modality is chosen for a particular texture design. Further on, if continuing to study this model we can see that people access the texture through these enabling interaction modalities. In turn, that also gives then potential access to the underlying structure of the texture, which might include standards for physical assembly of the materials into new forms of textures and new transmaterials, reconfiguration of the textures, as well as access to the core computational infrastructure that enable a certain texture, and which connect it to other computational elements – co-present in the same location, or located elsewhere but still instantly available over the network.

In a sense, these new textures make an interesting combination in our world beyond the most obvious one of connecting digital and physical materials in the same objects. Instead, and far more interesting I think is the combination of abstract textures (e.g. logical, graphical and semantic textures) with concrete textures (physical and tangible textures). In a sense, this creates a bridge, not only between the physical and digital world, but also a bridge between capabilities of reasoning and experiencing, and ultimately between thinking and being in the world!

As such, these new textures fill an important role of working as a unifying manifestation that link together abstract and concrete structures into new complex systems – in this book referred to as interactive architectures.

REFERENCES

Benyon, D. (2004). *Designing Interactive Systems*. Reading, MA: Addison-Wesley.

Brownell, B. (2005). *Transmaterial: A Catalog of Materials That Redefine our Physical Environment*. Princeton Architectural Press.

Brownell, B. (2008). *Transmaterial 2: A Catalog of Materials That Redefine our Physical Environment*. Princeton Architectural Press.

Bullivant, L. (2005). *4dspace: Interactive Architecture, Architectural Design*. Wiley-Academy.

Bullivant, L. (2006). *Responsive environments – Architecture, art and design*. V & A Contemporary Publications.

Bullivant, L. (2007). *4dsocial: Interactive Design Environments, Architectural Design*. Wiley-Academy.

Farrelly, L. (2009). *Basics Architecture: Construction + Materiality*. AVA Publishing.

Greenfield, A. (2006). *Everyware – The dawning age of ubiquitous computing*. Berkeley, CA: New Riders.

Indergaard, M. (2004). *Silicon Alley - The Rise and Fall of a New Media District*. Routledge.

Jones, Q. (2004). People-to-People-to-Geographical-Places: The P3 Framework for Location-Based Community Systems. In *J. Computer Supported Cooperative Work, 13*(3-4), 202–211. doi:10.1007/s10606-004-2803-7

Nelson, H., & Stolterman, E. (2003). *The Design Way: intentional change in an unpredictable world*. Educational Technology Publications.

Oosterhuist, K. (2007). *iA #1 Interactive Architecture*. Rotterdam: Episode Publishers.

Rheingold, H., et al. (2007). *Open 11: Hybrid Space*. NAi Uitgevers/Publishers.

Sengers, P., et al (2004). Culturally Embedded Computing. *Pervasive Computing, 3*(1).

Streitz, (2002). Roomware: Toward the next generation of human-computer interaction based on an integrated design of real and virtual worlds . In Carroll, J. (Ed.), *Human Computer Interaction in the Next Millennium. Addison-Wesley*. ACM Press.

Tietz, J. (1998). Geschichte der Architektur des 20. Jahrhunderts, Könemann Verlagsgesellschaft mbH.

Vallgårda, A., & Redström, J. (2007). Computational composites. In *Proceedings of CHI '07 - the SIGCHI conference on Human factors in computing systems*. ACM Press.

Zellner, P. (1999). *Hybrid Space – New forms in digital architechture*. Thames & Hudson.

ENDNOTE

[1]   I use the term "we" here to indicate that the development of this theoretical framework was done in close collaboration with Erica Robles at New York University.

Chapter 6
Interactive Architecture

Having discussed and theorized the concept of interactive architecture in general, and "interactive textures" in particular this chapter is devoted to applying the idea of *interaction through textures*, and to describe and analyze the movement towards interactive architecture as full-scale built environments that rely upon a complete blend of physical and digital materials, and which provide spaces for social interaction as well as computational interfaces for interaction with digital material in public places.

In this chapter several examples of interactive architectures will be reviewed and discussed from a viewpoint of a new kind of architecture as well as from an interaction design perspective.

The chapter follows a simple structure in terms of three movements in scale and one vision statement. These three movements include the movement from digital elements to interactive textures, the move from textures to architectures, and the move from architectures to environments. As seen from these three movements, the scale is increased from the basic enabling elements all the way up to our surrounding environment. Having passed through these three movements the chapter ends with the exploration of a vision of living systems, which include not only interactive architectures, but also new textures for landscaping.

DOI: 10.4018/978-1-61520-653-7.ch006

FROM DIGITAL ELEMENTS TO INTERACTIVE TEXTURES

Pieces of electronics do not make interactive textures happen. Instead, in order to make the move from pure pieces of technology to interactive textures several aspects needs to be carefully considered. With the same eye for quality in material selection when it comes to creating new physical textures that any skilled designer, artist or architect is used to we also need to carefully select the digital technology to be blended into these new textures. In the same way as any skilled designer considers the material properties of any physical material, some specific attention must be putted on the properties of the digital material in question.

Further on, as we are to bring these two elements together in the creation of new textures, the connections or relations between these two must also be designed as to fully make the two elements work together.

A source of inspiration for this complicated work can be found in the intellectual work by Oosterhuist (2007) on the components and nature of interactive architecture including his statement that:

"interactive architecture is not about communication between people, it is defined as the art of building relationships between built components in the first place, and building relations between people and the built components in the second place".

As noticed from this quote we need to think about integration of materials at different levels. We cannot only think about integration between the physical and the digital into one coherent structure. But we must also consider this integration in relation to its potential users.

In the movement from digital elements towards the creation of new interactive textures a guiding notion can then be the concept of "compositions" as described and outlined in chapter 5. Through this unifying concept equal attention is given to the creation of relationships between the elements of the composition and the relationship between the composition and an external observer via the concept of appearance as wholeness. Thus, in our efforts to design new textures we should critically ask ourselves whether or not a certain composition of physical and digital elements appears as a wholeness – and not only visually, but also functionally and in the interactional interplay in which both physical and digital aspects of a certain composition comes into play.

One of the hardest challenges to make this appearance of wholeness happens lies in the designers ability to texturize the computational in the physical, mostly because traditional materials are easier to carve out visually, and digital technology on the other hand, are typically a challenge to fully embed in the physical world.

FROM TEXTURES TO ARCHITECTURES

When we have the new textures in place, when we have access to new transmaterials and new architectural elements to play around with the next challenge is to move from these textures and elements to the level of architecture. This, both in terms of scale of installations, but foremost in terms of conceptual thinking on digital integration in our physical world.

Here, to make the move from textures to architectures require a mindset focused not on interactive textures and architecture as two separate elements, but instead, a thinking that directly takes a point of departure in a unified view on these two under the label of "interactive architecture".

The notion of "Interactive architecture" (e.g. Bullivant, 2005; Fox & Kemp, 2009) bridges in itself two design traditions, i.e. design of interactive systems (e.g. Benyon, 2004) on the one hand, and traditional architecture (e.g. Ching, 2007) as the tradition of designing our built environment on the other hand. As such, this emerging area, in which digital technologies are used as one design material (Vallgårda & Redström, 2007) amongst other materials in the creation of new built environments, challenges the traditional approach to systems design, as well as the methods applied to arrive at well-grounded digital solutions. More specifically, interactive architecture as an emerging design practice simultaneously calls for an architectural approach to interactive systems design, and for an interactive systems design approach to the design of our built environment. As described by Sengers, et al. (2004) the recent movement towards ubiquitous computing calls for such a practical and theoretical bridge between architecture and interactive systems design.

Most recently this challenge has been addressed in a number of papers in the area of participatory design and related design approaches including e.g. reports on design of immersive environments for public use (Robertson, et al, 2006), design of co-creative media environments (Watkins & Russo, 2005), and design of museums as interactive public places for cultural engagement (Watkins, 2007) and exhibition design (Taxén, 2004). While these studies document the design cases and the methods applied in these projects there is still a need for new studies that explicitly sets out to address this seemingly gap between architecture and interactive systems design and to contribute with new knowledge and specific insights related to methodological approaches to design in the area of interactive architecture. As to make the move from new textures to interactive architecture, this challenge needs to be addressed and carefully explored.

Research on methods and design for interactive architecture spans across several areas including approaches like ambient intelligence and ubiquitous computing from the interactive systems field, and a turn towards digital materials in the field of architecture. Below I will outline some of the most recent attempts made to bridge the areas of interactive systems design and architecture to create a knowledge base, and a point of departure for research in the area of interactive architecture.

Reviewing some of the current research on this topic within the field of interactive systems design we find documented research on design of ambient information systems (Pousman & Stasko, 2006) ambient intelligence (Ruyter & Aarts, 2004) i.e. computerized environments, and its use in everyday life (e.g. Cai & Abascal, 2006), as well as research into intelligent architecture and design of interactive places for architecture and entertainment (e.g. Sparacino, 2008).

From the field of architecture we find a similar movement into the area of interactive architecture including e.g. reviews and application of innovative digital materials and technologies in the creation of built environments under the notion of "living systems" (Margolis & Robinson, 2007), intellectual essays written on architecture from the perspective of virtual and real spaces (Grosz, 2001), reviews of new digital materials for architecture (Matério, 2007), i.e. partly digital fabrics and materials sometimes referred to as "transmaterials" (Brownell, 2005; 2008), or "smart materials" (Addington & Schodek, 2005). If moving further into the architectural research community we find examples of documented projects in the area of interactive architecture under the label of "disappearing architecture" (Flachbart & Weibel, 2005) in which the notion of "non-location" has been introduced to discuss how digital technologies not only add to the construction, form and function of a place, but at the same time makes the place dislocated through the geography-spanning character of digital technologies.

If reviewing the work done in-between these two strands of research, i.e. work specifically conducted to address "interactive architecture" as such we find some good examples including Bullivant's work on responsive environments (Bullivant, 2006), interactive architecture (Bullivant, 2005), and interactive design environments (Bullivant, 2007). Further on, Spiller's work on reflexive architecture (Spiller, 2002) and Kolarevic & Malkawi's work on performative architecture (2005) adds to our understanding of this phenomenon. Taken together, this strand of literature provides a very detailed overview of the practical and concrete initiatives taken right now in terms of design of interactive environments. Further on, McCullough's (2004) theoretical conceptualization of this movement in terms of the establishment of a new digital ground, and Greenfield's (2006) reinterpretation of pervasive computing, ubiquitous computing, and ambient informatics into the proposed notion of "everyware" serves as an important and fundamental point of reference for further research into this area.

Moving further into the literature in this area, and if also looking into current research on methods and design approaches to realize interactive architecture we find some good support in the area of participatory design as outlined above, including research conducted by e.g. Robertson (2006), Watkins & Russo (2005), Taxén (2004) and Roussou et al, (2007).

Having all of this said, however, it looks like we still lack some documented research that takes on an architectural approach to interactive systems design, and an interactive systems design approach to the design of our built environment, i.e., and approach that takes into account the broad range of "users" that an interactive environment includes. While this has been acknowledged in the area of participatory design as the need for a multi-voiced approach to design, and the acknowledging of the importance of diverse application of PD (Törpel, 2005) it has not yet been applied in the area of interactive architecture.

In this book two specific contributions are made to this current body of knowledge on interactive architecture. First, the concept of interactive textures as put toward in this book works as a concept with its roots simultaneously in the field of interaction design and architecture, thus contributing to the creation of a theoretical framework that spans across these two strands of research. Further on, through the case studies presented in chapter 7 in this book, some contributions in terms of methodological approaches to interactive architecture design are provided. Still, this is only small contributions and should be read as indicators of possibilities for the development of full-scale theories and methods capable of addressing this field of interactive architecture.

While the concepts and cases presented in this book might work as theoretical and methodological indicators there are also several very practical and real indicators of a movement from rather small-scale development projects of new textures towards the application of such textures in full-scale architecture, as the following examples will illustrate.

For instance, as illustrated in Figure 55, buildings might be covered with a digital "skin" that can make them appear as a typical static building (see Figure 55, left), and then dynamically change as to change its appearance, to communicate movement, animate patterns, attract our attention, or to serve any other purpose imaginable (see Figure 55, middle and right).

As we can see from this set of pictures the visual appearance of a building is crucial from our understanding of it. Further on, we can notice that when the texture is in line with our expectations and our previous experiences of similar buildings we immediately make sense of them, i.e. we tend to "read" them in a certain way. For instance, in the first picture (Figure 55, left) we understand the straight grid of light squares as floors and sections of the building, and the light seems to be aligned with the physical structure of the building. However, when the animation starts (see Figure 55, middle and right) a deviation between the animated light and the possible physical structure of the building happens which creates a confusing appearance of the whole building. A confusion that immediately catches our attention.

Figure 55. Dynamic building façade: The Uniqa tower in Vienna and the 'Twists and Turns' installation which is a playful work that responds to the implied structure of the building its 'situated upon

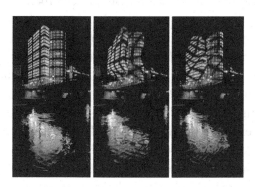

Another example of interactive architecture is displayed in Figure 56. Here, a set of public displays has been arranged as a series of lines in a public space. The displays thus appear to form a larger architectural structure, and the similarities in the representations on the screens also communicate that these screens are connected.

Here, this interactive architecture builds upon several architectonic ideas to make this public interactive installation work. As already mentioned, the repetition of the lines of displays gives the displays a unified architectonic appearance which makes the displays appear not only as a technological installation, but in fact as an architectonic installation in which the digital displays are important building blocks.

If analyzing this installation a little bit further we can also see how the notion of consistency as a focal concept in the notion of "textures" have been explored through not only the repetition of displays, but also through the recurring theme and style of visualization across all of the screens although each screen is not showing exactly the same image frame simultaneously. Also, this installation illustrate the

Figure 56. Interconnected public screens as a dynamic texture in the cityscape

architectonic concepts of "solids" and "voids" in a good way in which not only the displays work in concert, but in fact, the distances in between the displays fills an important role in the creation of a half circle formed "room" that also frames this space from the street lights in the background.

Further on, this installation utilizes from the use of a combination of light and darkness to make it appear as an effective installation. That is, the contrast between the light and glowing displays in contrast with the darkness in this public place. As a consequence of this, the installation does not only appear better, but it also contributes to making this place lighter and thus safer as a public space.

Contrary to this example which illustrate a dance between solids and voids we find several examples of whole buildings covered with display technologies including e.g. the building illustrated in Figure 57. This follows a trend in modern architecture right now to cover whole buildings with a digital texture that enable the building to dynamically change its visual appearance and potentially communicate a message to any potential observer outside the building.

From an interactive architecture point of view I find this examples exciting and boring at the same time. These new buildings are exciting to the extent that a new (digital) material is used for the façade, which open up for new possibilities in terms of dynamic appearances of buildings. On the other hand, though, this installation does not benefit much from architectural thinking. Instead, the physical architecture is almost replaced by the display technology covering the whole building. And, in doing so, it also loses its architectural dimensions for the favor of a building size display, which in turn make this more of an exercise in interactive systems design rather than an interactive architecture. This, due to the lack of architectural thinking blended with thinking on interactive textures.

Figure 57. Whole building covered with a digital texture

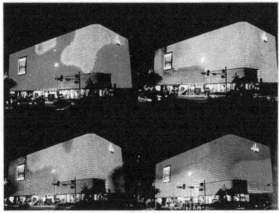

What becomes obvious from these examples is that for successful interactive architecture it is not only the scale of the installation that matters, but in fact how architectural thinking has been linked with interaction design thinking in the real world manifestation of the ideas and in the texturation process of aligning digital materials with physical materials.

As in the example above we can raise the question of where we draw the line between texturation of digital technologies into physical space, vs. the substitution of the physical in favor for the digital? In case we go for the second strategy here in which we replace the physical with digital material instead of working through a blending process of interlinkage between the physical and the digital we end up with a result leaning towards interaction design in public spaces rather than interactive architecture from an analytical point of view.

Here, we change the fundamental appearance of a building from being, in fact, a building to instead becoming a huge digital interface. If following this line of thinking we can then only reply on interaction design thinking in our sense making of the built environment as an interactive surface, or an interface. That would, from my perspective be a huge mistake since we would then miss the rich history and body of knowledge in the field of architecture on how to create functioning, meaningful and sustainable environments.

So, contrary to this, I suggest an interact architecture agenda that is open for technological explorations while at the same time making use of classical concepts from architecture in new innovative texturation processes of information technologies in physical spaces.

FROM ARCHITECTURES TO ENVIRONMENTS

Not only do we need to relate these new textures available to the concept of buildings, and not only can we rely on architectural thinking when introducing digital elements and technologies in physical spaces. Instead, we also need to scale our thinking one step further up from single architectures to environments.

In one sense, this scaling from architectures to environments is a matter of physical scale. We can easily think of a scale ranging from buildings to streets, to blocks of buildings, and even to suburbs and full-scale cities. This is an important perspective and intellectual exercise since it gives us a sense of how single architectures are situated in a bigger environment or landscape.

Working with the scaling of ideas from basic elements to large-scale environments is also conceptually challenging. As we move from the size of the building, in which concepts like openings, planes, edges and corners are at an appropriate level of conceptualization we now need to move into architectural concepts like "space within a space", "interlooking spaces", "clustered organizations", "circulation", "datum", "rhythm" and "transformation" (Ching, 2007) in order to fully understand architecture at the level of analysis where buildings are situated in formation of environments and landscapes.

In similar terms, we need to look beyond the notion of a "user" and private use of the digital, and direct our attention to public interaction, broadcasting, ambient information environments, crowd computing and interaction for the masses.

In a sense, the intellectual exercise of scaling from basic materials to complex environments is also a test on whether the ideas are sustainable or not. Any solution can function as a small prototype installation. However, when it is supposed to be part of a larger system, part of a larger structure, in frequent support of peoples everyday activities, and used, not only by one test person, but by hundreds, and potentially thousands of people then the sustainability of any design reveals itself.

TOWARDS LIVING SYSTEMS: INTERACTIVE ARCHITECTURE AND LANDSCAPING

As we reach the level of analysis that deals with our surrounding in terms of environments and landscapes we find some interesting support for our thinking on interactive textures in the recent work by Margolis and Robinson (2007) on living systems. In their book "Living systems – innovative materials and technologies for landscape architects" they take a point of departure in innovation in material technologies which enable new living systems (Margolis & Robinson, 2007) not only for designers and building architects but for landscape architects as well.

According to their view, in "living systems" technology becomes integral to the conceptual framework of landscape architecture. That is, through applying an organic perspective on landscaping in which the architectural systems in terms of performance criteria and operations facilitates and adapt to the cyclical processes of natural systems scaffolded by digital technologies we're facing a new agenda for landscape architecture.

In this new agenda new methods are needed in order to not arrive at technical solutions, but on the contrary take these new materials, textures and "living systems" as a point of departure. As formulated by Margolis & Robinson (2007):

"Living systems calls for a shift away from the traditional design process that initially identifies a landscape's behaviors and performance criteria and then offers a range of product/construction solutions that can accommodate such functions, toward a design process which integrates the function into the design from the outset" (Margolis & Robinson, 2007, p. 8)

As this quote illustrates it is the same case for "living systems" as for interactive architecture, i.e. there is a need for a unified perspective in which we no longer can separate issues related to technology from issues related to architecture. In this book, this is tackled through the notion of *interactive textures* as a theoretical concept that bridges the physical and digital divide simultaneously with a bridging of material properties and surface.

This is also an indication with some bearing on the theorizing on interaction *per se* as pushed forward in chapter 1 in this book. To the same extend as we cannot focus on either technology or architecture, but need a unified perspective we can neither focus on humans or digital technologies in the creation of new interaction spaces. That is, we cannot arrive at a good understanding of requirements on interaction technologies by looking at people and their activities. Nor can we imagine new interactive systems with a narrow perspective on digital technologies. Instead, we need to take a point of departure in the inner intersection of interaction per se, in the dance between technological capabilities and new forms of activities as to further explore the design space of interaction with and through digital materials.

Following the line of thinking related to the need for new methods to address "living systems" as put forward by Margolis & Robinson (2007) we can see a similar trend within the field of interaction design. For instance, in the paper "Concept-driven Interaction Design Research" the authors Stolterman & Wiberg (2010) argues that in the field of interaction design people do not only develop systems based on a human-centered design approach from problem identification to product in a similar process as criticized by Margolis & Robinson (2007). Instead, it is a common approach to also follow a concept-driven process in which guiding theoretical concepts, like the notion of "interactive textures" work as a vision and raw model for the practical efforts made to realize such installations.

Through one such approach in which a point of departure is taken in interactive textures in the first place both theoretical advancements and new products can valuable outcomes from the design process.

With a theoretical notion as a guiding tool it is also easier to know whether or not a certain piece is working or not in a certain composition. That is, through clear definitions of the composition at hand, the purpose, quality, function or properties of a given element can be discussed and evaluated in relation to the wholeness of the composition. In doing this exercise of relating pieces to composition we also redirect our attention from small scale ad hoc problem solving to design for wholeness. One such perspective is critical as to situate architecture in the design of whole environments, as to situate architecture in landscaping, and as to situate the montage of design solutions in any practical context.

In the next chapter we look into four such context in which we reports from our different projects conducted on texturing of information and interaction technologies in various public places ranging from wearable and mobile devices for dynamic social groups to large scale texturing of digital technologies in a public space.

REFERENCES

Addington, M., & Schodek, D. (2005). *Smart materials and technologies for the architecture and design professions*. New York: Elsevier, Architectural Press.

Benyon, D. (2004). *Designing Interactive Systems*. Reading, MA: Addison-Wesley.

Brownell, B. (2005). *Transmaterial: A Catalog of Materials That Redefine our Physical Environment*. Princeton Architectural Press.

Brownell, B. (2008). *Transmaterial 2: A Catalog of Materials That Redefine our Physical Environment*. Princeton Architectural Press.

Bullivant, L. (2005). *4dspace: Interactive Architecture, Architectural Design*. Wiley-Academy.

Bullivant, L. (2006). *Responsive environments – Architecture, art and design*. V & A Contemporary Publications.

Bullivant, L. (2007). *4dsocial: Interactive Design Environments, Architectural Design*. Wiley-Academy.

Cai, Y., & Abascal, J. (2006). *Ambient intelligence in everyday life*. Springer-Verlag.

Ching, F. (2007). *Architecture: Form, Space, and Order*. New York: John Wiley & Sons, Inc.

Flachbart, G., & Weibel, P. (2005). *Disappearing architecture – From real to virtual to quantum*. Birkhäuser. doi:10.1007/3-7643-7674-0

Fox, M., & Kemp, M. (2009). *Interactive Architecture*. New York: Princeton Architectural Press.

Greenfield, A. (2006). *Everyware – The dawning age of ubiquitous computing*. Berkeley, CA: New Riders.

Grosz, E. (2001). *Architecture from the outside – Essays on virtual and real space*. Cambridge, MA: MIT Press.

Kolarevic, B., & Malkawi, A. (2005). *Performative Architecture – Beyond instrumentality*. UK: Spon Press.

Margolis, L., & Robinson, A. (2007). *Living Systems – Innovative materials and technologies for landscape architecture*. Birkhäuser.

Materio (2007). *Material World 2: Innovative Materials for Architecture and Design*. Birkhäuser.

McCullough, M. (2004). *Digital Ground – Architecture, Pervasive Computing, and Environmental Knowing*. Cambridge, MA: MIT Press.

Oosterhuist, K. (2007). *iA #1 Interactive Architecture*. Rotterdam: Episode Publishers.

Pousman, Z., & Stasko, J. (2006) A taxonomy of ambient information systems: Four patterns of design. In *Proceedings of AVI '06 - the working conference on Advanced visual interfaces*. ACM Press.

Robertson, T., Mansfield, T., & Loke, L. (2006). Designing an immersive environment for public use. In *Proceedings Participatory Design Conference*, Aug 2006, Trento, Italy. ACM Press.

Ruyter, B., & Aarts, E. (2004). Ambient intelligence: visualizing the future. In *Proceedings of AVI '04 - the working conference on Advanced visual interfaces* ACM Press.

Sengers, P., et al (2004). Culturally Embedded Computing. *Pervasive Computing, 3*(1).

Sparacino, F. (2008). Natural interaction in intelligent spaces: designing for architecture and entertainment. *Multimedia Tools and Applications, 38*, 307–335. doi:10.1007/s11042-007-0193-9

Spiller, N. (2002). *Reflexive architecture, Architectural Design*. Wiley-Academy.

Stolterman, E. & Wiberg, M. (in press). Concept-driven Interaction Design Research. *International Journal of Computer Human Interaction (HCI), 25*(2).

Taxén, G. (2004) Introducing participatory design in museums. In *Proceedings Participatory Design Conference 2004*, Toronto, Canada.

Törpel, B. (2005). Participatory design: a multi-voiced effort. In *Proceedings of CC '05 - the 4th decennial conference on Critical computing: between sense and sensibility*. ACM Press.

Vallgårda, A., & Redström, J. (2007). Computational composites. In *Proceedings of CHI '07 - the SIGCHI conference on Human factors in computing systems*. ACM Press.

Section 3
Character:
Cases and Concepts

Making Cases and Seeing with New Eyes

As formulated by Marcel Proust, *"The real voyage of discovery consists not in seeking new landscapes, but in seeing with new eyes."* There are two aspects of consider when looking into the character of new interactive textures. We need both empirical examples of how this illustrates itself in our everyday world and new ways of seeing the things in our surrounding.

This section of the book is advocacy for these two needs. First, five different cases are introduced in the first chapter in this section which aims at illustrating a range of cases from IT-support to people moving around in places (almost independent of place) to the other extreme end of this scale, i.e. totally interactive environments, and everyday city textures in which the technology is not only embedded in our physical surrounding, but actually also highly embedded in the cultural life surrounding us as we experience the modern city nowadays. From the other strand of thinking, and as to also address the need for seeing with new eyes the second chapter in this section of the book takes us through several theoretical lenses through which we can look at our surrounding and start to see, analyze and understand how the digital is texturing itself in our everyday world, changing our conventions, and changing us from users of computers to inhabitant in general.

As a specific contribution to the *seeing with new eyes* dimension this section of the book also presents the IT- ("Interaction through Textures) framework as to further guide our thinking on this matter.

Chapter 7

Five Cases:
From Mobile Devices to Interaction Landscaping and the City

In this section of the book four of my own research projects in this area are be presented. The first four cases represent a spectrum of interactive services, prototype systems and installations developed as research prototypes over the last 10 years ranging from the design and implementation of novel handheld devices, to technologies for interactive landscapes. Some cases contain only one developed system and other cases contain several examples. However, the important thing here is not the number of systems presented, but the illustration of a design space in which our physical environment is becoming part of the interaction that modern IT will enable–an interaction landscape that spans across physical locations and digital services, and across mobile devices and embedded computational power in public places. As for the fifth case, it serves the purpose of a real life reference point in which we look into how our modern cities are developing through the adoption of new digital technologies, and through the texturing of these technologies in the public city space.

DOI: 10.4018/978-1-61520-653-7.ch007

CASE 1. MOBILITY: SUPPORTING PEOPLE MOVING AROUND IN PLACES

The first case presented in this section of the book contains the description and analysis of five mobile prototype systems developed which each of these systems demonstrate a different way of framing the physical environment and how it comes into use as a resource in design of mobile services and devices. These systems include:

RoamWare: A mobile system for dynamic group communication
FolkMusic: A peer-to-peer system for mobile music sharing
MoveInfo: A concept design for interaction landscape access
Negotiator: Availability management in the interaction landscape
Midgets: Concept for application mobility across interaction landscapes

In all of these five projects, the digital aspects of our surrounding is highlighted as to make us aware of this "interaction grid" laid out across our physical world, and how we potentially could benefit from this in the design of new products and services.

Given an understanding of our environment as a surrounding interaction landscape which we can move through, interact with others in, and get access to information-, and interaction services and computational power at anytime, anywhere we can also start to portrait digital services that live on top of this computerized environment. One such environment will enable us to interact with each other while moving from being co-located to geographically dispersed, across different interaction channels, and indirectly via the physical environment.

My first example, called RoamWare (Wiberg, 2001), enabled people to seamlessly "roam" between physical and virtual meetings. The RoamWare system supported smooth transitions from physical co-located mobile meetings to online group communication by relying on a novel dynamic group addressing technique enabled by mobile devices equipped with short range radio communication capabilities similar to Bluetooth to create dynamic contact/buddy lists depending on the persons present in the physical vicinity during a face-to-face conversation.

While the RoamWare system was build with mobile and dynamic work groups in mind, the FolkMusic system (2004) builds on similar technologies, in this case mobile devices and short-range ad-hoc networks, but is a system that support strangers to find new pieces of music that might be available at the current location or via nearby persons. The system support both identification of new music from other inhabitants in the environment as well as discovery of pieces of music left at a certain location by use of GPS coordinates.

My third example is called MoveInfo (Wiberg, 2008). In this project we conceptually explored the possibility to enable the carrying of information objects from one location in the interaction landscape to another location by use of mobile devices. In more concrete terms, the setting for this project was the control room in a process industry in which we explored how to seamlessly pick information objects from big control rooms displays and carry these "live data" objects out in the plant. Here relied on stationary computers, mobile devices and wireless networking as parts of the interaction landscape to realize this service.

From an interaction landscape point of view I think about this project in terms of enabling integrations across the interaction, and the challenge we tried to address in this undertaking can be thought of in terms of separated "computational islands" that can be bridged by wireless technologies and mobile devices. This project thus illustrated how we can make use of the digital material to overcome informational barriers in the current geography, i.e. in the traditional plant the machines were located in the factory and the information was location in the control room, but through the current digitalization of our environment this division is now no longer necessary. Instead, information objects can now easily be brought to any new location, accessed from anywhere, and redirected to any other device or computational resource across the interaction landscape.

As a forth example I take a recent project called Negotiator (Wiberg & Whittaker, 2005) in which we were interested in exploring how the access to several communication channels, including back-channels and feedback channels as constantly accessible in the modern interaction landscape could support more smooth and lightweight availability management on mobile phones. While the traditional model for availability management on mobile phones relies on a quite static view of availability (assumes a person to be available if the phone is turned on, and if the person is not available the means for dealing with incoming phone calls is to press the "no" button) we wanted to develop this model as to be more close to real life availability including seamless micro-negotiations of availability. In this project we thus relied on mobile phones data communication capabilities for enabling lightweight support for negotiating availability on mobile phones, a service in support for the mobile phone user, the caller, and anyone else present at the caller or the called site of the interaction landscape. This project thus also illustrate that the way we design and implement these kinds of services is of matter not only for the primary user, but also for every inhabitant in the environment. This project also illustrated that availability is often dependent upon the current situation (which often is associated with physical location) and in this view this project is related to current research into location awareness and context awareness systems which is an area with questions all related to the issue of environment interaction, design of ambient information environments and interactive architecture.

Finally, in one of my most recent projects called MidGets (Wiberg, 2007), I was interested in exploring what future media production, sharing, and consumption services could be like given the new interaction landscape. In the MidGets project we were inspired by the current development of P2P networks, file sharing communities, novel services like Joost, Yahoo pipes, and bit-torrent networks which all build upon the idea of easily accessible, shared, remixed and free media. In the MidGets project we were also inspired by the current interest in so called Widgets, i.e. small executable programs that are specified to provide small pieces of information (e.g. the current stock rate, flight information, etc.) and the idea behind Widgets on putting together ones own set of Widgets and also the ability to send any Widget to another person. In the Midgets project we have, based on these points out departure formulated a set of design criteria's for this kind of new media in which MidGets are defined as small, separable, executable and editable media objects that can live across heterogeneous media platforms that form one part of today's interaction landscape. In this project we envision that media objects with these characteristics form a kind of media that easily can be shared, re-mixed, and circulated across a multitude of devices in the interaction landscape. In a nearby future we can assume that media will move freely across different interactive environments, technological platforms, across different media formats and across different digital networks. Media will in this sense appear more as a liquid than solids (Wiberg, 2007) that can move/float freely across the interaction landscape. Traditionally, most media follow a life cycle that can be described as a one-way cycle from media production, to media editing, packaging, distribution and finally media consumption. With the current trend towards integrated, user-driven, interaction landscapes the typical life cycle for new media might be better described in terms of media that is circulated, shared, remixed and re-circulated between the inhabitants of the interaction landscape. Thus, media is accessible everywhere (in the interaction landscape), always on its move somewhere (in the interaction landscape), and most certain, always under constant redesign by the inhabitants of the interaction landscape. In this sense, new media becomes both the content, as well as the communicational glue that bring people together in the interaction landscape.

CASE 2. FOCUSING ON PLACES AND PUBLIC "INPUT GATES"

The second case presented in this chapter illustrates that although people are mobile that does not automatically imply that the technology needs to be mobile as well. On the contrary, the technology can be stationary, and situated in a place, and be used to monitor the mobility of people, i.e. monitoring technologies can be mounted onto the physical landscape to function as an "input gateway" to enable e.g. online

Figure 58. The WorldPortal: A physical online voting portal

voting by just passing through a physical installation of an online voting portal like the WorldPortal project as illustrated in Figure 58 below:

The question at the top of the portal in Figure 58 says: "Do you drink fair trade coffee?" (Swe: "Dricker du rättvisemärkt kaffe?"), and the openings is marked with "Yes" and "No". Inside the portal a computer with a light sensor counts each person that passes through the portal and add that vote to a counter on a web page by sending this information to a web server over the 3G network (see Figure 59, right).

In this project we explored new and novel ways of supporting online voting via a physical voting portal. The main idea here was to make the physical act of voting by walking through a portal accessible all over the world via the WorldPortal web mirror of the physical voting system (see Figure 59).

In more general terms this project was guided by our thinking around the concept of "environment interaction" (Wiberg & Stolterman, 2008) and from a research point of view we were interested in exploring new ways of blending, not only digital information into the physical world, but also an interaction modality, i.e. a mode of

Figure 59. The physical WorldPortal (left) and the online web mirror of the portal (right)

interacting with digital material, as to explore a full blend of a physical activity (in this case voting by walking through a portal) and an equal digital activity.

In this particular project we took a specific point of departure in the current trend of doing daily web surveys by use of simple "question of the day"-forms on the web. Further on, we have been inspired by the current development and widespread use of mobile devices that makes the Internet accessible "anytime, anywhere", current research into tangible UIs (e.g. Hornecker & Buur, 2006) and research into embodied interaction (e.g. Hill, 2002) which have illustrated how computational power can be effectively blended into our physical environment, and how we can rely on our whole body as a means for interaction with the world by use of body movement and gestures. These three aspects (the mobile internet development, development of tangible UIs, and embodied interaction) do all illustrate the need for good models of environment interaction.

In concrete terms, the WorldPortal is a physical portal for in situ voting through body movement. The physical installation of WorldPortal is illustrated in Figure 59, left. As the figure illustrate, the portal have two openings and a big question above it.

In technical terms, the portal consists of a physical portal made of plywood, which has then been covered with a black plastic film. Each opening of the portal is also labeled "Yes" (in Swedish: "Ja") and "No" (in Swedish: Nej"). Inside the portal an embedded computer is installed with a GPRS-connection to the Internet and two lasers connected to it.

Each laser cover an opening in the portal, and when someone passes through the portal the embedded computer counts that person and adds his/hers "vote" to the website for the portal. This is done automatically without any additional interaction needed by the voting person. This was an important requirement for this project as to fully realize the total blend of the physical and virtual voting procedure. Still, since we wanted the two to fully blend, and not just make the digital part

Figure 60. A picture illustrating the embedded computer inside the WorldPortal

disappear we wanted to acknowledge the person passing through the portal that it also was digital in some sense. We therefore added a loudspeaker inside the portal so that when a person passed through the portal the portal said "Thank you!".

The first field trial of the portal was held in collaboration with the Fairtrade organization (www.fairtrade.org) and the question in focus for the citizens of the city was: "Do you drink fair-trade marked coffee?" (in Swedish: "Dricker du rät-tvisemärkt kaffe?").

To make the portal as public as possible we put up the portal in the city center during a Saturday, and in only four hours more than 800 persons actively decided to leave their opinion by just passing through the portal. This was in our view a very positive result since it proved that people were actually ok with leaving their opinion in a public space 1) while being observed by others, and 2) by just passing through any of the two openings in the portal.

We could also during our field trial observe that the portal changed, or at least affected people's activities. While the typical, or most common behavior in this city center on a Saturday is strolling around we could see that the portal gained a lot of attention (probably just due to its physical form) and more importantly, how it also affected a lot of people to consciously move towards the portal and leave their opinion by passing through one of the two openings.

From an *interaction through textures* point of view the WorldPortal illustrate several important aspects of human-environment interaction. First, the portal is a physical manifestation that could on the one hand be thought of as just a traditional voting portal, but on the other hand, it could as well be thought of as a physical gateway to online voting. In this view, the physical world provides access to a digital reality. Further on, while the most common physical-digital integration is realized through public information displays, this portal combines something far more interesting which is the total blend of a physical activity (in this case "voting") with an equal digital activity ("online voting") while sticking to only one mode of interaction, which is the physically move through one of the openings in the portal.

We can thus think about the portal both as a physical gateway to digital inter-action, as well as an example of a total blend of two instances of interaction (i.e. voting on a physical place or voting online on the web) into only one interaction modality seamlessly integrated into our environment.

While the "physical gateway to digital interaction" aspect of the WorldPortal might indicate that the human-environment relation might be about being able to "send" information or commands to the digital world, we can on the other hand see how the "total blend of two instances of interaction into one interaction modality" illustrate that the physical world and the digital world is currently being blended in a bidirectional sense, i.e. digital information is not only presented on public places in the physical world, nor is it about sending information or commands from physical locations to online computers, but instead, this example illustrates how this complete blend of the physical and digital enable new kinds of activities in terms of human-environment interaction. Here, these new activities can be described in terms of encompassed physical-digital interaction with the world.

CASE 3. FOCUSING ON PLACES AND PUBLIC "OUTPUT GATES"

This third case illustrate that digital technologies can also be embedded in physical locations to function as "output gates" in public places.

Here, I will describe the OpenSpace project in which a 42" display was used to provide the visitors at ICEHOTEL with real-time information about the chance to see northern light (see Figure 61). In winter of 2008/2009 the display was mounted outside the entrance to the ICEHOTEL in a big block of ice and connected to an online database via the 3G network.

Project Background and Description

In the north of Sweden, in Jukkasjärvi, you find the ICEHOTEL (www.icehotel. com). This is the first hotel in the world build out of just snow and ice. At the time for this project it was the 16th year for the ICEHOTEL, and what was ones just a onetime tourism attraction is now a complete tourism industry with visitors coming from all over the world to spend a night or two in the ICEHOTEL. The snow and ice structure for the ICEHOTEL is solid throughout the winter and it also has

Figure 61. Public outdoor display embedded in ice in front of the entrance to the ICEHOTEL in Jukkasjärvi, Sweden

An online public outdoor "northern light" display

Figure 62. A view from the inside of the ICEHOTEL

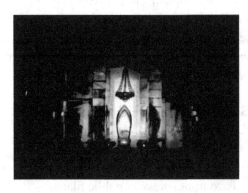

an isolating character that prevents the temperature within the ICEHOTEL to drop below minus 5 degrees Celsius.

While snow and ice is one thing that is characteristic for Jukkasjärvi, so is the northern light. Geographically, Jukkasjärvi is located very close to the polar circle, and since there is not so many disturbing lights from the little town with only 700 inhabitants it is quite easy to spot the northern light if you happen to know when to be outside and look up into the sky.

For several years space researchers have collected data about the solar activity and from that data they have been able to make quite accurate prognoses for when the northern light could be visible to the human eye at a certain location. So far however, these prognoses have 1) only been accessible by space researchers, and 2) and more importantly, at least from an environment interaction point of view, these data have not been accessible at the specific location from where a northern light could be observed, i.e., until now this data has not been blended into the physical environment. In our project we have therefore set out to bring this data about solar activity into the environment, to the specific place where northern light could be spotted, i.e. at a public meeting place just outside the ICEHOTEL.

In our project called ICE - an acronym for Interaction in Cold Environments, we have worked in close collaboration with the IT-company Apara and the computer display manufacturer MultiQ to realize a public display that could present a prognosis to the visitors at the ICEHOTEL about the likeliness to spot a northern light during their stay.

To implement this public display, and to fully make it part of or fully textured into the aesthetic and completely ice-based environment at ICEHOTEL, we needed a display that could run in very cold outdoor temperatures (down to minus 42 degrees Celsius), an ice-based design of the display stand that did not reveal that a networked computer was embedded inside the stand, a Plexiglas protection around the display as to prevent melting ice, from the heat of the display itself, to destroy the display,

Figure 63. A picture of a typical northern light in Jukkasjärvi, Sweden

and a colour schema for the digital interface adjusted to the colors of the ice (see Figure 64, right). From a technical viewpoint the computer display manufacturer MultiQ provided us with a display especially designed for rough environments, and the IT-company Apara provided us with the hardware client, a Teracom 3G computer, and client software for running a Linux-based public display. We then used online data provided by Alaska institute of Space Physics in an application that we programmed to view the chance, in percentage, for the ICEHOTEL visitors to spot the northern light in the region for the moment. Figure 64, left shows a picture of the hardware used as well as the software running on the display.

In relation to the concept of *interaction through textures* some specific issues are important to highlight here.

Figure 64. Two pictures of the northern light public display. Hardware illustration with the display running the northern light application (left), and the final montage of the display inside a solid block of ice (right)

First, the extreme environment, both in terms of extreme weather conditions for digital equipment, as well as the high aesthetical level of the ICEHOTEL were two challenges that we had to overcome as to make the technology blend into this special environment. While the importance of designing according to the context have been repeatedly highlighted in the area of HCI (see e.g. the literature on contextual design including e.g. Beyer & Holtzblatt, 1998) the challenge for us was not to make human-computer interaction to work in a certain environment, but rather to make the whole human-(digitally enhanced) environment interaction cycle work.

Second, we noticed that once it was installed, nobody asked any questions about the technical installation (e.g. questions like "From where comes the data that feeds this representation?" or "how is it connected to the internet?"). We took this as a proof of concept for our installation in terms of a total blend of the digital technology with the physical environment to the extent that the two were no longer separable.

Finally, and probably most importantly, the display was not understood in terms according to any traditional human-computer interaction model in which the focus is on the relation and/or interaction between the human and the computer. Instead, the display only provided an attention cue to something else, something bigger, outside the computer, that is, the display was only a guide for the visitor for to redirect his/her focus away from the computer screen to the open sky and look for the northern light. In this way, this northern light public display enabled the hotel visitor to be more aware of the northern light, and it also provided the hotel visitor with information not available before.

In this ongoing project we have until now identified that the role of this public display can be understood as 1) a visual attentional cue that informs and acknowledge the hotel visitors about the northern light, 2) a directional cue in that the display can redirect the hotel visitors attention towards the open sky, and 3) an augmentation of the physical world in that new information is provided in the physical environment itself. In all these cases, the northern light public display has changed the human-environment relation in this particular setting.

CASE 4. TOTALLY INTERACTIVE ENVIRONMENTS

At the end of this spectrum of digitalized environments I will in this forth case present our recent work on the creation of an interactive large-scale public environment.

For this particular project we took a point of departure in some current attempts to digitalize public places through the adding of ambient information cues, and another point of departure in some spectacular public places specifically designed to support social interaction in a public space.

The first place working as a source of inspiration for this project was the Stock-holm Airport – Arlanda in Sweden. In the passage between terminal 3 and 4 the hallway windows has been covered with plastics in different colors as to change the visual appearance of the hallway from a straight walkway to a more mystique "room". The colored plastics still allow for some light from the outside to go into the hallway, but the visibility of the outdoor environment is somewhat blurred (see Figure 65). Further on, a sound designer were hired to design a soundscape for this hallway based on natural sounds like the wind blowing, bird sounds, etc as to further scaffold another experience of this hallway.

In a sense, this example illustrates a low-tech interactive architecture in that it plays with both some basic electronics (in this case a sound system) and the archi-tecture of the hallway. However, the level of technical complexity is not the deter-mine factor. Instead, it is how these two elements of electronics and architecture come together to form a new space.

In this case, the goal was to change the appearance, and thus the experience of the hallway. To create a new atmosphere for this particular hallway – from being a passage that connects two terminals ultimately design to just transport people from point A to point B, the experience of this hallway is now more about the immersion in a space filled with colors and sounds. And, with quite simple means that specific goal was reached.

From a methodological viewpoint this example has important implications for the design of interactive architecture. If the idea is clear and good, then it might not be about huge technical challenges to overcome to create new spaces, or to change to appearance and experience of existing physical spaces. If we were asked to label this

Figure 65. Hallway with colored walls and with ambient sounds of nature coming from hidden loudspeakers

approach then would suggest Experience-centered Design as one candidate name for it. The basic reason for this is that a point of departure for the new design was taking in what kind of experience people should have from walking through this hallway. With a good understanding of that, the rest was just a matter of technical solutions.

There are other spaces that have been explicitly designed to address a certain experience of a place. One such example is the ICEHOTEL Icebars as the one shown in Figure 66, located in Stockholm, Sweden.

In these icebars the fundamental architectural elements are made of quite traditional materials with a big emphasis put on the use of raw ice from the Torne River located in the far north of Sweden as to also make the connection to the icehotel located in that geographical area.

In general, it is interesting to look at different purposeful designs of environments (being it cafés, theaters, office spaces, banks or in this case bars) for the purpose of understanding the use of different physical spaces, and to specifically study the relation between the architecture and the use of the space.

In our ongoing project focused on interaction design in extreme environments we have a long-term collaboration with the company ICEHOTEL located in the very north part of Sweden. As part of this project we explored how these icebars could be furthered developed through the adding of digital material to this public space as to turn it into an interactive architecture installation for the purpose of making the connection with the ICEHOTEL as located in the far north of Sweden even more clear, despite the fact that these icebars are located geographically far away from this exotic site with icebars in Stockholm, Sweden, Copenhagen, Denmark, Tokyo, Japan, Olso, Norway and London, UK.

Figure 66. Interior picture from the Icebar in Stockholm, Sweden

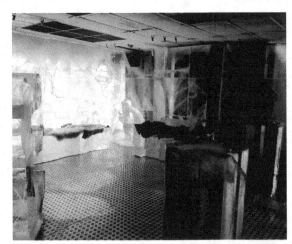

As for a short background, ICEHOTEL is situated in the village Jukkasjärvi, 200 kilometres north of the Arctic Circle in Sweden and 17 kilometers from Kiruna, the nearest town. The original company "Jukkas" (present day ICEHOTEL) has been a tourist operator in the northern region of Sweden since the 1970s. For many years the company focus was on the summer season and the magnificent outdoor experiences including hiking, fishing, and river tours. However, during the dark winter the river was frozen and the people of the small village of Jukkasjärvi went into hibernation. By the end of the 1980s it was decided to turn things around. Instead of viewing the dark and cold winter as a disadvantage, the unique elements of the arctic were to be regarded an asset. Inspired by the work of visiting Japanese ice artists, in 1990 the French artist Jannot Derit was invited to have the opening of his exhibition in a specially built igloo on the frozen Torne River. This first version of the ICEHOTEL measured 60 square metre. The building was named "Arctic Hall" and it attracted many curious visitors to the area. Since then the company have grown and today it has a turnover above 200 milj SEK per year and it attracts many tourist from allover the world to come and experience the wilderness and the exotic

Although ICEHOTEL has many local attractions to offer including attractions like the uniqueness of sleeping in a hotel made of just snow and ice filled with art and interior decorations also made of this simple but still elegant material, combined with hiking tours, hunting activities, ice fishing, snow mobile rentals, the Saab ice driving experience, and of course, the natural northern light to offer visitors from all over the world they also do several things to reach out and address an international audience. Today, ICEHOTEL is a player at an international arena through their collaboration with Absolut (http://www.absolut.com/) around the Absolut ICEBAR concept with ice bars nowadays located in Stockholm, London, Tokyo and Copenhagen and through bigger media events made together with international brands including e.g. Hugo Boss, Saab, Yves saint Lauren, Montblanc, etc.

Through the realization of the Absolut ICEBAR concept ICEHOTEL discovered the possibility of extending the spirit of ICEHOTEL in Jukkasjärvi to other locations as well, i.e. from a shorter extension down to Stockholm in Sweden, to Tokyo as a more distant location.

Right now ICEHOTEL is taking its next step to strengthen its position as a player on an international arena through a project with an explicit focus on interactive architecture. Together with Umeå University and Philips as a technology partner ICEHOTEL is exploring how the design materials of ice and digital material could be composed, or completely blended to create a unique interactive and entertaining environment that could communicate the spirit of ICEHOTEL across the globe to several new locations. This whole development project called ICEHOTEL X has as its goal to be a forerunner in interactive architecture through the unique combination of two materials that normally does not go well together, i.e. digital technology and water, in any form or state.

The design concept of ICEHOTEL X was however not a purely technologically driven project, and it is not intended to work as a technology showroom for the technology partner Philips. Instead, the guiding idea was that it should be an interactive environment totally designed inline with the vision of ubiquitous computing as stated by Mark Weiser:

"For ubiquitous computing one of the ultimate goals is to design technology so pervasive that it disappears into the surrounding [...] The most profound technologies are those that disappear. They weave themselves into the fabric of everyday life until they are indistinguishable from it." (Weiser, 1991, p. 66)

In order to reach this goal we realized quite early on in the project that we needed to address this challenge from two different perspectives. One of which we needed to focus on the environment as a whole and how it needed to be configured to support some unique experiences for its visitors, i.e. in the words of Oosterhuist (2007) how the relationships between the components of this environment (including the ice walls, art pieces, food, drinks, activities, etc) should be defined and linked together to then "build relations between people and the built components in the second place" Oosterhuist (2007), i.e. to create an unique experience of the spirit of ICEHOTEL. Thus, we needed to address this design challenge from multiple viewpoints including professional perspectives from architects, artists, chiefs and food designers, interaction designers, ice designers, computer engineers etc.

From the second perspective we needed to address several specific requirement related to the location and character of the environment. Since the vision was to create an ice-based environment similar to the Absolut ICEBAR we needed to have in mind the cold climate in the environment (minus 5 degrees celcius) and how to adjust the technology installations according to this requirement. Further on, we needed to plan for the activities in this environment given a floor space of about 100 square meters and a low ceiling (2,40 meters from floor to inner ceiling, and then another 60 centimeters for the cooling systems, ventilation etc.). Further on, the floor needed to be designed to carry the weight of the ice walls and for the trucks that bring the ice inside the environment each time the place is changing its theme (typically every 6-9 month). This idea of frequently updating the environment with a new interior also calls for another technical requirement, i.e. to design a flexible installation, or general platform that easily can be re-configured every 6-9 month to support new interactive themes, activities, events and experiences.

In general we envisioned an interactive environment rather than a reactive/responsive environment, i.e. the visitors should be able to interact with the walls, floors, things and the ceiling and not just passively watch it like an animated installation. In other words, we wanted to support the visitors' active exploration of, and interaction with the ICEHOTEL X environment.

From a technological viewpoint we opted for a design goal of a general flexible platform rather than a specific installation (compare the "general computer" vs. "information appliance" discussion a couple of years ago, e.g. Bergman, 2000). And in this vision we aimed for something like a "WIMP-standard" for an interactive physical, and social environment.

Through simple sketches as illustrated below we worked through the whole range of scenarios from only supporting one single user´s interaction with only one digital interactive wall (see the upper left sketch in Figure 67), via scenarios for "single-user, multiple walls"," single user, multiple walls + interactive floor", "single user, multiple walls + interactive floor + interactive ceiling", "multiple users, multiple walls + interactive floor + interactive ceiling", "multiple users, multiple walls + interactive floor + interactive ceiling + interaction via the environment with distributed friends", and finally "multiple users, multiple walls + interactive floor + interactive ceiling + interaction via the environment with distributed friends all equipped with tagged or digital objects + the environment equipped with tagged objects as well".

In relation to this schematic and systematic exploration we also had a graphical vision of the space as a source of inspiration (see Figure 68).

This early version of the project proposed creating an immersive representation of the north (see Figure 68).

The development of the simplest scenario was quite straight forward whereas the last scenario were inspired by the extended perspective on mobility proposed by

Figure 67. Sketches on the scenarios explored in design workshop No 3

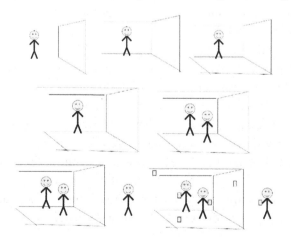

Figure 68. An early graphic sketch of Icehotel X as a fully digitalizaed and interactive space

(Kakihara & Sorensen, 2002) in which mobility is discussed in terms of the mobility of not only people, but also of symbols or signs (i.e. communication) and objects. Similarly, we wanted to explore not only a scenario with one person interacting with a single interactive object or wall, but explore the whole range of scenarios from that rather simple scenario to a "fully interactive scenario" in which several persons and objects interact with each other and with and via a fully interactive environment. This, to outline a sketch of the whole design space for the project at hand.

To bring some extra dimensions into this already complex picture we added the dimension of possible modes or degrees of interaction with the environment ranging from a *passive* environment that demands no activity from the visitor, but instead broadcasts some animations or information to the people in the environment, via design of *ambient* information displays which demands some attention from the visitor to acknowledge subtle changes in the environment, to more *interactive* installations that demand some action taken of a visitor to show some information or respond in any other way.

Here, we arranged this session as a typical brain storming exercise in which we started with an exercise in divergent thinking in which any idea that came up should be stated explicitly without any critique from any other design team member, followed by a session directed towards more convergent thinking in which we tried to sort out the best ideas and decide which ideas to move forward with in the design process.

While the on-site design workshops were quite easy to arrange and to carry out it was much harder to find good ways of dealing with the in-between workshop activities for a fruitful, creative, and effective design process.

In order to combine different design perspectives and to continue the convergent process towards a concrete design small two party meetings were arranged over phone, via email, and through the exchange of sketches, drawings and Powerpoint illustrations. Via these meetings the profession could be mixed but with a much more specific agenda than in the larger design workshops, e.g. a meeting between the lightening designer and the interaction designer were arranged to discuss if a wall display could be realized with a grid of OLED lights and what kind of resolution one such display could deliver. Another meeting were arranged between the artist and the market manager to discuss activities to be held in the environment. Through these multiple design meetings over a distance several new links were made within the design team, which created a network of personal relations within the design team.

During 2008 and 2009 we were collaborators on this multi-professional design team charged with creating "Icehotel X", a full-scale public interactive environment placed in the city center of Copenhagen. The design challenge of "Icehotel X" was intended to communicate "the spirit of Icehotel" in an urban location 2000 kilometers south of its actual location.

Although raw ice was transported from the Arctic Circle to the center of Copenhagen, and then placed in a refrigerated indoor environment approximately 100 m^2 (1076 ft^2), Icehotel X still did not effectively communicate the experience of encountering the far north. Thus, we chose to texture the environment by integrating digital technologies into the composition. We believed the transparent qualities of ice and the animated luminosity possible via large displays would better evoked the experience of the Icehotel.

Concerned with the relation between ice and computational power we *integrated* these materials into a single composition. We rejected high-resolution displays and high-speed networking in favor of a large low-resolution LED display whose luminous properties better aligned with the qualities of the ice. Although cinematic representations of the far north, streaming videos, or broadcasting literal real-time interaction between the spaces might provide an experience of the Icehotel, we felt these options might detract from visitors' engagement in their actual location, or risk drawing attention to the computational power and thus turn Icehotel X into a sort of technological showroom.

Two walls covered with LED-pixels (see Figure 69, left) formed an 8 m long and 2.4 m high interactive wall inside of Icehotel X. These "pixel walls" contained bulbs mounted in a grid and spaced 5 cm apart. The resulting low-resolution display (160 x 48 pixels) was designed specifically to support abstract images and animations (see Figure 69, middle and right). We smoothed the raw pixels by covering them with 4mm opaque plastic film. The resulting installation appeared as a continuous wall of light rather than an isolated piece of equipment (see Figure 70).

With two pixel walls and an ice-based interior in place we began aligning the materials into a desired texture. An iterative design process, carried out by engineers,

Figure 69. Low-resolution pixel walls (left) depicts abstract representations of the northern lights (center) and open fire (right)

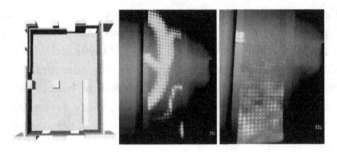

Figure 70. Icehotel X pixel wall: covered in opaque plastic (left); viewed through a wall of ice (right)

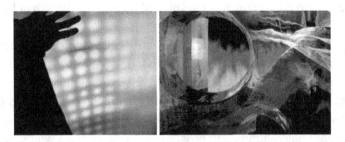

light designers, and film editors produced a final composition of abstract animation and ice (see Figure 70).

The final composition communicated the spirit of Icehotel by blended ice and computational power. Bringing the raw ice to life meant crafting an environment that evoked wilderness in the north. We included common tropes like open fires, northern lights, blizzards, and glowing stars (see Figure 71). Still, we just wanted the basic properties of these elements to be present in this unique interactive environment we were envisioning.

Figure 71. Animation frames from the Icehotel X installation

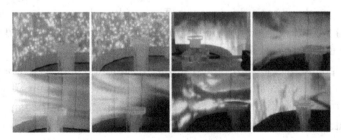

Icehotel X opened to the public in April 2009. Though digital technologies were omnipresent in the environment, visitors awarded them no particular attentions. No one even looked directly at the pixel wall (see Figure 72). Unlike public installations of televisions of large high-definition screens, these displays helped visitors experienced the room. Rather attention on the other persons co-present in this space. From an interactive architecture point of view this was a huge success, since ultimate, any architecture should remain in the background of our attention, while still working as a scaffold for the social interaction in that particular place. This result were also in line with the theoretical point of departure taken from the work by Weiser (1991) in which we aimed for the texturing of digital technologies into this environment to the extent that it would "disappear" and weave itself into the fabric of everyday life until they it is indistinguishable from it (Weiser, 1991, p. 66).

CASE 5. EVERYDAY CITY TEXTURES: TIMES SQUARE, NEW YORK

Moving from the first case focused on small mobile devices via indoor architecture it is now time for the fifth case to move along this axis of scale and address texture as being an important aspect of the modern cityscape.

As discussed in this book texture serve us in our everyday lives as a navigational aid. However, a danger with the modern cityscape as pointed out by Greenfield (2006) is that we have not deliberately considered this aspect which has now lead us into a situation where we allow the texture of a city to start repeating itself (e.g. through store chains putting of their signs along ever block around a city until almost nothing differentiate one city block from the next one. According to Greenfield (2006) this leads humans into a so called "withdrawal behavior" typically manifested by people plugging in their iPods and just stop carrying about their surroundings.

An alternative approach this trend is to work actively with the textures in the city. Architects can partly do this. When they design a new building they can give it an

Figure 72. Opening day at ICEHOTEL X

interesting form and play with the textures of the building to create an interesting visual appearance of the building. But foremost, and if we look around any modern city it seems to be the case that the texturing of the cityscape is mostly done by the people inhabiting the city, ranging from people renting the buildings, and living and working in those buildings to the people strolling the streets.

The picture as shown in Figure 73 provides a good example of how people have worked with the texture of this cityscape beyond the imagination of the architects that once drew the buildings. In this book I think about these activities in terms of landscaping, i.e. an act of modifying an area of land. This particular picture is from the famous Times Square in New York City. This particular place has become work famous just because of this enormous work put into the texturing of messages (mostly advertisements) around this pretty large intersection of two major roads on Manhattan (i.e. at the intersection of Broadway and the 7th avenue).

An interesting dimension of this picture, from the perspective of ubiquitous computing, is that the digital dimensions of this cityscape is not coming through. Instead, in this particular picture it needs to be highlighted on a big sign telling that there is also free wifi available at this particular location.

Going back to the initial discussion in this book, this is an example of digital technology not working in concert with the physical space. Instead, the physical and the digital are competing for the same space creating a tension between the digital and the physical. This is also a good example of the difference between ubiquitous computing and interactive textures. Going back to the vision by Mark Weiser (1991) the ultimate goal of ubiquitous computing was to blend technology into the background of our attention until it disappears. That has in fact been realized here, to the very extent that there was a need to put up a sign telling about this invisible

Figure 73. A picture showing signage as city texture at Times Square, New York City

wireless networking infrastructure. Interactive textures on the other hand work with digital and physical materials in concert, creating spaces where these two materials form interesting unifications that together enrich a space.

In the next figure we can see how an attempt has been made to also introduce a digital element (the horizontal pixel display) to work in concert with the painted signage on this particular building (see Figure 74).

Ultimately, it is possible to work deliberately with the textures of the city, to create more interesting places, inform people about the buildings, the location and activities going on and also to engage us as humans as active contributors to the city life.

There are many approaches to the texturation of the cityscape as a landscaping activity. The most obvious approach is of course the one as shown in Figure 74. There is however other approaches taken as to create a more unique texture with the potential of standing out as a unique landmark in the city. One such example is shown in Figure 75 in which the added covers follow the same thematic format thus creating a unified wholeness across several placards placed next to each other.

This focus on coherence make the total impression less cluttered compared to the picture in Figure 74.

Figure 74. Digital and non-digital elements working in composition to form the texture of this building façade

Figure 75. Several placate following the same theme and arranged within close proximity of each other forms a texture that communicates coherence

There are also other examples of landscaping of the city textures, and some of the most interesting ones are not even on the visual textures, but more related to the cultural textures of the cityscape. One such example that I have is from my study visit to New York where I was walking from New York University across Washington Square Park. As I was walking across the park I suddenly passed by a man sitting in the very middle of the park playing his piano (see Figure 76). Sitting in the park he was playing the theme song for the "Oceans 11" Hollywood movie. Although it was more like a performance played out in this particular park that particular day it still added to the whole experience of the park, i.e. it added to the texture of the park. In other terms, the adding of the piano, and a skilled person playing the piano did not just add the piano as another material of the park. Instead, and far

Figure 76. A man sitting in Washington Square Park playing his piano as an important aspect of the materiality and the city texture of this particular place

more important, it redefined the context and the materiality of the park as a place for social activities as well.

Moving from examples of cultural textures in the modern city landscape we should also all the current efforts made to blend digital technologies, especially electronic displays into the modern cityscape. In Figure 77 one such example is shown in which a large scale public display has been put up close to Madison Square Garden. This particular display is put up by the DB Climate Change Advisors in collaboration with www.know-the-number.com/ to make us aware of the current amount (in tons) of greenhouse gases in our atmosphere. As such, it works as a physical installation of something that is hard to "see" if just looking around, at the same time as it illustrate itself as a very dynamic installation in constant connection with the sensors that measure the current pollution of our atmosphere.

To make this kind of installation possible a number of technologies needs to be combined in order to have it running on a day-to-day basis, including processing of sensor data capable of reading greenhouse pollution of our atmosphere, network technologies to transfer the processed data to this particular location, and a large weather resistant display to represent the data and let the inhabitants of the city become aware of the current figures related to this particular issue.

Figure 77. A new city landmark in the form of a physical manifestation of a dynamic aspect of our atmosphere possible to present to the city inhabitants through the unification of processing of sensor data, network technologies and large public displays

Figure 78. Digital display covering part of a building in New York City

These kinds of digital installations are not only visible as new dynamic landmarks in the cityscape. Instead, and as illustrated in Figure 78 these displays now comes in almost any form and are placed on all sorts of buildings.

Right now there is a big trend going in this direction. A problematic aspect of it though is that it is competing with the underlying architecture of these buildings. However, working in parallel with this development we can now see an even more interesting development, which is less about covering the world with digital technologies. Further on, it is not about "ubiquitous computing" in the sense of making the technology disappear. Instead, there are many examples now in the modern cityscape of what I like to think of as "texturation approaches" to digital technologies for the modern cityscape. One such example is shown in Figure 79.

Here, a clear movement in thinking is obvious. Instead of trying to hide the technology or going for covering the physical buildings with a "digital skin" the aim here has been to make these two materials come together and work in concert with each other. As seen in Figure 79 the façade and the street becomes integrated with each other via this dynamic LED screen enabling the building to attach to and play with the street and vise versa. Simultaneously the display give life to this intersection at the same time as the street and the building scaffold the otherwise kind of simple low-res display. From the perspective of this book, this is a good example of different materials and different architectural elements working together in concert to form a new dynamic texture in the modern cityscape.

As we move away from competing materials towards unification into coherent textures we open up a new fascinating design space in-between the area of traditional architecture and interaction design. When moving away from façade coverage towards digital technologies being part of the facades we can start to experiment

Figure 79. Integrated LED displays as part of the architecture and street design across the street from Madison Square Garden in New York City

with and play around with the very appearance of a building, and play around with different ways of letting people experience and engage themselves with the built environments surrounding them.

Probably this is just the beginning of a new area of development but already today there are a few examples out there which have started to play around with this new design space. One further example is shown in Figure 80. In this photo, also from the Times Square in New York City we can see a wall size display mounted on the outside of a skyscraper. The most interesting aspect of this display is however not the size, even though that aspect is pretty impressive by itself. Far more interesting is the interplay going on between the architecture and the digital technology. Here, the display has not been installed to simply cover the building facade. Instead, there is openings in the display for the windows of the building not only enabling the people inside of the building to have a nice view of the Times Square, but also, it let the architecture and the digital technology co-exist thus creating an interesting texture possible to play around with to show information, change the color and appearance of the building, etc.

Figure 80. Interactive texture aligned with the architecture of this particular building on Times Square, New York City

With these examples in place in different public spaces it is now likely to imagine that these particular examples will also inspire further development in this direction. In a sense, it is the start of an interesting process that explores the interplay and intersection between traditional architecture and interaction design.

As illustrated in Figure 80 the interactive texture works in concert with the architecture of the building. But also, if zooming out from this picture we can see how this interactive element is also working in concert with other added textures in close vicinity of this particular installation (see Figure 81)

As interactive textures start to find their way into areas of art, architecture and the cultural life in the city a new design space is opening up as an interesting canvas to be further explored by any established design profession (ranging from artists, interaction designers, architects, etc.) and this development will probably also give rise to new design professions that will situate themselves at the very intersection of the physical, the digital and the social, i.e. with a focus on the crafting out of new interaction practices.

FIVE DIFFERENT CASES: SOME CONCLUDING REMARKS

In this chapter I have presented five different cases, which taken together have illustrated the texturing of information and interaction technologies into our physical and social world in several different ways.

Figure 81. Digital texture working in concert with the architecture of the building and in concert with other kinds of signage used in this particular place

I am not claiming the work as reported in this chapter to serve as a complete description of the different types of projects that can be done in the area of information technology texturation. Instead, these five cases are intended to serve as points of departure and as sources of inspiration for thinking about the evolving interaction landscape and the opportunities for blending computational power into our everyday activities, social rooms, and physical spaces. As such, the first four cases can be thought of as "demos" of the interaction landscape in the making and how we might align different computational materials to our physical and social world. Further on, the fifth case demonstrate the rise of new everyday city textures composed of physical as well as digital materials. An opportunity forming a design space yet to be fully explored.

In the next chapter I present a complementary theoretical portfolio intended to stimulate our thinking around these new textures and material compositions. With a point of departure taken in some basic concepts the next chapter is intended to complement the empirical projects presented here with some theoretical notions capable of labeling, describing and analyzing these kinds of real world installations.

REFERENCES

Beyer, H., & Holtzblatt, K. (1998). *Contextual Design*. San Francisco: Morgan Kaufmann Publishers.

Greenfield, A. (2006). *Everyware – The dawning age of ubiquitous computing*. Berkeley, CA: New Riders.

Hornecker, E., & Buur, J. (2006). Getting a grip on tangible interaction: a framework on physical space and social interaction. In *Proceedings of the SIGCHI conference on Human Factors in computing systems (CHI '06)*. New York: ACM Press.

Kakihara, M., & Sorensen, C. (2002) Mobility: An extended perspective. In *Proceedings of the 35th Annual Hawaii International Conference on System Sciences*, 1756-1766.

Oosterhuist, K. (2007). *iA #1 Interactive Architecture*. Rotterdam: Episode Publishers.

Weiser, M. (1991). The computer of the 21st century. *Scientific American, 265*(3), 66–75. doi:10.1038/scientificamerican0991-94

Wiberg, M. (2001). RoamWare: An Integrated Architecture for Seamless Interaction In between Mobile Meetings. In *Proceedings of GROUP 2001, ACM 2001 International Conference on Supporting Group Work*, September 30-October 3.

Wiberg, M. (2007). Midgets: Exploring the Design Space for Truly Liquid Media. In *Proceedings CMID '07, 1st international conference on cross-media interaction design* - 22-25 March, Hemavan, Sweden.

Wiberg, M. (2008). Re-Space-ing Place: Towards Mobile Support for Near Diagnostics . In Hislop, D. (Ed.), *Mobility and Technology in the Workplace*. Routledge.

Wiberg, M., & Stolterman, E. (2008). Environment interaction: Character, Challenges & Implications for Design. In *Proceedings of the SigMobile and ACM conference "MUM 2008 the 7th international conference on Mobile and Ubiquitous Multimedia."* ACM Press.

Chapter 8
Interaction through Textures

In this chapter I present a complementary portfolio to the range of real world projects as described in chapter 7. In doing so, my intention is to also stimulate our intellectual thinking around these new textures. With a point of departure taken in concepts this chapter is intended to complement the empirical projects presented in this book with some theoretical notions capable of labeling, describing and analyzing these kinds of real world installations. Further on, these concept are not only formulated to describe these new textures, as already done in the previous chapters, but to also provide us with some conceptual tools for thinking about interaction with and through these new textures at hand.

In particular I will go back and reflect upon the notion of "interaction through textures" from a number of alternative perspectives and in relation to the topics of e.g. so called P3-systems, the issue of interacting vs. being in these new environments, public interaction rituals, conventions for interaction with and through interactive textures, and the texturing of interaction knowledge in the world.

DOI: 10.4018/978-1-61520-653-7.ch008

P3-SYSTEMS (PEOPLE-TO-PEOPLE TO GEOGRAPHICAL PLACES)

In the emerging interaction landscape people nowadays make use of a multitude of digital services, devices and channels to communicate, collaborate and interact with each other. This is typically described as CMC – Computer Mediated Communication, CSCW – Computer Supported Cooperative Work, or simply digital technologies for online social networking.

In a recent framework aimed at framing so called P3-systems Jones et. al (2004) address this behavior as people-to-people interaction. However, people do not only interact face-to-face, or via online channels. People also make use of the physical environment in their communication with others. People make use of both symbolic resources in the environment (including papers, whiteboards, notice boards, etc) as well as the physical character of a specific place (e.g. a lecture room, or a stage) as a scaffold for human communication.

Besides the use of these symbols and physical resources available in the environment people are also starting to adopt digital services that make use of our physical surrounding. Such services are typically labeled e.g. context-aware systems and location-aware applications. Following this line of development we can also see an increase in applications that reply on e.g. RFID-tags, network triangulation techniques, GPS and other location based positioning techniques. We can for sure say that geographical places are becoming an important aspect to consider, and in line with the P3-framwork this development is addressed through the notion of People-to-People-to-geographical Places, i.e. P3.

Still, this is mostly focused around the individual and how he or she makes use of various mobile devices and systems to communicate and interact with others with geographically situated data as an important input factor. Further on, the notions of context-aware applications and devices as well as the notion of location-aware systems is mostly about a mobile device and how it should be able to relate to resources in the physical environment (including position, nearby objects, access to computational resources, etc).

It is a promising start and a valuable perspective. However, to enrich our understanding of interactive architecture and new interactive textures we also need to twist this framework around and take an explicit point of departure in the physical environment and ask the critical questions about how we will engage ourselves in interaction with and through these new textures and environments? How we will be able to discover, access and make meaningful use of these new textures? And what vocabulary we need to develop in order to talk specifically about interactive textures and interactive architecture?

In the following sections a first attempt is made to carve out a perspective and approach for developing one such register for the area of interactive architecture.

DISCOVERING THE INTERACTIVE TEXTURE

While I have in this book addressed the different ways in which we might be able to "read" and "write" these new textures, we still have not come down to the ultimate question of how to discover them as embedded in the materials of our physical surrounding.

As these new materials will start to find their way out in the physical environment it will probably be a phase in which these interactive textures will be quite easy to discover for two different reasons. First, it is likely that the digital technology will not be fully mature and will be rather clumsy (or in other terms not fully texturized in relation to other materials) meaning that for technical reasons such new textures will be rather easy to recognize. These installations will also be quite rare meaning that we will probably know where these installations are made. At the other hand of the spectrum we find the fully matured textures. These textures are also easy to recognize since they are elegantly aligned with the purpose they fulfill, with the other materials from which they are realized, and with appropriate interaction modalities associated with them. However, in the development from early clumsy prototypes to the future of interactive textures we will probably struggle to discover interactive textures, and if we do, we might run into various troubles related to understanding how to access, operate and make meaningful use out of them.

As we're approaching a future with well functioning interactive textures broadly embedded in our physical world the classical notion of being "down to earth" will probably change in its fundamental meaning. Traditionally, this notion was about connecting to the pure nature, and the raw materials, and to experience the wilderness of e.g. free flowing water, growing threes, and beautiful flowers. However, and as pinpointed in chapter 3 the very concept of "nature" is changing as we move into the world of the artificial. More and more, the "nature" around us is man-made, i.e. artificial. In this new world, the expression down to "earth" might as well be a synonym for "down to the man-made," i.e. down to the artificial, and as such, also down the things that are designed.

An important implication from this line of reasoning is that it highlight nature as designed, and it highlight a perspective in which we not only acknowledge design, but also develops our sensitivity for the designed world, including how new textures are purposely integrated in our physical world.

INTERACTING VS. BEING (USER VS. INHABITANT)

As already mentioned and addressed in chapter 1 a shift that I see as both useful and unavoidable is the move away from the notion of the "user" when it comes to interactive systems in general, and interactive textures in particular.

Instead there must be a focus on the human, on people, or maybe inhabitants. This is a change that is not only a consequence of focusing on the environment instead of artifacts, it is also an intentional move where the human experience as a whole becomes the core of any design. An individual person is living his or her life moving in and out of environments, some are work related, some family related, some offers other activities, and many of them are or will be blended environments. This means that the designer is not only faced with the challenge of designing one specific environment, there is on top of that the challenge of making that design fit with other environments the individual will inhabit and frequently move between.

In these new interactive environments it might be more appropriate to leave the notion of user behind as people will constantly occupy these settings and it will be virtually impossible to distinguish sessions of "usage" from non-usage, and even to separate many of these sessions.

Further on, from a human-centered point of view, people might not necessarily experience that they "use" their environment. We all know that we seldom talk about our homes as something we "use". Instead we live in our homes. We live, move, stay, and travel in cities and environments, we don't use them, except in extraordinary cases. An understanding of these new environments will probably have to shift the focus from use to being or living. As a result of this, I believe that the recent interest in experience in HCI research is highly appropriate when it comes to understanding this shift. We can see promising attempts in this direction (e.g. Croon Fors, 2006; Rogers, 2006).

In this movement from the notion of a user towards notions of just people, humans or inhabitants we will also acknowledge that more and more, our interactions with and through digital textures will happen in public places.

PUBLIC INTERACTION RITUALS

Interaction in public places is becoming part of our everyday lives. Already today we see people using their mobile phones and laptops in public places, we see people using automatic door openers without even thinking about their very existence, and electronic door cards are to many of us just everyday objects and sort of old news. People are really getting used to operate digital devices, services and systems in public places.

However, there are also examples of technology use in public spaces that has been cumbersome for their users as well as for other co-present individuals. One such example is the introduction of the wireless headset for mobile phones. In many cases, unthoughtful adoption of this rather simple technology led to some strange situations. People could no longer judge whether or not someone was talking to someone else over the phone, or if they were just talking to themselves. The technology was small, wireless, and thus quite hard to see, so it was more or less up to the user of this piece of electronics to act out the meaning of speaking loud by him- or herself in a public place and to make that act appear as meaningful to any potential observer of one such act.

As we embed digital technologies in our physical world, to the level of real texturization of information technology, we will be facing additional challenges to overcome in relation to interaction in public places. Although a single individual might be able to find, understand, and operate an interface situated in an architectural structure it must also appear as meaningful to any other co-present individual. The public space is also per definition a social space. As such, we must design these environments with a focus not only on the individual, but also on the social level of human co-existence.

If we take a point of departure in the work by Goffman (1959) on the representation of self in our everyday lives we can think about these new spaces in terms of "stages" on which we are actors in front of an audience, i.e. we're (inter-) acting in front of other co-present persons.

Through the development and adoption of new technologies new "stages" will be developed on which we're expected to perform in public. Such stages will consist of both physical and virtual elements as the following example tries to illustrate.

If just talking the current digitalization of bus tickets as a simple example of a new interaction stage we can now see how the physical setting of bus riding meets a new practice in public interaction behavior. Traditionally, you got onto the bus, paid for a ticket and took your seat. Now, some bus companies are starting with e-tickets in which you, while waiting for the bus, sends an SMS to a certain service to get a virtual bus ticket, which you're then supposed to show to the bus driver as you're about to enter the bus. In theory this sounds like a rather straightforward and simple maneuver. However, in practice this simple use case unfolds as follows:

First, to make use of this service people need to know about it in the first place, i.e. they need to know about the very existence of the SMS-service and that they are supposed to use it *before* the bus arrives at the bus stop. This can be rather tricky in case there is no sign telling about this online mobile service. This, due to the fact that it is a pure digital service with no other physical manifestation of it in the physical world (compare with ATM machine which is also typically mounted on a wall in the physical world, though a lot of its services are also digital and networked).

The other alternative is to know about it from experience or being informed about it from other co-present persons. As for the SMS-technology there is no such thing as service discovery (as in Bluetooth) nor any location-based notifications of available SMS-services.

Second, having gained knowledge about the existence of the SMS-service the persons need to have the proper technology available and configured to access and use the service (in this case a mobile phone and a subscription that allows for SMS purchases of services from the phone).

Third, and with the technical resources available, the person needs to know how to access and use the service (i.e. in this case to know which code to send to a certain number to buy an accurate e-ticket).

Forth and finally, having used the service for the purchase of the ticket, the person needs to know that he or she is supposed to ensure the bridging, or make the linkage, between the virtual world and the physical world by showing the bus driver the e-ticket on the screen of the mobile phone.

As illustrated in this rather simple case there are new stages evolving which spans across the world of the digital and the world of the physical. On these stages people are supposed to act in public and appear as rational in the activities they engage themselves in. We can also easily image how this simple example of the SMS service could be developed to include a wider interaction landscape that modern bus riders should be familiar with, including anything from transportation related services that could e.g. inform the bus rider about delays in the schedule, and traffic jams along the route, to value-adding services including e.g. virtual points systems for sustainable traveling choices, etc.

As inhabitants of these interaction landscapes highly situated in public contexts we need to develop our knowledge on how to navigate and tap into these systems of services and flows of information situated everywhere around our everyday activities.

In my previous work (e.g. Wiberg, 2006) I looked into the notion of graceful interaction in intelligent environments. In this work I pinpointed the need to understand this dimension of interaction in public places, especially when it comes to "invisible" or highly integrated digital services in our physical environment. In this work I pinpointed the need for a third person perspective on interaction (as further described in chapter 1) and the need for conventions in order to be able to discover and "read" interfaces and interaction modalities that have been highly embedded in our world.

This challenge will also grow when we move from simple interactions with the built environment towards interaction through these new textures available. As we engage ourselves in such activities we do not only engage ourselves and other co-present persons in the close vicinity. More radically, this will also include and engage remote participants and they will be part of the interactive textures *per se* as they manifest aspects of their dynamic character in our physical world.

Adding to this complexity we will find that the interactive textures will not only form themselves in relation to the materials from which they are made, and to the individuals' interaction with and through these textures. Instead, the appearance and functioning of these textures will also be set and affected by the interactions of others. As such, public interactive textures will manifest themselves through the collective engagement with these textures.

From this, new behaviors for interaction in public places will evolve and new practices will establish themselves. Over time, new cultures, new interaction rituals, and new social conventions will find their way into our built environments.

CONVENTIONS FOR INTERACTION WITH AND THROUGH INTERACTIVE TEXTURES

How we behave typically follow certain social protocols so called "conventions" (Lewis, 1969). These conventions can be thought of as customs and traditions, i.e. series of actions that we have learned to follow in various occasions, and in different particular situations. As such, conventions are rooted in our culture and they work as guiding principles for social behaviors and individual activities.

For us to understand how we should train persons to use and relate to new textures in architectural spaces we should also think about existing conventions and how we could align these new textures with the conventions that people are already familiar with, and in case we are to develop new conventions we should carefully consider how we aim to relate and associate such conventions with the already established ones.

In relation to the adoption of new interactive textures we need to further develop, adjust, and sometimes challenge the existing conventions that we live by. In essence, we need to develop our sensitivity and our conventions for interactive texture discovery, -exploration, -usage, and –engagement.

The conventions we live by not only affect how we view the world, and how we act in the world, but also the language we use to describe and talk about the world. Here, I previous example of our need to shift from the notion of "user" to inhabitants or persons is just one example of how we are affected by the common understanding, and common conventions around objects in the world. If moving further along this line we might also notion that the term "with" might be another such concept rooted in our understanding of traditional human-computer interaction activities in which we typically "interact with" a computer. However, as we shift from "users" to "inhabitants" we might also drift from "interaction with" to something closer to how we're engaging ourselves in the digital services available and how we make interactional commitments to the interactive textures that will occupy parts of our built environments.

PUTTING "INTERACTION KNOWLEDGE" INTO THE WORLD

While social conventions are about the socially trained, or experience-based approach to understanding how to read and make sense and use of our surrounding, there are also possibilities of working from the other end of the spectrum with the appearance of the physical environment *per se* and how it could invite and guide interaction with, and potentially and through, it.

In particular, we can think about the *placement* of interactive textures in relation to other textures in the composition of full scale built environments. We might also think about various ways of explaining, through the very texture of an object or an architectural element, how it is intended to be read, thus leading us in the direction of cues and support for *reading* textures. Through a similar process we can also think about ways of inscribing how a certain interactive texture can be modified, changed, and in other ways edited thus leading us into thinking on *writing* cues for textures. Through careful thinking around these three basic dimensions we can take various actions to inscribe ambient instructions into the very appearance of the textures on how they could be engaged in our interactions in the world.

Looking around for some support in the academic literature we can easily find several strands of research in support of this view. For instance, if looking in the field of ergonomics (e.g. Kroemer, et. al., 1994) we find good support I how the physical form and appearance of an object can inform its user about its functions, and ways to operate it, etc. Also, in the field of architecture (e.g. Ching, 2007) we find architectural guiding principles telling us about how the physical outline of a building can support e.g. way finding, circulation, and usage. In architecture there is even a language, or at least a set of concepts developed to talk about how such inscriptions can be made into our built environment including the concepts of e.g. circulation, paths, etc. (Ching, 2007). If now switching over the area of interaction design we can find similar support in concepts like affordance (Norman, 1993; 2002), which describe how a product, service or an interactive system might communicate its abilities and usage to a user. In this theory Norman (ref) also make a lot of connections to the area of product design and everyday objects and through several empirical examples he is able to illustrate that this line of reasoning holds for physical products, and architectural elements, e.g. doors, as well. From the field of psychology we find additional support, not at least from the field of environmental psychology (Bechtel & Churchman, 2002) which provide us with knowledge on how the layout the physical spaces affect us and our behaviors, and how the use of physical cues can guide us in different ways. Also, if looking into current theories on socio-technical systems, including e.g. ANT – Actor Network Theory (e.g. Callon, 2001) we find good support for our thinking on how guidance for usage and meanings can be inscribed in objects. In this theory it is even described how everyday object can contain not only inscribed meanings, but also how these objects might be interlinked as human and non-human actors organized in socio-technical networks across our social, physical and digital world.

THE IT- ("INTERACTION THROUGH TEXTURES") FRAMEWORK

As we envision the future of interactive architecture as built environments that on the one hand stands on a stable foundation in architecture as *communicated persistent structures*, and on the other hand are realized through deployment of innovative interactive textures that enable people to engage themselves with and through these structures in a graceful and elegant manner, we should at the same time also envision a framework and a method to further develop concepts capable of informing the design of such environments that will be situated in between the field of architecture and interaction design.

As described in chapter 1 and 3 of this book we need one such language or semantics (Krippendorf, 2005) to develop our thinking in this area, to expand our current body of knowledge, and to guide design projects in this area. In other terms, there is a need for "an architectural register for interaction" capable of coping with the emergent area of interactive architecture.

One such semantics should be able to describe, analyze, and even inspire and guide design of new interactive architectures through concepts like *"textures for momentary escapades"*, *"Interaction landscapes"* and *"interaction datum"*[1].

In our approach to create one such architectural register for interaction, and to start our work on the construction of a method and approach for generating one such semantics we set out to interlink architecture with interaction design through a cycle that start out in the borrowing of a set concepts from the field of architecture to discuss and address interactive architecture (see arrow 1 in Figure 82).

Following this simple model as outlined in Figure 82 I then challenge this set of concepts from an interaction design perspective (arrow 2) in an attempt to refine concepts with roots in both the field of architecture, and in interaction design, i.e. an architectural register for interaction (arrow 3). Through this interlinking of architecture and interaction design we seek to establish a foundation for interactive architecture in which no separation of digital material is made apart from other materials that constitute parts of our built environment. This, in the same sense as

Figure 82. An interlinking approach to the development of an architectural register for interaction

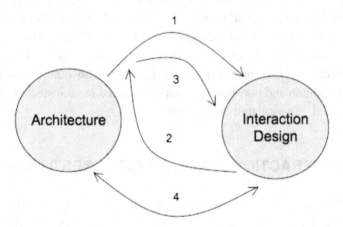

Greeenfield (2006) argues that the concept of ubiquitous computing, i.e. the complete blending of computational power into our everyday lives, looses its power as an analytical concept capable of addressing specific computational aspects of such computers at the same time as computational power actually gets completely blended into all of our everyday objects, activities, and surroundings. As such, this approach enables us to take on an interaction design perspective in architectural planning, and to address interaction design issues from the viewpoint of architecture.

In doing so, this demonstrate how this cycle enable us to carry out a wide set of different projects which all set out to blend interaction design with architectural thinking, and how this cycle enable us to frame this blended phenomenon of interactive architecture through notions like "interactive textures" and "interaction through textures" in terms of design, and as "interaction landscaping" in terms of these textures in use.

As to exemplify this cycle of linking architectural thinking with interaction design reasoning I use the core recurring concept in this book, i.e. the notion of "interactive textures" and I illustrate in the following how this notion is simultaneously anchored in the areas of architecture and interaction design, and how this concept has developed through the different stages of this interlinking approach.

In this case, the conceptual exploration started out with a need for a richer understanding of the notion of "surfaces", a concept that is almost always in focus in any interaction design project. As described in chapter 1 we are right now in a general development cycle that moves us away from traditional GUI designs towards new interaction paradigms including e.g. tangible user interfaces, embedded computers, etc. In line with this development we thus wanted to move away from the flat screen as the main "surface" for interaction and think broader about what kind of "surfaces" we have in the world, how these "surfaces" related to other surfaces, how these surfaces express themselves, and how these surfaces relate to the raw materials from which they are made.

So, in my development of the notion of "interactive textures" I looked into the literature within the area of architecture as to learn more about different kinds of surfaces. From this strand of literature I came across the notion of textures as further defined and outlined in chapter 2 of this book.

Following the arrows as outlined in the model above (see Figure 82) I then borrowed this notion of "textures" as a richer concept than "surfaces" from the field of architecture (arrow 1, Figure 82). Having put a specific focus on this new concept I then delivered a critique from the perspective of interaction design (arrow 2) arguing that textures might not only be a concept that can describe the relation between a physical material and a surface, but might in fact also be a functioning term for talking about the "skin" of physical/digital materials as well. Through this interplay between the notion of textures coming from the area of architecture, and its relation to digital materials as well a new term, i.e. the term of "interactive textures" grow out as a synthesis from this interplay (arrow 3). In doing so, it both grow into an applicable term for talking about the "surfaces" of new computational materials as well as it added itself to the vocabulary or semantics needed to build a conceptual foundation for the area of interactive architecture (arrow 4, Figure 82).

While this was just one example of concept development following this model there is still a lot of work to be done in this area. Both in terms of concept development, but also in terms of concept validation through the practical work of building and evaluating new interactive architectures.

As for a start, similar concept developments can probably be done for architectural concepts like e.g. datum, rhythm, repetition, awareness, interlocked spaces, etc. and from the interaction design perspective, notions of "awareness", "modalities", "embodiment" and "mobility" might be interesting to further explore via this framework.

In general, there is a lot of research needed to be conducted in this area. In particular, there is a need for definitions, cases, demo installations, user studies, etc. in order to get a sense of the general character of this phenomenon and the design space the meeting of architecture and interaction design brings about beyond the technology-driven agendas typically find in the areas of e.g. location-, and context-aware applications, intelligent environments, and ambient information spaces. Instead, with a true focus on the mechanisms at work in architecture, carefully blended with digital technologies new innovations are just around the corner. Further on, there is a need to explore this new design space systematically, and to validate efforts taken through user studies. Here, the framework presented above might work as a method for a systematic approach to the exploration of this area. Further on, the building of an architectural register for interaction could also function as a vehicle for the development of theories that could help us to understand, describe, analyze and even form principles and guidelines around this area. By doing this, we build a body of knowledge around this area. We explore the area systematically, and we develop a vocabulary for working in this field – as such, this model proposed might work both as a process or method to approach to area of interactive architecture, as well as a vehicle for theory development.

In the next section of this book I will take a point of departure in this method for building an architectural register for interaction in an exploration beyond these "cases and concepts" that has been the general theme for this section of the book. In doing so, we should now move ahead and not merely "think outside the box" as I suggested in section 1 of this book, but more radically, we should also question the very existence of a "box" in our exploration of interaction landscaping activities. This, for the purpose of identifying new sustainable solutions and opportunities for real innovations in the area of temporal forms and new spatial engagements.

REFERENCES

Callon, M. (2001). Actor Network Theory . In Smelser, N., & Baltes, P. (Eds.), *International Encyclopedia of the Social and Behavioral Sciences*. Oxford, UK: Elsevier.

Ching, F. (2007). *Architecture: Form, Space, and Order*. New York: John Wiley & Sons, Inc.

Croon Fors, A. *(2006). Being-with Information Technology: Critical explorations beyond Use and Design. Umeå University: Department of Informatics. (PhD thesis)*

Goffman, E. (1959). *The Presentation of Self in Everyday Life*. GardenCity, NY: Doubleday.

Greenfield, A. (2006). *Everyware – The dawning age of ubiquitous computing*. Berkeley, CA: New Riders.

Jones, Q. (2004). People-to-People-to-Geographical-Places: The P3 Framework for Location-Based Community Systems. In *J. Computer Supported Cooperative Work*, *13*(3-4), 202–211. doi:10.1007/s10606-004-2803-7

Krippendorff, K. (2005). *The semantic turn: A new foundation for design*. CRC Press.

Kroemer, K., Kroemer, H., & Kroemer-Elbert, K. (1994). *Ergonomics: How to Design for Ease and Efficiency*. Englewood Cliffs, NJ: Prentice Hall.

Lewis, D. (1969). *Convention: A Philosophical Study*. Cambridge, MA: Harvard Univ. Press.

Norman, D. A. (1993). *Things that make us smart*. Reading, MA: Addison Wesley.

Norman, D. A. (2002). *The Design of Everyday Things*. New York: Basic Books.

Rogers, Y. (2006). Moving on from Weiser's Vision of Calm Computing: Engaging UbiComp Experiences. In P. Dourish & A. Friday (Eds.), *Ubicomp 2006* (LNCS 4206, pp. 404-421). Berlin/Heidelberg: Springer-Verlag.

Wiberg, M. (2006). Graceful Interaction in Intelligent Environments. In *Proceedings of the International Symposium on Intelligent Environments*, 5-7 April, Cambridge.

ENDNOTE

[1]   These where concepts explored during the creation of the icehotel x interactive environment as case nr 4 which was further described in chapter 7.

Section 4
Exploration:
There is no Box

Getting Real and
Realizing Where to Go

The title of this section of the book is "Exploration: There is no box". This is an ontological statement, and a statement actually inspired by the Matrix movie in which the lead figure in the movie, Neo, (which in this movie lives his life in a virtual world overlaid across the physical world) gets a simple but elegant advise when training himself in a simulator in which he is supposed to bend a (virtual) spoon only with his thoughts, but constantly fails to do so. The advise reads as follows: -*"There is no spoon. Do not try to bend the spoon — that's impossible. Instead, only try to realize the truth: there is no spoon."* In similar terms, what this book has aimed at explaining, from section 1 in which "the box" was challenged as the way we frame the computational today we need to not only "think outside" the box, but we actually need to think along an alternative line, in which we do not introduce "the box" in the first place. Introducing the computational in terms of boxes leads us in the direction of a specific focus on the boxes, its applications etc. Instead, and as introduced in this book, the computational is becoming peripheral today and we need compositional thinking that integrate the computational in our everyday world instead of isolating it as an area in itself.

The "getting real" is therefore related to section 3 of this book, i.e. the "seeing with new eyes" perspective. Getting real is also about leaving our boxes related conceptions about the computational behind and switch to another ontological basis in which we take a point of departure in IT as an embedded element and interaction landscaping as our main focus for understanding this new world. To help our thinking along this line this final section of the book provides an overview of this new ontology in which IT is embedded and how it now operates as an installed base, followed by a closing curriculum in which I outline a new agenda for approaching this new materiality, while at the same time pointing even further ahead, towards temporal rooms and new spatial engagements.

Chapter 9
Interactive Architecture and Interaction Landscaping

In this final section of the book I will contrast "Interactive architecture" as an infrastructure, system, structure, and "installed base", designed with a particular planned use in focus, with the concept of "interaction landscaping" as a framing concept for the actual use of interactive environments.

Here, *Interaction landscaping* is viewed as an important conceptualization for understanding the core concept as outlined in this book, i.e. "interaction through textures". By its current definition the concept of "Landscaping" refers to:

..."any activity that modifies the visible features of an area of land, including but not limited to: 1.living elements, such as flora or fauna; 2.natural elements such as landforms, terrain shape and elevation, or bodies of water; 3.human elements such as structures, buildings, fences or other material objects created and/or installed by humans; and 4.abstract elements such as the weather and lighting conditions." (Wikipedia on "landscaping")

As such, this section of the book is an exploration of the tension between the careful planning and co-construction of the physical and the digital built environment (including electricity, projection areas, placement of buttons and handles, etc.) with the modifications that users do to the interactive textures of their surroundings.

DOI: 10.4018/978-1-61520-653-7.ch009

This last section of the book is inspired by the recent bottom-up approach to design that is significant for e.g. the Web 2.0 development and the "Lifehacking" phenomenon (see e.g. Bernstein, et. al., 2007), and in this last section of the book a discussion around IT – "beyond the box" is initiated as to address the hardest challenges related to this area, including issues of sustainability and how to work with innovations around new emerging interactive textures. In an attempt to take a truly fresh point of departure for one such discussion the whole notion of "the box" needs to be erased. Thus, the guiding theme for this fourth and final section of the book is titled "There is no box".

In the following two sections a traditional architectural perspective is applied to the current development of IT as to contextualize these technological developments even further in the context of architectural thinking. Then, this view is critically examined from a use perspective that is growing within the field of interaction design, i.e. the understanding of how people not only use digital technology in the form and in the shape it has from its design origin. Instead, people always try to adjust, change, modify and alter the technology either to fit some slightly different purposes, or just for the fun of turning it into something else. Sometimes this is described in terms of technology drift (e.g. Ciborra, et. al., 2000). In other more recent cases this has been described in terms of "lifehacking" (e.g. Bernstein, et al., 2007).

In a sense, these two blocks of sections in this chapter represent two different paradigms, i.e. an architectural paradigm, and a paradigm rooted in interaction design more closely related to what people do with their everyday digital technology. Still, in practice these two paradigms melt together and as it will be shown these two perspectives taken together work as a stable ground for understanding new digitalized environments.

IT AS EMBEDDED ELEMENT

Over and over again, this message has been repeated in this book. IT is soon part of everything. We have all the examples needed to exemplify this movement, and we can totally see this in the current development of various research disciplines targeting everything for computers in cars to computers in medicine. Just to mention a few areas we're right now watching the raise, development and establishment of the areas of telematics, bioinformatics, museum informatics, mobile informatics, social informatics, and industrial informatics (Holmström, Wiberg & Lund, 2010), all related to different application areas of IT in our modern society.

In a sense, IT has become texturized in several different application areas, in different organizations, and in different social systems. Following the ubiquitous computing paradigm, it will soon also be texturized in virtually any physical environment as well. Through this development IT changes from being about simple applications and pieces of technologies to becoming an infrastructure and an installed base at the same scale as other architectural systems.

IT AS INFRASTRUCTURE AND INSTALLED BASE

In chapter two when I started to look more specifically at textures and the mechanisms and operations around textures I focused heavily on representations. The book was in a sense guided by our understanding of digital "surfaces," and to some extent I argued that we "read" textures in terms of surfaces. In the beginning of this book we also looked at how textures related to materials similar to how representations relate to sets of information. This was an understanding of textures at the level of the artifact, the object, and the architectural element.

However, architecture is about whole systems. Accordingly, our understanding of embedded IT, or interactive textures must scale to this level of analysis. In the following, one attempt is made to exercise this scaling from textures as representations to textures as installed base (see Figure 83).

Taking "texture as representation" as a point of departure we can on the one hand think about this in terms of surfaces and information as previously outlined. However, we can also think about this specific notion of representations and think about how representations relate to the notion of semantics. Any representation "represents" something. In semiotics, this "something" is a sign, and a representation is a code system for the signs. We apply these code systems to formulate messages. As such, representations are very much about semantics, and thus about communication as well. Any chosen representation communicates as message. If representations are about semantics and communication then we can also think about different discourses in this communication, and think about this in terms of a language. These languages belong to larger (typically cultural and social) structures, and these "soft" structures are typically supported by technical and physical structures, or infrastructures. As these structures stabilize over time, they become rooted in the physical, digital, and social world as an installed base. As this line of reasoning illustrate, textures scale to the level of architecture, and the two are highly intertwined in this hierarchy and cycle from the small scale installation to the backbone infrastructures.

So, from an architectural perspective, we can surely work with embedded IT and interactive textures at the whole range from simple small scale installations to the incorporation of this element in the fundamental complex of intertwined systems that are focal to any modern piece of architecture.

Still, how people will actually use these complex systems is another question.

Figure 83. Model of IT and how it scales from small-scale textures to large-scale infrastructures

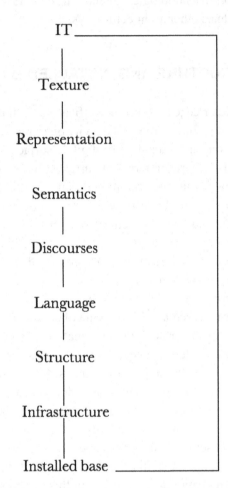

LIFEHACKING

As stated above, people love to change things either for good reasons, or just for the fun of doing it. It does not matter how well we plan and how much we try to fit technology and our built environment to various human needs. People will still want to change, adjust, and in other ways affect the spaces in which they live.

In the area of interaction design, a quite recent development is the trend towards so-called "lifehacking". According to Wikipedia (2009) (http://en.wikipedia.org/wiki/Life_hack) the term life hack refers to:

"productivity tricks that programmers devise and employ to cut through information overload and organize their data."

The original definition of the term life hack referred to quick-and-dirty shell scripts and other command line utilities that filtered and processed data streams like email and RSS feeds. Examples of these types of life hacks might include utilities to synchronize files, track tasks, remind you of events or filter email.

As the meme spread, the definition of the term expanded. Today, anything that solves an everyday problem in a clever or non-obvious way might be called a life hack. The term became popularized in the blogosphere and is primarily used by computer programmers who suffer from information overload or those with a playful curiosity in the ways they can accelerate their workflow.

"Life" refers to an individual's productivity, personal organization, work processes or any area the hacker ethic can be applied to solve a problem. The terms hack, hacking, and hacker have a long (and troubled) history in the computing and geek communities, particularly within the open source crowds.

While the whole movement in life hacking was technology related in the beginning (see e.g. http://www.lifehacking.net/oldblog/) it is now quickly becoming life-style centered, and currently there is a "hacking your life" movement in terms of being more productive under the popular label GTD – an acronym for "Getting Things Done" and there are several forums growing rapidly on the Internet in which people are sharing ideas about how to tap into the information streams, and how to apply modern interaction technologies to make their lives easier, richer, more productive, etc. For one such example see e.g. the online community at: http://www.lifehack.org/

INTERACTION LANDSCAPING

Given that we understand this movement towards life hacking we should then also try to draw some conclusions from this movement, and we should think carefully about how we could further develop technologies and our built environments in line with this movement. If this is the current practice, then we could also provide people with the tools to make these adjustments easier for anyone.

In forming a vocabulary for the *life hacking* and *interaction landscaping* activities currently taking place the follow lens including 6 different "uses" of the interaction landscape might be possible to identify and work in relation to:

1. The service landscape (offered use)

    Any understanding of the interaction landscape needs to pay attention to "offered use", i.e. what kind of services that are available in the interaction landscape.

2. Drift (change in use)

    Second, we need to understand how the services offered changes over time, and what we can do to tweak digital services into what we want them to do for us.

3. Workarounds (change of use/the alteration of use)

    The practice of tweaking these services, or to find ways around mal-functioning services is the act of crafting new paths across the interaction landscape. Ultimately, this is the meaning of workarounds.

4. The Do it yourself trend (invention of use/establishment of specialized use)

    Forth, the invention of new use and establishment and initiation of personal ways of doing a particular thing in the interaction landscape should never be underestimated.

5. Service combinations (the integration of use)

    As a fifth lens we can see how people combine and integrate different services in the interaction landscape to work in concert. Open standards, open protocols, and open formats enable information to float freely across different applications, platforms and devices adding flexibility not only in terms of device choices, but also in relation to how different services can be combined in new ways. This is sometimes also referred to as mesh-ups.

6. Service sharing (the "extragration" of use)

    Finally, the sixth lens offered here is about the sharing of services not only across the technical landscape, but also across the social landscape working on top of the services available and the ways in which these services has been integrated into larger sociomaterial structures.

An important overall message behind these 6 lenses is that this shows a movement from simple use of available technologies towards the forming of what the use and the use landscape should be about in the first place. In that sense, interaction landscaping is less about applying what is available, but more about adjusting, changing and assembling the resources necessary to do whatever one actually want to do.

Since interaction landscaping is so much about the assembling, integration and adjustment of different services into working collages we might soon see the rise of the "nano-use" as a complement to the digital interaction imperials. The new nano-uses of digital services are about specialized services that are narrow in their focus and thus perfect for anyone working across the interaction landscape. For instance, the DropBox service offer syncronization of a folder between different computers, Etherpad offer straight to the text online writing, picknik offer online editing of photos, Flickr online sharing of Photos and Google offer internet search. Of course, these services also offer a lot of other things, but for the interaction landscaper these are the core functions that when considered as nano-use services with ease can be integrated into a larger interaction landscape.

Given the fast growing interest in this kind of nano-use where you probably will not spend 2 years on editing a whole book manuscript on EtherPad (but more likely 15 minutes to just compose a draft to be shared with a couple of friends) it is likely that we will is a growing market for the "long-tailing of interaction" (following the long-tail principles outlined by Anderson, 2006). I.e. we might see a market for online services which people might not use throughout their whole workday but maybe only once a week (but there might be hundreds of millions of people using the service world-wide). In that sense it is likely that in terms of development actors and service providers in the interaction landscape we might see a movement from "monuments" occupying a large space in the interaction landscape (following a spatially oriented paradigm of being the "biggest" actor on the market) towards actors working under the paradigm of interaction support for "moments" (following a temporally oriented paradigm) in which fast services are instantly made available to anyone who occasionally happen to need a particular service. In other terms, this is a movement away from "the gigants" (representing the stable structures) in the interaction landscape towards "the gigahertz" (representing fast dynamic alterations and alternatives).

Two further, and kind of obvious implications in relation to this development as outlined above are *flexibility* and *openness.* We need to design for change, adoption and innovation, and we need to design not only for use, but also for the adoption process itself. Flexibility is crucial, and an open access to this flexibility is also crucial. Therefore, we should stimulate initiatives on open source, open standards, open protocols, open APIs, etc. Things that allow for the masses to further innovate the use of modern computational resources.

From a design perspective on interactive architecture we can think along the line of the design of environments that will inform, react and respond to human needs and present itself through its services, protocols, access methods and standards. Ones one know how to work the interaction landscape one can also find new or alternative ways of working a way through it. And, depending on the equipment at hand and the level of understanding of how to read and make use of the interaction landscape different results will come of these creative processes.

As formulated in chapter 1 interaction is today very much about interactional commitments and about how we can engage various computational resources in our interactions. To support this, we need to develop environments that are truly open for those people that want to engage them in their lives and everyday activities. Just think about it for a second. If everyday truly means "every day" then it is crucial that the engagement is simple, straightforward, seamless and fun since this is activities that will be acted out every single day.

Open environments can also stimulate and promote open innovation and promote co-creation of new services, applications, new environments, new businesses, and even new use practices.

Still, no matter how flexible we build our systems and interactive architectures people will still use them in new ways, which we can never be truly prepared for. Instead, we are probably now facing an evolutionary and user-driven development of the interaction landscape, i.e. the everyday interaction landscaping activities that continuously challenges and modifies the built interaction landscape.

So, if we accept a view of modern computing, not as isolated computational islands, but as a wide-ranging complex network of intertwined digital networks, services, and platforms, which are seamlessly mixed with, and blended into our physical environment we can see an emerging interaction landscape taking form – partly designed and partly evolutionary built.

To build good services for the inhabitants of these new environments we need new thinking on, for instance, session management models. For a traditional application the session could be restrained to a single user, or a small number of users, one stationary computer, and a limited amount of uptime for one particular session. In the modern interaction landscape on the other hand, this model is challenged. In the modern interaction landscape, the inhabitants move around, change location, meet each other, share sessions, join each other's sessions, or create new sessions as they go along. Thus, modern session management models needs to reflect this behavior and support computational sessions that can for instance grow, shrink, change, expand, split, and transfer to another media, device or carrying network. Thus, it is needed to adopt an almost ecological, or biological perspective on session management to cope with the current development of the interaction landscape and the landscaping activities there within.

Indeed, the innovation power is great when adding people and the use dimension to the new landscapes we're creating in the borderland between the physical, the social and the digital. In the next chapter we summarize this under the notion of "a digital world" and outline a new agenda for interactive architecture with one foot in current issues on sustainability and innovation, and with one foot already in the future of temporal forms and new spatial engagements.

REFERENCES

Anderson, C. (2006). *The long tail*. New York: Harper Collins.

Bernstein, M. S., Van Kleek, M., Schraefel, M. C., & Karger, D. R. (2007). Management of personal information scraps. In *CHI '07 Extended Abstracts on Human Factors in Computing Systems* (San Jose, CA, USA, April 28 - May 03, 2007). (pp. 2285-2290). New York: ACM.

Ciborra, C., Braa, K., Cordella, A., Dahlbom, B., Failla, A., & Hanseth, O. (2010). *Industrial Informatics Design, Use & Innovation*. Hershey, PA: Information Science Reference.

Monteiro, E., & Simon, K. A. (2000). *From Control to Drift: The Dynamics of Corporate Information Infrastructures*. Oxford University Press.

Chapter 10
Conclusions

A DIGITAL WORLD

As outlined in this book, "interactive textures," and built environments that integrate digital components with physical materials, will increasingly constitute the settings for social life.

In thinking about what these settings will look like we could probably come up with dozens of scenarios and examples and most of them will be wrong. Not because of lack in our imagination, but because this question is probably not correctly formulated or timely situated in the first place. In my view, the change has already happened; we're already living in a digitalized world.

In this book I have presented interactive architecture and interactive textures as a concrete possibility, but foremost as an eye opener to a digital world that is already here. Even more directly, and from the horizons of today, the complexity of the current blending of our physical built environment with modern computational materials – ranging from traditional information technologies to recent developments in area of ubiquitous computing, mobile devices, and ambient intelligence – not only provide us with new ways of accessing and interacting with information and other persons, but ultimately it challenge us in our thinking on integration of the physical and the digital.

DOI: 10.4018/978-1-61520-653-7.ch010

With a point of departure taken in an ordinary working day for me I can easily picture the following scenario: With the tip of my finger I can have access to almost any information in the world through the applications and services on my mobile phone. As I walk into work I unlock the doors with my key-chain RFID-tag. When I flip up my laptop the files are synchronized with my other computers, and when I drive home from work, street signals are switching from red to green when they notice that I am approaching a cross road. Back in my home I enjoy tapping into the latest tweets from twitter, check a few blogs, and reply to a few network invitations before tuning in some good music from the online streaming service Spotify as recommended by a friend. It's a landscape of services and technologies and I am navigating it seamlessly.

Through these computational materials of objects, services, applications, networks, and media spaces the interaction landscape is in place, and it is already situated in my everyday world.

As we develop new interactive textures we will see a great involvement of our physical world in the simple scenario outlined above. We will be able to offload information to the environment, and seamlessly hide and integrate the raw technologies and interfaces as to make them truly blend with the textures of our homes, cars, workplaces, etc. Still, the digital dimension of these textures will not "disappear", nor be "embedded". Instead, they will be highly integrated and part of the new textures that we will adopt and develop for different purposes, or as outlined in chapter 9, just for the sake of it, or just for fun.

For these new textures we will invent new interaction modalities as to make good and effective use of these computational resources, and we will learn how to operate these new textures efficiently, rationally, and gracefully. However, in order to further develop this area in a systematic manner we need an agenda, and a mission statement for our work.

A NEW AGENDA

Any agenda needs a method and an approach for reaching the goals and mission statements formulated in the agenda. If the mission statement here is to further develop this area of interactive architecture, then the method proposed in this book goes via the development of an architectural register for interaction. As formulated in this book we have, on the one hand, the traditional field of architecture which provides us with a rich register of concepts to describe and analyze our built environment. On the other hand, the field of interaction design enables us to do the same, but with a focus on digital technologies as the design material in focus, thus creating a knowledge gap in between interaction design and architecture which makes it hard to fully address this phenomenon of interactive architecture.

The method as proposed in this book is not a tool for addressing this gap. However, it juxtaposes perspectives from the fields of architecture and human-computer interaction. By borrowing a set concepts from the field of architecture to discuss and address interactive architecture, we can challenge a set of architecturally rooted concepts from an interaction design perspective in an attempt to refine concepts with roots in both the field of architecture, and in interaction design, i.e. an architectural register for interaction. Through this interlinking of architecture and interaction design we seek to establish a foundation for interactive architecture in which no separation of digital material is made apart from other materials that constitute parts of our built environment. The conduct of this interlinking process is the core mission for this new agenda.

With this register at hand we hand the tools for talking specifically about new fully digitalized environments and can, as a next step set out to tackle two of the most challenging questions right now, i.e. the issue of sustainable development, and the issue of innovations. In the next, and final section of this book I will try to elaborate upon these two areas in relation to what I see as the next step of development for the field of interactive architecture.

In this following final section I will address these two challenges of sustainability and innovations through a mixture of the classical time-space dimensions so fundamental to our built environment, and thus to the area of architecture, with the two dimensions of forms and engagement so crucial to the area of interaction design.

In general terms, this notion of "innovations" is typically addressed from the need to "think outside the box". As indicated in chapter 9, when it comes to IT this "box" as representation of the computer has become so rooted in our minds that it is becoming increasingly hard to think about any other possible form for computational materials.

To think outside of this box, which typically frames the notion of a computer, might lead us into thinking around how it relates to other resources "outside of the box", including online resources, online services, other computers, grid computing, and so on. However, such reasoning is still not actually questioning the box *per se* as a conceptualization of the computer. In this book I have tried to actually get rid of the box. In fact, the theme for this final section of the book is titled "there is no box!". The form is free and all we have is computational materials that can be assembled in any way to engage itself in the emerging interaction landscape.

TEMPORAL ROOMS AND NEW SPATIAL ENGAGEMENTS

As described above, the temporal and the spatial are the two must fundamental aspects of our built environment. The old Greek philosophers use these two dimensions in their reasoning about the world and even nowadays these two dimensions are popular e.g. in descriptions of "anytime, anywhere" computing.

Further on, temporal form and the notion of interactional engagements as outlined in chapter 1 are fundamental aspects to understand interaction *per se*.

In an attempt to sketch out the next step to take in the area of interactive architecture we need to go back to the purpose of understanding "textures". In this book, this fundamental concept was deliberately chosen since it represents a unifying perspective capable of uniting the digital with the physical, and surface with material. To me, the next step follows the orientation of this reasoning.

If the temporal and the spatial are fundamentals to architecture, and if forms and engagements are fundamental to interaction we need to follow the same approach as outlined in this book and explore ways of integrating this two perspectives. In this last section of the book I therefore suggest that "temporal rooms" and "new spatial engagements" might be a way forward for developing this area.

As already mentioned in chapter 1, Mazé (2007) describes temporal form as an important aspect of any interactive material. This line of reasoning can be extended to the thoughts outlined in this book on how to make interactive surfaces integrated, and still visible, in the physical world through the notion of interactive textures. The adding of a dynamic character to the physical world, and a true focus on this enabling dimension will probably open up for a new area of innovation when it comes to new "temporal rooms". Innovations that will have huge implications for service design, technology development, and interaction design projects as we used to know them.

Further on, as we engage ourselves in interactions we will at the same time engage ourselves in spaces. Today, we engage ourselves mostly in virtual spaces and physical spaces separately, but as these two to start to blend we will engage ourselves in these blended environments. A new spatial engagement will in turn also lead us into innovative thinking around sustainable solutions for the spaces we're engaging. This, due to the fact that we do not only engage places in our interactions with others, but equally the other way around, we engage ourselves in the places we occupy.

For quite a few years now we have had a specific research interest in technologies capable of sensing the environment under labels like location-based services, context-aware systems, etc. This acknowledges our physical world from a technical perspective.

From another perspective, and as a short anecdote, I was involved in a project a couple of years ago in which we built a new web site for traveling people. For one of the persona descriptions in this particular project we created the "I am a location" character. This was to acknowledge how people build expectations around places, how people experience places, and how people keep memories of places and fill places with meanings.

No matter from which perspective we look at places, they are important to us, and we should careful consider how we texturize typical distance-spanning technologies like IT into these places of our everyday lives.

In the end, we might also want to reflect upon how we might benefit from this book from a research point of view. Well, in the same way as AI – Artificial Intelligence has lead to, not only new technical innovations, but also new knowledge on how our brain works, and new knowledge about human intelligence *per se*, we will for sure follow a similar learning cycle for IA – Interactive Architecture in that we will not only arrive at novel, innovative, and sustainable solutions, but we will simultaneously learn more about our built environment and about how we engage ourselves in our physical, digital and social world. Although the big difference this time around is that for IA the built environment now also equals the digital environment, and in this book the notion of "interactive textures" are not purely a theoretical construct, but also proposed as the practical ways and the means through which these two are becoming one.

REFERENCES

Mazé, R. (2007). *Occupying Time: Design, Technology and the Form of Interaction.* PhD Thesis, Malmö University, Sweden.

About the Author

Mikael Wiberg is a chaired professor in human-computer interaction at the Department of Informatics and Media at Uppsala University in Sweden and Research Director for Umeå Institute of Design, Umeå University. He received his Ph.D. in Informatics at Umeå University in 2001. The topic for the thesis was design of mobile CSCW (Computer Supported Cooperative Work) systems for ongoing interaction. In his current research he is focused on the emerging Interaction Society with related issues including e.g. research into mobile CSCW, ubiquitous computing, ambient intelligence, availability management, interactive architecture, and interaction design. Wiberg is the editor of the book *"The Interaction Society"*, and he has published his work in a number of international journals including e.g. ToCHI, BIT, IEEE Network, IEEE Pervasive Computing, WebNet Journal, *International Journal of Educational Technology & Society, Journal of HCI, International Journal of Design*, and at international conferences including e.g. TEI – Tangible & Embedded Interaction, CHI, GROUP, Mobile HCI, HCI, etc. Mikael Wiberg has participated in many projects in social mobile interaction & ubiquitous computing. His current EU-project is titled *"[x]ID – Interaction Design in eXtreme environments"*. Mikael Wiberg has previously served as an editor for another book published by IDEA-group, i.e. Wiberg, M. (ed.) (2004) *"The Interaction Society: Practice, Theories & Supportive technologies"*). Mikael Wiberg has co-edited the book *"Industrial Informatics Design, Use and Innovation"* and has also contributed to another book published by IDEA-group (i.e. Wiberg, M. & Ljungberg, F. (2000) Exploring the vision of anytime, anywhere in the context of mobile work, in: Knowledge management and Virtual organizations: Theories, Practices, Technologies and Methods, Yogesh Malhotra (Ed.).

Index

A

Activity theory 37
Actor Network Theory (ANT) 179, 182
ad-hoc networks 143
adjacent spaces 76
affective interaction 15
ambient informatics 11, 12, 40, 41, 42, 131
ambient information 131, 136, 139, 144, 152, 158
ambient information spaces 62, 69
ambient instructions 178
ambient intelligence 2, 18, 50, 61, 62, 130, 131, 196
Ambient Orb 6
Ambient Umbrella 6
architectonic structures 98
architectural approach 130, 132
architectural composition 98
architectural element 96, 98, 114, 178, 189
architectural paradigm 188
architectural perspective 188, 189
architectural planning 180
architectural register 179, 180, 182
architectural spaces 177
architectural structure 175
architectural systems 189
architectural textures 76, 79, 84

architectural thinking 188
articulation 55
Artificial Intelligence (AI) 200
artistic eye 102

B

basic materials 101, 102, 103
bioinformatics 188
blended environments 174, 199
blogosphere 32, 191
Bluetooth 143
bottom-up approach 188
built environment 54, 55, 62, 63, 66, 70, 73, 74, 75, 76, 77, 78, 79, 81, 87, 113, 115, 130, 132, 135, 176, 177, 178, 179, 187, 190, 191, 196, 197, 198, 199, 200

C

C6-principles 118
clustered organizations 136
coherent structure 56, 129
combinations of professions 41
communities of practice 41
computational aesthetics 122
computational capabilities 124
computational composition 120, 122
computational grid 15

computational infrastructure 125
computational interfaces 128
computational islands 144
computational material 14, 15, 16, 17, 18, 19, 26, 35, 36, 38, 40, 42, 60, 62, 63, 68, 69, 96, 97, 99, 117, 118, 124, 181, 196, 197, 198
computational materiality 118
computational power 4, 5, 6, 7, 11, 12, 14, 15, 17, 19, 30, 35, 40, 43, 59, 61, 62, 69, 72, 89, 90, 97, 124, 142, 143, 147, 159, 160, 169, 180
computational resources 193
computational surfaces 115
computational textures 115, 124
Computer Aided Design (CAD) 77
Computer Aided Design tools 77
Computer Mediated Communication (CMC) 3, 172
Computer Supported Cooperative Work (CSCW) 3, 23, 50, 51, 52, 53, 172, 182
computing paradigm 188
conceptual level 74
conceptual tools 171
co-present individual 175
crystallization 58
crystallographic 58
cultural engagement 130
cultural life 168
cultural textures 164, 165

D

data communication 144
design loop 99
design material 130
digital activity 147, 148
digital artifacts 43
digital augmentations 113
digital built environment 187
digital channels 15
digital clock 115
digital components 196
digital design 1, 9
digital devices 174
digital dimensions 162

digital elements 78, 79, 85, 128, 129, 135
digital environment 200
digital fabrics 131
digital facades 63
digital footprints 26
digital information 87, 146, 148
digital installations 166
digital instrument 9, 10
digital interaction 148, 149, 192
digital interactive 157
digital interface 85, 135, 151
digitalized environments 60, 63, 152, 188
digitalized interaction 23
digitalized world 196
digital landscape 97
digital material 1, 2, 12, 18, 19, 21, 25, 34, 36, 41, 60, 63, 79, 80, 81, 82, 84, 87, 90, 99, 100, 101, 102, 104, 110, 116, 128, 129, 130, 131, 135, 137, 144, 147, 154, 155, 169, 179, 198
digital networks 145, 194
digital places 78
digital services 13, 15, 35, 142, 143, 192
digital signage 79, 83, 91
digital skin 166
digital solutions 130
digital technology 1, 2, 3, 4, 9, 13, 17, 23, 24, 25, 32, 33, 34, 35, 43, 46, 62, 65, 78, 79, 82, 84, 87, 96, 102, 113, 114, 129, 130, 131, 135, 136, 137, 138, 142, 149, 152, 156, 159, 161, 162, 165, 166, 167, 172, 173, 175, 181, 188, 197
digital texture 60, 134, 174
digital tools 25, 77
digital world 26, 27, 30, 32, 33, 34, 35, 39, 54, 60, 114, 124, 125, 196
diverse application 132
down to earth 173
dynamic texture 81, 82

E

elements 95, 96, 97, 98, 99, 100, 102
embedded computational power 142
embedded computing 61
embedded internet 5, 6

embedded IT 189
embodied interaction 15, 147
empirical projects 171
enabling fabrics 97
enclosure system 73
environment interaction 144, 146, 147,
    148, 149, 150, 152
everyware 1, 4, 124

F

Facebook 15, 72
face-to-face 172
face-to-face conversation 143
face-to-face interaction 68
feedback-loop 22
finished materials 96
FolkMusic 143
FolkMusic system 143
functional behavior 10

G

gene-manipulation 70
Getting Things Done (GTD) 191
graphical user interface (GUI) 3, 17, 22,
    61, 180

H

hacking 191
hands-on interaction 124
horizontal connections 118, 119
Human-Computer Interaction (HCI) 1, 3,
    16, 18, 19, 20, 21, 22, 23, 26, 28,
    29, 30, 33, 34, 36, 41, 49, 50, 51,
    52, 53, 60, 61, 152, 174, 177, 198
human-environment interaction 148, 149
hybrid spaces 114

I

immersive environments 130
indoor architecture 161
industrial informatics 188
information appliance 157
information architecture 115
information ecologies 40
information spaces 115

informative textures 82
input gateway 145
installed base 187, 189
integration as transition 9
integration of architecture 113
integration of materials 129
intelligent architecture 131
intelligent environments 176, 181
interactional commitment 10, 34, 35, 193
interactional games 38
interaction datum 179
Interaction Design (IxD) 1, 3, 12, 18, 19,
    20, 23, 24, 28, 29, 30, 32, 34, 36,
    38, 41, 42, 50, 52, 53, 59, 60, 61,
    65, 78, 80, 81, 82, 87, 88, 91, 112,
    113, 114, 115, 128, 132, 135, 137,
    154, 166, 168, 170, 178, 179, 180,
    181, 188, 190, 197, 198, 199
interaction ecologies 40, 41
interaction grid 60, 62, 143
interaction knowledge 171
interaction landscape 3, 4, 11, 13, 15, 16,
    17, 31, 32, 35, 40, 142, 143, 144,
    145, 169, 176, 179, 191, 192, 193,
    194, 197, 198
interaction landscaping 180, 182, 187,
    191, 192, 194
interaction modalities 15, 16, 18, 22, 44,
    80, 97, 114, 124, 125, 173, 176
interaction paradigm 10, 11, 18, 180
interaction rituals 36, 38, 171, 177
interaction society 3, 4, 11, 12
interaction technologies 3, 14, 17, 18, 24,
    29, 40, 41, 42
interaction through textures 128, 148, 151,
    171, 180
Interactive Architecture (IA) 2, 4, 12, 41,
    42, 59, 61, 62, 63, 70, 72, 73, 88,
    90, 98, 113, 114, 125, 128, 129,
    130, 131, 132, 133, 134, 135, 137,
    144, 153, 154, 155, 161, 172, 173,
    179, 180, 181, 182, 187, 193, 194,
    196, 197, 198, 199, 200
interactive design 131
interactive environment 2, 3, 15, 16, 41,
    42, 52, 131, 156, 158, 159, 160, 187

interactive installations 158
interactive landscapes 142
interactive scenario 158
interactive sculptures 63
interactive services 142
interactive surfaces 199
interactive systems design approach 130,
    132
interactive technologies 28
interactive textiles 60
interactive texture 81, 82, 83, 85, 86, 88,
    89, 90, 95, 97, 99, 100, 101, 104,
    105, 111, 112, 113, 118, 119, 122,
    128, 129, 130, 132, 134, 136, 137,
    162, 168, 171, 172, 173, 174, 177,
    178, 179, 180, 181, 187, 188, 189,
    196, 197, 199, 200
interactive themes 156
interlocked spaces 76
interlooking spaces 136
interpersonal interaction 124

L

life hack 190, 191
life hacking 188, 190, 191
Linked 72
live data 144
living systems 128, 131, 136, 137

M

material appearances 107
material blending 62
material properties 100, 107, 111, 129,
    137
materials 95, 96, 97, 98, 99, 100, 101, 102,
    103, 104, 107, 109, 110, 111
material science 54, 57, 58, 60, 61
Media districts 113
media environments 130
Media spaces 113
MidGets 145
MidGets project 145
mixtures of professions 41, 42
mobile blogs 4
mobile computing 5
mobile informatics 188

mobile interaction 15, 20, 50
mobile system 143
MoveInfo 143, 144
multi-touch interaction 124
museum informatics 188

N

navigational aids 112, 114, 122
Negotiator 143, 144
non-digital materials 101, 104, 110

O

online channels 172
online community 26, 191
online data 6
online group communication 143
online interaction 26, 31, 37
online services 27, 60
online social networking 172
online streaming 197
online voting 145, 146, 148
online world 26, 27, 30
open protocols 192, 193
open source 191, 193
open standards 193

P

P2P networks 145
P3-systems 171, 172
passive environment 158
peer-to-peer system 143
people-to-people interaction 172
People-to-People-to-geographical Places
    (P3) 171, 172, 182
People-to-people-to-places systems 16, 42
perceptual level 73
Personal Computer (PC) 2, 13
pervasive computing 2, 131
physical/digital compositions 99
physical-digital integration 118, 148
physical/digital materials 181
physical material 117, 124, 125, 135

R

raw material 95

reading textures 178
reflexive architecture 131
responsive architecture 114
responsive environments 114, 131
responsive texture 82
RoamWare 143, 170
RoamWare system 143

S

semi-finished materials 96
service landscape 192
smart environments 2, 52
smart materials 131
smart textiles 80
SMS-service 175, 176
SMS-technology 176
social city design 4
social informatics 188
social interaction 3, 20, 26, 40, 51, 128
Social Interaction Design 1
social landscape 192
social life 196
social networking 4, 15, 26, 27, 31, 35,
    37, 172
social networking services 4, 15, 26, 27
social networks 72
social protocols 177
social systems 188
social world 3, 4, 17, 39, 44, 189
sociomaterial structures 192
socio-technical networks 179
socio-technical systems 179
spatial engagement 194, 199
spatial layout 18
spatial system 73
state-of-the-art 112
structural system 73
systematic approach 182

T

tangible interaction 124
tangible user interfaces (TUI) 2, 15, 34,
    60, 147
telematics 188
temporal character 19

temporal dimension 19, 28
temporal form 19, 32, 182, 199
temporal rooms 199
texturation approaches 166
texture as representation 189
textures 54, 55, 56, 57, 58, 59, 60, 61, 63,
    64, 65, 66, 67, 68, 69, 70
time-space dimensions 198
transmaterials 54, 80, 81, 89, 124, 125,
    130, 131
true blending 112

U

ubiquitous computing 1, 2, 4, 11, 12, 18,
    43, 48, 50, 61, 71, 113, 126, 130,
    131, 138, 156, 162, 166, 170, 180,
    182, 196
ubiquitous interaction 13
ubiquitous internet 8, 10

V

vertical connections 118
virtual elements 175
virtual meetings 143
virtual online worlds 62
virtual points systems 176
virtual spaces 199
virtual voting 147
virtual worlds 26, 27
visual appearance 56
visual qualities 54, 56
voting portal 146, 148

W

Web 2.0 188
Widget 145
WiFi network connection 5
WiFi networks 34
WIMP-standard 157
Windows, Icons, Menus and Pointers
    (WIMP) 3, 22, 49, 51
wireless technologies 144
WorldPortal 146, 147, 148
writing cues 178